Local environmental policies and strategies

Edited by

Julian Agyeman

and

Bob Evans

Series editors: John Benington and Mike Geddes

Published by Longman Information and Reference
Longman Group Limited, 6th Floor, Westgate
House, The High, Harlow, Essex CM20 1YR
Telephone: Harlow (0279) 442601; Fax: Harlow (0279) 444501;
Telex: 81491 Padlog

A catalogue record for this book is available from the British Library.

ISBN 0–582–22938–3

Printed by Bell and Bain Ltd, Glasgow

Longman Local Government Library

The Warwick Series on Local Economic and Social Strategies

This series is designed to contribute to the ability of policy makers and managers in local government to meet the challenges of the 1990s. The focus is on strategic questions of local economic and social change. The series deals with issues which confront local government (and local public services more widely) at the level of corporate or inter agency strategy (for example, industrial restructuring, Europeanisation, ageing, poverty, transport, the environment). These issues are challenging local government to move beyond its traditional and primary role as a distributor and deliverer of services and to explore the potential for influence in new economic roles (as a major employer, investor and purchaser within the local economy) and in its political and ideological roles (as a democratically elected body, with a mandate to represent the interests of the whole community).

The series will present the results of applied research and innovative policy initiatives in key areas of local government strategy, policy making, organisation and management. Its primary aim is to contribute to the development of good practice in local government policy making and corporate management, but it will also contribute to a better conceptual understanding of the role and functioning of the local state.

We hope this series will stimulate a lively and critical exchange of ideas and experience about policy making in the public sector. The editors welcome contributions to the debate from local policy makers, managers and academics.

John Benington and Mike Geddes

Contents

Preface

The idea for this book arose from a series of discussions at South Bank University in early 1992. We were concerned that, despite the existence of a large number of books which addressed a wide range of environmental issues, very few of these appeared to be aimed at what we believe to be a fertile and idea-laden ground — the development of local environmental policies and strategies and their implementation, management and monitoring.

This seemed to us to be a major omission for two reasons. Firstly, it is apparent that, in Britain at least, it is local government, rather than national government which is the focus for environmental initiative, policy and action. During the last decade, local authorities and local and national pressure groups have been setting the pace in the field of environmental policy. Today, they are at the forefront in developing what has come to be termed the 'new environmental agenda' with its focus on sustainability and sustainable development. By way of contrast, activity at the level of central government has been minimal.

Secondly, a fundamental principle of environmental action and politics is that national and global change can only result from action at the local level. The maxim of 'thinking globally and acting locally' is therefore central to environmental policy. Concerted and sustained action at the local level is seen by all serious commentators and policy makers as a prerequisite for the achievement of global sustainability.

In this book we have sought to address these issues by focusing upon 'the local' as the major source of environmental drive, initiative and enterprise in contemporary Britain and we have been fortunate in being able to bring together a group of highly regarded and experienced environmental practitioners to contribute to this debate. Most of the chapter authors have been involved in writing the policy documents and reports which have been bench marks in the development of UK local environmental policy — for example, several were involved in the Local Government Management Board's acclaimed *Environmental Practice in Local Government*.

However, it is an inevitable fact of life that official reports and publications cannot always be as frank as their authors would wish. Moreover, speculation over future policy direction and critical evaluations of existing policy do not usually feature in such documents. A book such as this is therefore an opportunity for experienced practitioners to reflect on policy achievements so far and on possible future courses of action, without reference to the constraints usually associated with official or institutional publications.

We hope that this book will stimulate a debate about local environmental policy and practice, and that it will serve to demonstrate what has been achieved during the last few years at the local level and to indicate the directions which future policy might take. We wish to foster this debate amongst practitioners and policy makers, and also amongst the academic community of teachers, students and researchers since we are certain that the future of environmental policy will involve a closer co-operation and partnership between these groups. It is for this reason that this book has been written to serve both these groups, and we believe that the following chapters will prove invaluable to the ever increasing numbers of academics, from a variety of disciplines, to students at undergraduate and postgraduate levels and to practitioners who wish to join in shaping the new environmental agenda.

Finally, we need to offer a disclaimer. Environmental policy is a fast developing area, and we are conscious that in the space available to us, we have been unable to provide a comprehensive review of all aspects of policy, although we hope that our chosen focus upon the strategic dimensions of environmental policy making at the local level will set a context for further debates and action. Furthermore, we are victims of time, in that the post-Rio and post-Maastricht policy process trundles on apace, and like all authors and editors we have to draw a line and go to press.

In our particular case, the Government's *Sustainable Development: The UK Strategy* (HMSO 1994) was released after the main body of this book was submitted to the publishers. Given the nature of our project it would be reasonable to assume that this might be an important document. However, it is a measure of the insignificance of this 'Strategy', breathtaking in its triviality and irrelevance, that we have not felt it necessary to alter our manuscript in any way. On the contrary, the publication of the Strategy has reinforced our view that local action and initiative is ever more important, given the current environmental policy vacuum at the national level.

Julian Agyeman
Bob Evans

Centre for Local Environmental Polices and Strategies,
South Bank University, London
March, 1994

Foreword

Jonathon Porritt

The 1992 Earth Summit in Rio de Janeiro created many expectations, the majority of which have yet to be met. Between then and now, recession in the world economy and a sequence of security crises from Somalia to Bosnia have driven the challenge of achieving genuinely sustainable development back down the agenda. Particularly here in the UK.

But that somewhat gloomy outlook is belied by what has been going on at the level of local government. Here things are buzzing, additional resources are being found *despite* restrictions on funding, new policies are being formulated and solutions advocated. There is still a fair amount of empty rhetoric reverberating around the place, but in stark contrast to what is happening nationally, that rhetoric at the local level seems to lead more often than not to real action.

And that's how it now has to be. Two-thirds of all the recommendations in Agenda 21 (the catch-all policy document signed up to by more than 100 world leaders at the Earth Summit) requires the involvement of local authorities. Forty per cent of the European Union's Fifth Environmental Action Plan can only be delivered through the involvement of the local authorities. Even more importantly, one suspects that it is only local authorities which can begin to translate the alienating jargon that besets our business (sustainable development, biological diversity, environmental impact assessments etc.) into a language that actually makes sense to people by relating those abstractions to the daily reality of their lives.

All the authors in this timely and excellent review of environmental initiatives at the local level stress the crucial significance of building a broader constituency of support through 'community environmental education'. Far too many environmental activists take it as read that the rationality and desirability of the changes they are proposing are self-evident. For the majority of people, that is often not the case. Environmental change is still relatively new territory, involving not just mechanistic changes in policy implementation, but changes in lifestyle, mind set and expectation. In such a context, the *explaining* is at least as important as the *doing*. Together with schools and colleges, local authorities find themselves on the cutting edge of the process of change through participation, participation through awareness-raising.

It is that hands-on approach which defines the editorial tone of *Local Environmental Policies and Strategies*. Whatever people mean by 'sustainable development' (loosely defined by John Gummer, Secretary of State for the Environment, as 'improving the quality of life today without cheating on our children tomorrow'), it cannot be achieved without strengthening local democracy or without removing the inherent inequities that now lie at the heart of almost all industrialised nations. It is all very well going on about a higher quality of life through higher environmental standards, but the linkage between this admirable aim and social justice within a revitalised democracy has to be made absolutely explicit.

Substantial common ground has already been established in adopting this approach. Local Environmental Forums (or even Round Tables) have been springing up all over the place, with enthusiastic participation from the voluntary sector, business community and professional bodies. Interestingly, however, it tends to be the local authority that is now taking the initiative in bringing those parties together, and demonstrating the benefits of practical partnerships for change at the local level.

This book brings out many of those benefits in clear and compelling terms: clean air, safer streets, reduced waste, greener cities, better housing, renewed community spirit, lower energy bills, different patterns of co-operation etc. Perhaps the only element that it consistently underplays is the growing convergence between regenerating the local economy and improving the local environment. A 1993 study done for the Local Government Management Board (entitled *Greening Economic Development*) broke new ground in demonstrating the enormous potential for creating wealth and new work opportunities through a strategic commitment to sustainable development.

Environmentalists today are both heartened and impressed by what is going on within local government — notwithstanding the threat of swingeing reorganisation and yet more budget reductions. As a measure of this I can't help but think back to the time when I was at Friends of the Earth in the late 1980s and we rather ambitiously threw down a gauntlet before local authorities in exhorting them to adopt our own 'Environmental Charter for Local Government'. That gauntlet has been seized on with considerable determination since then, and enormous progress has been made by literally dozens of local authorities in developing their own charters and initiatives.

In that respect, they no longer depend on that kind of external pressure to take the first steps down the road towards a local version of Agenda 21. The logic of sustainable development is starting to create its own momentum at the local level, and there are millions of people in the UK today whose lives will be the richer and the better for it.

Jonathon Porritt
March 1994

Note on contributors

Julian Agyeman is a consultant in environmental education and policy and was previously Environmental Education Advisor to the London Boroughs of Islington and Lambeth. He has published and broadcast widely on environmental issues and has written a publicity guide for the Central/Local Government Environment Forum.

John Carr is Director of Promotion and Passenger Facilities for Metro (the West Yorkshire Passenger Transport Executive). He has wide experience of public transport, transport planning and local government. As transportation policy advisor to the Association of Metropolitan Authorities he has been closely involved with responding to recent transport legislation, with environmental issues and with promoting better bus services.

Jeff Cooper is the Waste Reduction and Planning Officer for the London Waste Regulation Authority, and is responsible for the production of the waste disposal plan for Greater London. He has worked for the Greater London Council and as a lecturer in resource science at Kingston University. He chairs the Local Authority Recycling Advisory Committee and the Council of Management of Waste Watch.

Dr Bob Evans lectures in the School of Land Management and Urban Policy, South Bank University. He has worked as a town planner in the public, private and voluntary sectors and is author of *Experts and Environmental Planning* (Avebury 1994). He is co-Director of the Centre for Local Environmental Policies and Strategies at South Bank.

Dr Paul Fleming is Energy Manager for Leicester City Council and energy advisor to the Association of District Councils. He is a Chartered Engineer with extensive experience of local authority energy efficiency, policy development and implementation.

Albert Golding is General Manager (Policy and Strategy) of the London Borough of Tower Hamlets and has specific responsibility for strategic policy, including regeneration and environmental issues and a Director of Bethnal Green City Challenge Company. He has over twenty years experience of planning, environmental and strategic policy development covering some of the most significant development and environmental programmes in London in recent years.

Professor David Goode has 25 years experience as an ecologist working with central and local government. Since 1982 he has played a key role in bringing an ecological dimension to the planning and management of open spaces in London as Director of the London Ecology Unit. Recent work has included policy development for strategic planning, new approaches to the design of urban green space and implementation of Local Agenda 21. Professor Goode is President-elect of the Institute of Ecology and Environmental Management, and President of the Trust for Urban Ecology. He is Environmental Advisor to the Association of Metropolitan Authorities.

Tony Hams is currently Environmental Advisor to the Local Government Management Board where he is co-ordinating the Local Agenda 21 UK Initiative. He is also responsible for developing post-Rio activities for UK local government both in this country, in Europe and at the United Nations Sustainable Development Commission. He was responsible for drawing up UK local government input to the Earth Summit and was a member of the UK delegation to Rio and the CSD.

Denise Hill is a planner who has worked in local government and has taught in England and overseas. She directs the MSc programme in Environmental Impact Assessment at Brighton University and is a member of the University's Earth and Environmental Sciences Research Unit. Her research and lecturing interests are in the field of environmental management.

Helmut Lusser is Assistant Chief Planner with the London Borough of Sutton. He is actively involved in a wide range of national environmental working groups contributing to many new initiatives, including the EcoManagement and Audit scheme for local government and the Sustainable Indicators project. He is a Council Member of the Town and Country Planning Association and a member of their Sustainable Development Working Group.

Anne Simpson is Joint Managing Director of Pensions & Investment Research Consultants Ltd, which provides investment advice, research and co-ordination of shareholder activity on issues of corporate responsibility for local authority pension funds with assets over £15 billion. Among other publications she is the author of 'Greening Local Investment' (*Economist* 1991) and is a Fellow of the Royal Society.

Trevor Smith is Assistant Director of Environmental Services at Brighton Council. He is Head of the Development and Support Group and Lead Professional Planner. Between 1990 and 1992, as Assistant Chief Executive, he engineered the major re-orientation of the Council's Services including the development of an environmental service and the Council's corporate environmental agenda. He has extensive experience as a practising planner.

Dr Philip Webber is head of Kirklees District Council's Environment Unit and has co-ordinated the Authority's environmental work since 1990. He worked on the LGMB's *Environmental Practice in Local Government* and *A Framework for Local Sustainability*. He contributes to various national environmental policy working parties including the AMA Environment Forum and the Local Authority Sustainability Indicators project.

1 The new environmental agenda

Julian Agyeman and Bob Evans

During the last few years, 'the environment' has developed into one of the most important policy areas for local government. Moreover, policy and legislative agreements currently pending will ensure that local environmental policy will rapidly expand as a central arena of action for British and European local authorities. The agreement to Agenda 21 at the Rio Conference; the implementation of the EU's Fifth Environmental Action Programme; the requirements of the 1990 Environmental Protection Act; the UK Government's National Sustainability Strategy — these and other developments will all place substantial obligations and responsibilities for environmental policy and action upon British local authorities. It is these agreements and initiatives which are at the heart of what is coming to be known as 'the new environmental agenda'. Central to this new agenda is local action, policy, and practice.

Local environmental policy is thus beginning to emerge in Britain as a discrete area of public policy which is distinctive in many ways. Firstly, in contrast with some other areas of local policy, such as housing or economic development, environmental policy development has been substantially driven in the UK by the stimulus of European and international agreements. It has been these agreements, and the policy message that they embody, which has been the driving force behind UK environmental policy at the national level, rather than the autonomous initiative of British governments.

Paradoxically, the environmental policy development that has occurred in Britain has been substantially due to the local initiatives taken by pressure groups such as the Friends of the Earth, and by local authorities. Drawing upon their wealth of experience in a variety of policy areas, including local economic development, land use planning and environmental protection, local authorities have initiated and experimented in a number of creative and innovative ways, to the extent that they can collectively be described as constituting the greatest repository of environmental knowledge and experience currently existing in Britain. Together with local and national pressure groups, they have set the pace in local environmental policy development during recent years as the extensive examples cited in the recent Local Government Management Board's Environmental Practice in Local Government clearly demonstrate (LGMB *et al.* 1992c).

It is important to note, however, that most of these initiatives are not simply a consequence of statutory responsibilities and obligations set by central government. Rather they represent a deeply held belief amongst councillors, officers and members of community organisations that to 'think globally, act locally' is a fundamental tenet of environmentalism. Thus, in Britain at least, environmental policy is distinctive in that much of it has arisen principally from local initiative and international agreement. To date, the role of central government in this arena has been minimal.

The second distinguishing element of environmental policy, at any level of government, is the implicit commitment to the notion of sustainability. This is clearly a contested and sometimes imprecise concept, and we discuss this in more detail below. However, the significance of sustainability is that it represents a substantial, and potentially unitary and unifying policy objective, based upon an increasingly commonly held view that: 'sustainable development is development that meets the needs of the present without compromising the ability of future generations to meet their own needs' (World Commission on Environment and Development 1987, p. 49).

As a policy objective, sustainability is, by definition, long term and all-embracing. In contrast, many other areas of public policy are by implication transitional and specific. The policy objective of sustainability has the potential to provide a robust and theoretically vigorous set of principles to guide and inform action. As we argue below, this cannot mean that all shades of political opinion will uncritically adopt identical policies for sustainability. Nevertheless, the necessary link between sustainability as a set of ideas, theories and prescriptions, and the process of environmental policy making and implementation distinguishes this area of policy in an important and enduring manner.

Finally, and unlike most of the more traditional areas of local policy, environmental policy requires a more integrative and holistic approach if it is to be effective. It is obvious that 'the environment' cannot be compartmentalised for the purposes of policy development and implementation. Questions of waste disposal, pollution or energy usage for example, require policy makers to think imaginatively across traditional departmental and professional boundaries, and in many local authorities this is now happening.

As we show below, the 'new environmental agenda' is demanding that local authorities adopt new structures — the reorganisation of departments for example — and new policy instruments — such as the publication of environmental action plans and programmes, and state of the environment reports. However, the complexity and diversity of this new agenda, linked with a changing economic and political climate, is also compelling local policy makers, politicians and activists to think and act in more creative and original ways, actively encouraging the involvement of agencies and individuals from the community and the private sector in initiatives to secure policy objectives. The very breadth of the environmental agenda is likely to ensure that the processes of local environmental policy making and implementation will extend much more widely than has hitherto been the case.

'Environment' as a concept

'Environment' is a continuum, a system which permeates all aspects of our lives. The continuum is huge, ranging from the microscopic scale of the sub-cellular environment of living organisms, to the cosmic scale environment of space. Along this environmental continuum, humans have developed, and continue to develop an increasing influence. The scale at which local environmental policy becomes operative, that is, where local authorities and others have an influence, is correspondingly large, ranging from the prevention and spread of diseases within the sub-cellular environment of humans (and other organisms) to the regulation of atmospheric emissions and pollutants.

Consequently, the scope of local environmental policy, which has, since Victorian times, been developed to improve the quality of peoples' lives, must be broad enough to encompass this range. Interpretations of the scale and scope of environmental policy are only now being clarified through developing ideas and practice. Alongside these developing ideas and practices, is the growing realisation that reductionist attitudes which split the environment into its constituent parts, are in part responsible for some of our present problems. It is only through a vision of the environment as a whole that we can begin to assess, evaluate and modify the negative distributional effects of our actions and redirect them towards sustainable environmental management.

One small example may suffice to illustrate the problems inherent in the administrative division of environmental responsibility. In 1987, in a London borough which was probably typical of most, the upkeep of trees was split, according to whose land the trees were on. If they were on school land they were the responsibility of the Inner London Education Authority; trees in parks were the responsibility of the amenities department; streetside trees were the responsibility of the civil engineering and public services department; trees on private land were the responsibility of the planning department, and if the trees were on a housing estate, they were the responsibility of the housing department.

In October 1987, the Great Storm blew holes through this particular authority's reductionist environmental policy. Trees fell everywhere, including one which fell from a street, through a garden and into the park beyond. Who was responsible for its removal?

The environment is in a greater or lesser mess precisely because policy makers have split it up into chunks, to be allocated to different committees, quangos and companies with different ideas, attitudes and agendas. This has, thankfully, within local authorities, begun to change as ideas about environmental policy making and management have been infused by more holistic ideas from, amongst others, environmental pressure groups such as Friends of the Earth, who have carefully manipulated public opinion towards greater care, sensitivity and awareness.

The local authority and the environment

It was not until the mid-1980s that historically discrete local authority policy areas, such as planning and development, environmental health and consumer protection, parks and leisure, housing, and highways and transportation began to converge under the corporate banner of 'environment', and the increasingly powerful 'environment committee'. There are, however, in the development of the local authority environment committee, two important caveats which need to be noted:

- Local authorities are at an early stage in developing 'environ-ment' as a corporate concept, and environment committee remits, in terms of their coverage of policy areas, vary between authorities. However, with increasing legislation and awareness of the interconnectedness of environmental services and issues, committee remits are growing.
- The influence of the environment committee varies between local authorities and, in terms of other committees' policy areas, influence is a key word. For example, environment committees may develop policy on the use of tropical hardwoods, CFCs or on energy efficiency, which will influence policy and purchasing decisions by the housing committee, but will not affect the decision to build (if it were possible). In short, most environment committees are primarily regulators rather than providers.

Once local authorities developed environment committees or, in some cases before, they began to recruit 'environmental co-ordinators', officers whose role it was to convene 'environmental co-ordination groups' or 'green teams'. These are meetings of officers and members from different departments who have a remit to co-ordinate environmental matters across the authority. This co-ordination has generally been of two types:

1) internal co-ordination of environmental statements, charters, policies and strategies;
2) external co-ordination of information to the community and schools.

By the mid-1980s, and without any statutory reason for doing so, authorities had begun to develop key documents which aimed to encapsulate their rapidly developing environmental policy frameworks into more comprehensive strategies. These 'environmental strategies' were broadly based statements of priority, principle and intent. Starting off as internal documents, subject to ratification by the environmental co-ordination group of officers and members, and then by the environment committee, they were often long, complex and relatively meaningless to the public.

With increasing public interest in the environment, especially so after Mrs Thatcher's 'green' speech at the Royal Society of Arts in September 1988, it became obvious that external co-ordination of information was needed. This took the form of environmental 'charters' or 'statements'— a distillation of the environmental strategy. One of the earliest was that of the London Borough of Sutton, who, in 1986, produced an environmental statement in the form of the alphabet, with each letter corresponding to an area of environmental policy and action.

The community information role of environmental co-ordinators frequently, and increasingly involved functions, such as 'green fairs', 'environment weeks' and school projects. Not only did these events create a window, through which the public could see what the authority was doing as regards the local environment, they also created an opportunity for publicity in the local media (Agyeman and Tuxworth 1994).

By the late 1980s, most authorities were endeavouring to be seen to be green, whether they actually were or not. As part of this growing environmentalism, many authorities began to set up community fora, often called an 'environment forum', whereby the views of interested individuals, pressure groups and amenity societies could be fed into the policy process via the environment committee or its satellites.

Increasingly during the 1980s, it became obvious that if authorities were serious about improving their environmental performance, they needed baseline data against which they could monitor and evaluate positive and negative change and propose improvements where necessary. In order to have an accurate measure of their environmental impacts in terms of both the impacts of their policies and practices (Policy Impact Assessment/PIA or Internal Audit/IA), and the state of the local environment (State of the Environment report or SoE), 'environmental auditing' was used. The earliest local authority environmental audit was carried out collaboratively by Friends of the Earth and Kirklees Metropolitan Council in 1989.

It is important to note that a major influence in local govern-ment and its interest in becoming more environmentally sensitive, was brought about by a pressure group, Friends of the Earth. Their publication *The Environmental Charter for Local Government* in 1988 defined auditing and acted as a guide to good practice, and many authorities 'adopted' the charter, often encouraged, advised and supported by local FoE groups in their area (FoE 1988).

Co-ordination and the local authority associations

Whilst co-ordination of environmental matters at the individual local authority level were taking place through environmental co-ordinators, developments were also occurring at the level of the local authority associations. Keen to channel this range of environmental initiatives, the Association of Metropolitan Authorities (AMA) appointed an environmental policy officer in 1989. The Association of County Councils (ACC) and Association of District Councils (ADC), and later, the Local Government Management Board (LGMB—formerly the Local Government Training Board LGTB) followed suit. Once in post, the officers began to develop position statements: *Action for the Future: Priorities for the Environment* (AMA 1989) and more recently *The AMA and the Environment* (AMA 1993); *County Councils and the Environment* (ACC 1990); *Pollution: Controlling the Problems* (ADC 1990) and *The Environmental Role of Local Government* (LGTB 1989) which in turn, further informed policy development.

The Associations also co-ordinated conferences on the environment for members and interested officers, the first being co-ordinated by the AMA in 1989 in Newcastle upon Tyne, 'Caring for the Future'. Since then, environmental co-ordinators' conferences have provided an opportunity to discuss and share ideas and try to maintain a common direction.

Another significant milestone in the development of environmental awareness amongst local authorities was the publication, in 1990, of *Environmental Practice in Local Government* (LGMB *et al.* 1990) by the local authority associations, and funded by the Corporation of London. It was published in response to the government's White Paper on the Environment, *This Common Inheritance* (DOE 1990). This guide to local environmental practice consists of case studies and covers many environmental service areas ranging from energy conservation to education. It impressed many people, both inside and outside local government, including the then Secretary of State for the Environment, Michael Heseltine.

The second edition of the guide, published in 1992, with funding from the Corporation of London, the Department of the Environment and the European Commission (DGXI), built on the successes of its predecessor and had a broader coverage, with more case studies.

It is interesting to note that the Department of the Environment was keen to be associated (financially and therefore also editorially) with the second edition of the guide, reflecting the impression that the first edition had made at a senior level within the Department. Indeed the guide seemed to open eyes within a Government not generally noted for its support of local authorities, to the extent of local authorities' non-statutory environmental endeavour, creativity and inventiveness.

By the early 1990s, environmental co-ordination with regard to local authorities occurred at three levels:

- the environmental co-ordinator (or same) in an authority;
- the co-ordinator in the local authority associations;
- the Central/Local Government Environment Forum

The latter forum was set up to exchange environmental information and to attempt to co-ordinate environmental messages (in the case of the publicity working group) or to develop policy and practice in relation to, for example, the trialling and implementation of the EC 'Eco Management and Audit Regulation' and BS 7750.

The 1990s, as far as environmental policy making and co-ordination at the local authority level are concerned, we have seen a refinement of the earlier 'let's be seen to be green' days. It is no longer acceptable to pass off a thin and insincere green veneer as total commitment. The public are increasingly sophisticated (and this will increase markedly when the present junior school population reaches adulthood), so are the issues and so are the management tools for dealing with them.

The emergence of the 'new environmental agenda' has brought with it a new vocabulary and a set of fresh principles, attitudes, theories and values. Within the general 'concern for the environment' there is, of course, a wide range of political opinions and positions. Moreover, as local environmental policy takes on an increasingly substantial profile, new challenges and problems are presented to the local agencies involved in policy formulation and implementation.

We feel that it is possible to broadly describe the main themes and problems of the contemporary environmental debate under three main headings. Firstly there is sustainability, a contested concept which is potentially far more radical than many suppose, and which is inevitably destined to be *the* core policy objective. Secondly, there are the issues of democratisation, equity and involvement which we have headed up under the somewhat ill-defined concept of subsidiarity. And finally, we look at strategy — the political and managerial processes which are directed towards the achievement of a sustainable society, looking particularly at the processes as they relate to local environmental policy.

Sustainability

Since the publication of the Brundtland Report (World Commission on Environment and Development 1987), the concept of sustainability has become pivotal to the development of environmental policy at local, national and international levels. It has become both an organising concept for policy development, and a political rallying cry for the environmentally conscious. However, as academics, politicians and policy makers regularly point out, sustainability is difficult to define. More importantly perhaps, sustainability is paradoxically both a contested concept and, at the same time, one which can be seen to span the divisions between different economic and political interests. Nevertheless, the centrality of this notion demands that all those who are concerned with environmental policy actively address the contradictions and conflicts inherent within it.

As Jacobs and Stott (1992) rightly point out, the two terms 'sustainable development' and 'sustainability' tend to be used interchangeably, whereas in fact they represent two distinct approaches:

> Sustainable development is not simply about the environment. The concept of 'development' also incorporates other indicators of human welfare; incomes (and their distribution), employment, health, housing, perhaps crime levels and so on. Sustainable development is therefore a more rounded policy goal than 'economic growth'. Certainly its concern with social as well as environmental factors means that it cannot be reduced (as some have supposed) to mere 'green growth' (Jacobs and Stott 1992, p. 262).

Conversely, 'sustainability' implies a much stronger commitment to the environment above other factors, principally economic growth.

> An economy is sustainable when it can be sustained; that is when the environmental capacities on which it depends are maintained into the future. . . . A sustainable economy is a *constrained* economy (Jacobs and Stott 1992, p. 263).

This distinction between an environmentally 'weak' sustainable development and an environmentally 'strong' sustainability is one which reflects the divisions which have existed throughout the development of environmental politics. On one level this may be seen simply as a question of degree. An individual (or a government) may support certain environmental measures and policies — the recycling of paper and glass or the improvement of facilities for cyclists for example — whilst still accepting the need for economic growth even if this may impose some longer term environmental costs. This is usually referred to as a 'light green', 'conservationist' or 'environmentalist' position.

Environmentalism is 'a concern for the environment' which is largely based upon a belief in the capacity of humankind to develop a managerial approach to environmental problems, without the need to make any fundamental changes in life-styles or patterns of production and consumption. It is an implicit assumption of environmentalist perspectives that protection of the environment is based in self interest. Pollution must be controlled, whales saved and glass recycled, because not to do so will damage our health, limit our capacity to enjoy our surroundings or unnecessarily exhaust our supply of raw materials.

This contrasts with the 'dark green' or 'deep ecology' position which Dobson terms 'ecologism' and which describes an altogether more radical position.

> Ecologism makes the Earth as physical object the very foundation-stone of its intellectual edifice, arguing that its finitude is the basic reason why infinite population and economic growth are impossible and why, consequently, profound changes in our social and economic behaviour need to take place (Dobson 1990, p. 15).

Ecologism represents a set of beliefs which are in the main oppositional to existing values and assumptions and which insist upon a radical re-ordering of the relationships which exist between humankind and the environment. Inevitably associated with this re-ordering, it is argued, will be a fundamental restructuring of existing social, economic and political relationships.

These two perspectives represent positions on the boundaries of the current environmental debate, and clearly there is a range of opinion between the two. However, this does serve to emphasise that despite the fact that sustainability is a contested concept, it has, as Murdoch points out, the ability to span the divisions between environmentalists and a wide range of economic and political interests who may not have immediately obvious environmental concerns. It is the very ambiguity of the term which makes it attractive, so that 'while sustainability is a concept with the potential to build a bridge between environmentalism and development, it may also serve as a convenient "cover" allowing traditional practices to continue' (Murdoch 1993).

As an illustration of the wide interpretations which may be placed upon sustainability, Jacobs (1991) remarks on how the British Government's official published response to the Brundtland Report claimed that British economic policy in 1988 already conformed to Brundtland's demand for sustainable development. Widespread agreement with this position is not evident at present. Moreover, the Government's recently published *UK Strategy for Sustainable Development* (HMSO, 1994) whilst implying support for sustainable development, offers a bland and non-committal response.

There are three further issues which require consideration. Firstly, it is important to clarify the links between growth and sustainability. It has been frequently asserted that there is a causal link between economic growth and the despoilation of the environment, and therefore the principle objective of green political action should be the achievement of 'zero growth'. However, as Jacobs (1991) and others have pointed out, there is no necessary correlation between economic growth, understood as annual increases in Gross National Product, and the increased consumption of natural resources or increased levels of environmental degradation. Although it may be correct to argue that *current* patterns of economic growth are causing environmental problems, it is also perfectly possible to envisage a situation where different patterns of production and consumption continue to stimulate economic growth but with a substantially reduced environmental impact.

Secondly, it is important to recognise that virtually all interpretations of sustainability incorporate or at least imply some element of *equity*. At the international level, for example, Agenda 21 is 'profoundly democratic and egalitarian in its outlook' (Levett 1993). This document not only emphasises the need to adopt policies and strategies which meet the needs of disadvantaged groups, but it also stresses the importance of encouraging such groups (women, youth, indigenous peoples) to participate in decision making and the implementation of policy.

Jacobs argues this point forcefully, pointing out that if sustainability is collectively agreed and enforced, it may actually win wider approval than if it is expected to rely on individual choice and action. Moreover, the 'free rider' problem means that many individuals will not be prepared to change their own lifestyle for the sake of the environment unless they know that everyone else is doing so as well. 'In this sense' concludes Jacobs, 'democracy is fundamental to sustainability' (Jacobs 1991, p. 128). We return to this theme below when we discuss subsidiarity.

Finally, sustainability has both a global and a local dimension, and these two are, it is argued, inextricably linked. The belief in the need to 'think globally, act locally' (a phrase originally coined by the Friends of the Earth) has been central to the development of environmental politics, and has increasingly been enshrined in much contemporary environmental policy. Although there must be reservations as to the extent to which national governments are prepared to countenance the widespread devolution of power, it is nevertheless the case that both of the current major environmental policy programmes of Agenda 21 and the EU's Fifth Environmental Action Plan depend heavily upon action by local authorities and other local organisations to secure implementation of policy goals.

This commitment to local action is in part a reflection of the long term green belief that sustainability may only be secured through local action, which for many has meant the development of some kind of communitarian or alternative community lifestyle, often based upon a rejection of individualism, capitalism, industrialism and the perceived environmental consequences of these. However, although such initiatives have demonstrated the viability of many green practices and policies, for example recycling or the development of alternative sources of energy, in the current political and policy climate, 'acting locally' increasingly refers to local authority action, and the process of increasing citizen involvement, perhaps through some notion of 'active citizenship' or through some kind of local 'capacity building'. Both of these notions are examined later.

Most writers on sustainability, for example, Jacobs (1991) and Mellor (1992), quite rightly argue that sustainability should be sought at as small a scale as possible, and as we have indicated above, this is also the general thrust of European and international policy. However, what is local sustainability, and given the differing views on the nature of sustainability discussed above, how can local policy makers interpret this concept? One solution which has been mooted is to identify what is *not* sustainable, rather than what is (Williams 1993), but it is difficult to see why this might be easier to specify.

One major difficulty for UK local authorities is that there is as yet little guidance and co-ordination emerging from the national government. Local authorities are being forced to take the initiative and to establish their own definitions of sustainability. Where central government guidance does exist, it is often contradicted by practice. Ruff (1993) for example has detailed how one local planning authority was prevented by the Department of the Environment from incorporating sustainable policies in a local plan, on the basis that such policies contravened the 'presumption in favour of development'. This was in spite of the fact that the most recent government guidance on the subject, Planning Guidance Note 12 (DOE 1992a) specifically requires local authorities to incorporate policies for sustainability in new local plan documents.

Nevertheless, as the chapters in this book clearly demonstrate, local authorities are currently the leading actors and agencies in environmental policy and practice in Britain, and in the absence of clear guidance from Westminster, they are in effect building UK local environmental policy from the bottom up. Inevitably, most of these initiatives fall into the category of environmentalism or 'weak' sustainability. Despite the fact that many local authority officers and members might wish to press for stronger action, as the examples in this book indicate, the constraints are often still substantial. Nevertheless, as Geddes (1993) points out, the need is for local authorities and local public service providers to emphasise their role as leading actors and models of good practice, and not simply to act as regulators of, or enablers for, the private sector.

It is often claimed that sustainability is difficult to define, and therefore, by implication impossible to achieve. Such claims imply that clarity of definition must precede action, but much intellectual effort could be devoted to the inevitably fruitless task of striving for one, unifying, precise definition of sustainability. Instead, sustainability should perhaps be regarded as an organising and guiding principle in decision making which may alter in character, degree or emphasis as time and circumstances change.

The principles embodied within the oft-quoted (and disputed) Brundtland definition are clear and enduring, representing a call to this generation to act as stewards of the environment on behalf of future generations, and although it is necessary to recognise the salience of definitional clarity, it is equally important to understand that an over concern with the definition of sustainability may result in environmental paralysis. Sustainability should be an organising and guiding principle rather than a definitional obstacle.

Subsidiarity

Subsidiarity is a concept of the early 1990s which has become prominent firstly as a consequence of the European Community's negotiations over the Maastricht Treaty, and secondly because it is increasingly becoming enshrined as a political goal to be achieved in tandem with sustainability. For example, as Helmut Lusser makes clear in Chapter 7, the Town and Country Planning Association is currently making the case for a new form of environmental planning which they argue must be linked with subsidiarity, defined as 'taking decisions at the lowest level compatible with attaining required objectives' (Blowers 1993, p. 16).

Subsidiarity may therefore be interpreted as a programme for devolving decision making down to the most 'appropriate' level, whether this be national government, regional or local government or non-governmental agencies. This is the interpretation incorporated in the EU's Fifth Action Programme *Towards Sustainability* (Commission of the European Communities 1992a) and might be termed the 'institutional' view of subsidiarity. However, there is also a more 'qualitative' and more political interpretation which views the drive to subsidiarity as a necessary and desirable process which will provide greater democratisation.

The difference between these two interpretations is a matter of emphasis, but, as we have noted earlier, the connections between sustainability, democratic processes and, implicitly, some notion of equity, form the essence of the new environmental agenda. Whether it is identified as subsidiarity, decentralisation, empowerment or participation, some component of democratisation is widely viewed as being integral to the achievement of an environmentally sustainable future. There are, however, a number of intertwined concepts here which require clarification, not least because although they appear to be similar in their character and objectives, there are often quite different underlying political agendas.

During recent years, central government has been increasingly concerned with the idea of **empowerment** as a way of enabling citizens to take greater responsibility for their lives and localities, and this concept has formed a substantial element of recent initiatives in the field of urban regeneration, notably the City Challenge programme. However, as Golding points out in Chapter 6, the achievement of a measure of empowerment of local communities requires substantial levels of political investment and organisational restructuring, and it is not clear that the Government's rhetoric is matched by a commitment to the implementation of policies for extensive democratisation of decision making in the field of, for example, local services.

While there have been some initiatives in certain policy areas — the changes in the arrangements for the constitution of the governing bodies of state schools for example — the general trend in government during the last decade has been to centralise rather than localise political power. Attempts to 'open up' government or to make it more accountable to the public have resulted in initiatives like the much-vaunted Citizens' Charter which in general have tended to have a high public profile, but a negligible impact in terms of increasing public accountability. Moreover, these initiatives cast the individual as a 'consumer' rather than as a 'citizen'. The former is, of course, a much more restrictive, and politically less powerful role.

A longer term component of government policy has been the commitment to establishing **partnership** arrangements to make and implement policy. These have been established most frequently in the field of urban policy and have usually referred to partnership agreements made between the public sector institutions and private sector companies. However, more recently, and specifically in the case of the City Challenge programme, partnership arrangements have been extended to include the 'local community'. It is still too early to tell whether these arrangements will result in delivering benefits and greater political control over policy to the residents of these areas, but past experiences suggest that this will not occur easily (Deakin and Edwards 1993).

If subsidiarity has an institutional form at the local level it is manifested in the drive to the greater **decentralisation** of control of local services. Several local authorities have sought to pursue democratisation and accountability through a restructuring of their administration and services, and in some cases of their political arrangements. Perhaps the best known initiative is that undertaken by Tower Hamlets Council in London's East End, described by Golding in Chapter 6. The breaking down of existing, large scale local government into smaller, more responsive 'parish' sized units of government has occurred before in Britain, though in most cases it has involved either voluntary, non-statutory neighbourhood councils, or town or parish councils with comparatively limited responsibilities and resources. The introduction of decentralised smaller scale neighbourhood local government offers the possibility of developing local environmental initiatives in tandem with the development of the principle of subsidiarity.

The belief that there should be some degree of public **participation** in decision making became popular in British local government in the 1960s and 1970s, in large part stimulated by the publication of the Skeffington Report (1969). However, it soon became clear that, in most cases, the citizens who chose to respond to invitations to participate in decision making and policy formulation, for example in matters of land use planning or road construction, were usually the articulate and educated middle classes, now sometimes described as the 'service class'. Moreover, such invitations, although often referred to as participation, more usually involved some form of consultation, a rather less positive level of involvement (Boaden *et al.* 1982)

Many writers, such as Pateman (1970) have argued that political participation is to be encouraged because it develops a stable society in which people feel they have a 'stake'. However, participation as described above and practised in Britain has tended to encourage the participation of those who are already 'stakeholders' in society, whilst doing little to empower other hitherto excluded groups. For these reasons, and given the wide-ranging and integrated nature of contemporary environmental issues, there seems little doubt that single issue participation programmes will not satisfy those who argue for subsidiarity and democratisation as necessary components of the drive to sustainability.

The final concept to be considered in this review of subsidiarity and democratisation is the notion of **capacity building** which has a particularly prominent place within Agenda 21 in that it is identified as a 'means of implementation' in most of the programme areas. Capacity building, like most of the concepts outlined above is open to interpretation. At its most basic it implies developing the capacity of people and organisations to help themselves and to undertake and implement policies which will contribute to sustainable development. The approach implicitly rejects the assumption that governments can and should exclusively provide services, facilities and resources, instead maintaining that long term, effective policy for sustainability can only be secured if there is widespread mobilisation of people, their energy and assets.

However, as Levett (1993) points out in his review of Agenda 21, the process of capacity building may be as important as the outcomes that it generates. 'It [capacity building] is as much concerned with enabling people and organisations to make the necessary changes as with the changes themselves' (p. 5).

All of this underscores Jacobs' view quoted above that 'democracy is fundamental to sustainability', and whilst he is probably correct, it also has to be recognised that at present, public opinion in countries like Britain is still substantially distanced from many of the positions, values and attitudes that are taken as common currency by those actively involved in environmental politics. Greater democratisation and public involvement in policy making will therefore need to be associated with substantial programmes of public environmental education, awareness and information, if policy is to progress beyond minimalist 'environmentalist' initiatives.

Moreover, although it may be splendid to support greater equity as an integral part of a sustainable society, it is quite clear that groups possessing political and economic power are unlikely to surrender this on the basis of some kind of naive environmental altruism. In this sense, environmental politics can be as reflective of social and economic inequalities as any other politics, and are potentially as radical and as threatening to the existing social order as any variety of traditional political radicalism.

Strategy

So far we have focused upon some of the ideas which underpin and inform environmental politics, but what of the process of policy making and implementation? In particular, how can local authorities and other local organisations interpret the often imprecise agreements of Agenda 21 or *Towards Sustainability*, and what mechanisms and arrangements are likely to be needed to implement them?

We have already noted that the environment cannot be compartmentalised, and that environmental policy must reflect this reality. This axiom therefore demands that new forms of organisation and new approaches to decision making and policy formulation must be established if local environmental policy is to be effective. As Lusser and Webber argue later in this book, policy processes need to be both *holistic* and *integrative* in order to reflect the cross cutting complexity of the new environmental agenda. In particular this must mean that the traditional local authority division of labour into professional departments, with the associated processes of compartmentalised decision making, has a limited lifespan.

These changes are currently occurring as some local authorities have begun to respond to the new environmental agenda. However, it is interesting to note that a somewhat similar form of organisation is beginning to emerge in some authorities as a consequence of the processes of 'market testing' and compulsory competitive tendering. These requirements of central government tend to encourage the formation of a more centralised form of local authority administration and decision making as the work of peripheral departments becomes a potential candidate for some kind of privatisation. Power and policy making is likely to become centralised in these circumstances as policy makers and administrators move towards a model of contract management.

As the authors of the chapters in this book frequently point out, the new environmental agenda demands new ways of working. Not only is there a need for local authorities to develop cohesive and integrative environmental programmes, plans and strategies, as many are currently doing, but also there is a need to abandon many of the old divisions of labour and professional and departmental boundaries which do not necessarily conveniently correspond to contemporary environmental problems and policies.

It is equally important to recognise that new agendas require new skills, and it is becoming apparent that these are being rapidly developed within local authorities, government and pressure groups. The fusion of the skills of policy making, formulation and analysis with an understanding of the traditional scientific knowledge bases of, for example, physics, biology, or chemistry is increasingly a necessary part of environmental policy making.

This does not mean, however, that there is a need for a new 'environmental' profession with the attendant diplomas, degrees and professional accreditation (although these are already developing) (Evans 1993). This would not obviously improve the quality of environmental decision making or policy advice. Rather, this fusion of skills is a reflection of the diverse and cross-cutting nature of environmental problems, and of the resulting policy prescriptions which are needed to address them. There is no one professional knowledge or skill which can legitimately claim superiority or exclusivity in the environmental arena. On the contrary, environmental strategies are likely to continue to demand the application of a whole range of skills, attitudes, talents and competencies.

Thus, to emphasise the point which we made at the beginning of this chapter, the environment represents a policy area which is qualitatively different. Nevertheless, the environmental policy *process*, of policy formulation, implementation and monitoring is currently not dissimilar to most other areas of governmental activity at central and local levels, in that most decision making and policy formulation is of the 'top down' variety. But, as we have already demonstrated, some component of democratic involvement in the policy process is integral to virtually every serious environmental perspective, and it is this element which has yet to become part of many local environmental strategies.

It is quite clear that, to be anything like effective, environmental policy will inevitably involve policies and decisions which will threaten current lifestyles, for example by restricting mobility and car usage, or by reducing levels of consumption and consumer choice. Such decisions (and these are mild 'environmentalist' examples) would presumably be taken on the basis of securing the future of the planet and protecting the interests of unborn generations. This raises the difficult issue that sustainability is potentially an inherently undemocratic principle, in that it is likely to generate policies which run counter to the immediate short term objective interests of the populations of both developed and underdeveloped societies.

Thus, there is a substantial potential conflict to be addressed as part of the process of environmental policy making. On the one hand there is a commitment to wider public involvement whilst on the other, it seems likely that comparatively few people in a country such as Britain will actively support policies which will reduce their perceived living standards or limit their immediate choices. It also seems probable that it would be possible for individuals to object to such policies whilst at the same time declaring support for an, albeit vague, 'green' agenda.

Given this potential conflict, the argument for a comprehensive programme of what has been termed 'community environmental education'(CEE), as an integral part of a local environmental strategy, is a powerful one. This has been called 'Education for Sustainability' (ES) by the United Nations Environment Programme (UK) (UNEP-UK 1992). There is a clear need to accompany environmental policies with an explanation of why such policies are necessary and indeed desirable. Clearly, this is a major task which will need to involve schools and other educational establishments (Toyne 1992), but is also likely to extend to youth organisations, pensioners' groups, adult education (NIACE 1993) and other voluntary and workplace organisations. The general point is that increased citizen participation will need to go hand-in-hand with CEE/ES if environmental strategies are to have any chance of long term and widespread acceptance.

A programme of CEE/ES is unlikely to become a statutory obligation for local authorities in the immediate future, and, as with so many environmental programmes, implementation is only likely to occur if authorities decide to voluntarily exceed their statutory duties.

Before leaving this discussion of strategy it is necessary to comment on the monitoring of programmes. Whilst it is to be expected that most attention will be focused on the future – new policies and initiatives and the means for their implementation, it is equally important, as Reade (1987) has so clearly argued, to be 'backward looking'. The continual evaluation of past policy decisions in terms of their effectiveness is obviously crucial, and it is in part a concern with this which has prompted the contemporary debate on 'sustainability indicators'. There is a need to have mechanisms which will assist in policy evaluation in terms of whether or not agreed programmes are contributing towards the elusive goal of sustainability. Monitoring, with all its attendant difficulties and complexities (Walker and Bayliss 1993) should be regarded as an integral part of the policy process, rather than an 'add-on' accessory.

The chapters

The following chapters of this book, we believe, make a substantial contribution to the development of local aspects of the new environmental agenda which we have sought to introduce in this first chapter. All the chapters draw upon current policy and practice, and emphasise how local authorities and environmental pressure groups have been at the forefront of environmental policy making and development during the last decade. They have set the pace in Britain by far exceeding their statutory obligations. Moreover, despite the declared intention of governments to define the role of local authorities as 'enablers' or 'regulators', the experiences recounted in this book demonstrate their real capacities as innovators and instigators of good environmental practice.

Each of the chapters deals with a different aspect of local environmental policy and strategy, but all focus upon the central issue of sustainability and its achievement at the local level. Within this key theme of sustainability there are four 'contributory' themes which recur throughout the book. Each of these linked themes is a facet of the overall policy goal of sustainability, in the sense that they are all integral to, and essential for, its achievement. We define these contributory themes as community environmental education; democratisation; 'balanced partnership'; and integrated/holistic policy making.

We cannot understate the importance of our first theme, community environmental education or education for sustainability. The involvement of people in what O'Brien (1993) has called 'the environmental culture', will require continuous action at all levels of government to improve not only the quantity and scope of environmental information, but also its quality and access to it. Tony Hams notes that this is a prerequisite for the improvement of policies and practices, whilst Helmut Lusser argues that consumer behaviour and attitudes will need to change through a process of community environmental education if environmental planning is to be effective. In a similar vein, Paul Fleming identifies increased awareness amongst the public and local authorities as the key to achieving greater energy efficiency.

We have already discussed our second contributory theme of democratisation in some detail earlier. However, its importance is clear, and this has been recognised by virtually all of the chapter authors. Albert Golding for example, shows how the processes of decentralisation can serve to achieve a measure of subsidiarity by bringing decision making and administration down to the level of the neighbourhood, whilst at the same time investing the notion of 'empowerment' with some substance. Philip Webber also emphasises empowerment, but he argues that this should properly apply both to local government and to 'ordinary people' if environmental policy is to be productive. Anne Simpson, in her discussion of green finance similarly illustrates how democratisation can permeate financial policy, through her discussion of the concept of the active shareholder.

We have chosen to call our third theme balanced partnership, and by this we mean the partnerships which will have to be established at the local level if environmental policy is to reflect local needs and aspirations, and if it is to be effectively delivered. We have emphasised 'balanced' partnership in order to distinguish this from the more usual kind of one-sided partnership which has tended to favour more influential or powerful interests. Local environmental organisations; citizens; the private sector; local government; educational establishments — these and other groups and agencies will need to combine and co-operate in effective partnership if the programmes and agendas outlined in this book are to have any substantial chance of success. For example, John Carr in his discussion of transport policy emphasises this point. He argues that if transport is to become more sustainable, a new partnership is required between national and local government and between public and private authorities.

Our final theme is that of integrated and holistic policy making, which we have identified as an essential process in our discussion above. All of the chapter authors concur with this view, and the arguments for new ways of working within local authorities and for strategies which reflect the multi-levelled and interdependent nature of environmental problems recur throughout the book. Denise Hill and Trevor Smith explore these issues within the particular requirements and constraints of the Eco-Management and Audit regulations and BS7750, whilst several authors, for example Lusser, Hams and Webber argue that holistic and integrative policy approaches are the only way forward. The significance of these issues can be seen in the chapters by David Goode and Jeff Cooper. Goode calls for far greater links between the different professionals concerned in the process of ecological planning, whilst Cooper demonstrates how waste disposal and reduction policy must be viewed in the context of policy for integrated waste management.

In our view, these four 'contributory themes' are integral to the organising and guiding principle of sustainability, and in our final chapter we take the opportunity to reflect on the importance of these themes as part of local environmental policy into the next millennium.

2 Local environmental policies and strategies after Rio

Tony Hams

The 1992 United Nations Conference on Environment and Development (UNCED) was a significant stepping stone in the slow move towards sustainability, not only for national governments but, as we shall see, for all major groups and particularly for local government. However it is important to look back a few years before those days of heat and hype in Rio de Janiero and to consider what UK local authorities had achieved before Rio, and what had influenced them in making their considerable progress.

The green years — the late 1980s and onwards

For many years local authorities in the UK had been carrying out environmental duties, solving environmental problems and creating innovative environmental solutions perhaps without realising the corporate context within which they could work. The environmental health officer was dealing with air pollution, the planning officer with structure and land use planning, the countryside sections were beavering away at habitat protection, the engineers, surveyors or technical services departments struggling to find holes in the ground for the ever increasing volumes of domestic waste. In most cases these separate activities were not seen as 'environmental' as we have come to understand the term, but as the normal day to day activities of a local authority.

In 1988 The Friends of the Earth released their *Environmental*

Charter for Local Government (FOE 1988). This had a far reaching effect on many local authorities. Whilst some had started to realise that environmental issues actually permeated further than the planning and environmental health departments into purchasing, grounds maintenance, education and even into the hallowed sanctuaries of the transport or surveyors department, many had their eyes opened for the first time to the fact that environment was a corporate issue in every sense. The Charter, like most seminal documents, had its faults and in some quarters it was dismissed as too far-reaching, but it did spawn a large number of charters and similar corporate statements — again of varying quality.

Alongside the development of the Charter, FOE had been encouraging Kirklees Metropolitan Council to produce the country's first State of the Environment Report (Kirklees MC/FOE 1989). Again this was a significant turning point in local authority approaches to environmental issues. State of the Environment Reporting has now become part and parcel of a forward looking local authority's work programme. From the sophistication of Lancashire County Council's approach (Lancashire CC 1992a) to the 'smaller' scale but exciting work being done in Mendip Borough Council for example (Mendip BC 1993).

Also in 1989 the Association of Metropolitan Authorities (AMA) organised 'Action for the Environment' in Newcastle, which was the first major environmental conference for local authorities. There was a real feeling then that the environment had arrived on the local authority scene. There was talk of environmental auditing being corporate, but the issues have progressed considerably since then. As a direct result of the Newcastle conference the AMA appointed its first environmental policy officer who was charged with developing corporate environmental advice to metropolitan authorities and with putting the message across to government that local authorities had a fundamental role to play as the local arm of environmental protection and enhancement. At a time when the government were making early noises about a National Environmental Protection Agency (EPA), the AMA coined the notion of a Local Environment Protection Agency (LEPA) — local authorities in partnership with government being allowed to deliver real solutions at a local level.

Around the same time as the message of corporate approaches to local authority environmental activity began to gather momentum, the first wave of local authority environmental co-ordinators were being appointed. Some were new posts — Stockport and

Kirklees were among the first — while other officers had the new environment portfolio lumped onto their existing duties. Very quickly we became used to seeing environmental co-ordinator posts being advertised in the Friday Guardian and a new brand of local authority officer was born. Now a network of some four hundred people exists — many of whom are still called environmental co-ordinators, but all are carrying out the co-ordinating environmental role in local authorities. Three national conferences specifically for the co-ordinators have been held and from lowly beginnings the network is beginning to bear fruit.

1990 saw the Government's first Environment White Paper, *This Common Inheritance* (DOE 1990) and local government's first Guide to Environmental Practice (LGMB *et al.* 1990). In developing the White Paper, Chris Patten the Secretary of State for the Environment invited local government to contribute a chapter on good practice in local government. Reacting positively to the invitation, the local authority associations in England and Wales decided that they would not produce something solely for government but would develop a guide which would be written and owned by local government. The White Paper was published in September 1990 and the Guide in December 1990. The White Paper in its very short section on local government recognised the importance of local authorities in environmental protection and enhancement, but the Guide put a considerable amount of flesh onto the bones of the White Paper as far as the world of local authority activity was concerned. Not only was the Guide a success in that it had the Local Authority Associations speaking with one environmental voice for the first time — something which the DoE thought would be difficult to achieve — but it also presented solid arrangements for a corporate approach to local authority environment activity.

A small number of the one hundred or so case studies were perhaps not 'best practice' (and Friends of the Earth told the world about this in no uncertain terms), but it was the first compilation of case studies which showed the world what local authorities could and should do as local environment protection agencies, and as such it was hailed as an important stepping stone. The second edition of the Guide (LGMB *et al.* 1992c) was published in October 1992 and exemplified good environmental practice in local authorities successfully.

Specific criteria were prepared against which the case studies were assessed and new sections on emerging issues were included — like environment strategies, management systems and purchasing, whilst the crucially important chapter on environmental education was expanded to include public information and awareness.

An indication of the growing awareness of local government's role in achieving environmental goals both nationally and locally was that the Department of the Environment and the European Commission (DGXI) made significant contributions to the preparation of the second edition of the Guide while the relevant Secretary(s) of State for the Environment were pleased to launch both editions.

Local and central government as partners

As part of the White Paper process the Department of the Environment set up three fora. The Central and Local Government Environment Forum (CLGEF) first met towards the end of 1989. Similar fora were established for the business and voluntary sectors. The CLGEF has met on average twice a year since then and whilst the interface between ministers and the many and varied leaders of the local authority associations has not always proved to be as productive as might have been hoped for, the work produced by the sub-groups of the Forum has been extremely useful.

The most important outputs have included a common agreement between DoE and the Associations to encourage government and local authorities to reduce energy use in their buildings and day-to-day activity by 15 per cent over a three year period. This exhortation came from a working group on energy which is now to be reformed to look at CO_2 reduction programmes in the UK.

Perhaps the most significant of the working groups has been the one set up to consider the EC Ecoaudit Regulation. This subject will be covered in detail in the later chapters but it is worth mentioning here as it represents an innovative venture both in output and process.

As mentioned above, local authorities have for some years been getting to grips with aspects of internal and external auditing. By examining their own performance and measuring results it is easier to record progress across a whole range of local authority environmental activity. In response to numerous requests from individual local authorities, The Local Government Management Board called together a dozen or so key local authority officers in 1991 to advise consultants in the production of a *Guide to Environmental Auditing for Local Authorities*. This publication together with the excellent chapters on auditing in the Environmental Practice Guides, written by Derek Taylor of Lancashire County Council, rapidly became the prime source of advice for environmental auditing activity for UK local authorities. The Department of the Environment and Friends of the Earth were involved in the preparation of the guidance and Michael Heseltine, the Secretary of State for the Environment, was prevailed upon to launch it.

In so doing, he formally invited central and local government to carry out further work on the subject and particularly to examine how the emerging EC Regulation on Ecoaudit — later to be named Eco Management and Audit — might be adopted for use by local authorities. The significance of this was not so much that this very important piece of EC legislation might be used to create a framework for local authority environmental management systems, but that here was government inviting local government to be equal partners with them in the process. The DoE and the LGMB provided the joint funding while DoE provided all the secretariat and back-up services. The DoE and the Local Authority Associations have recently agreed the final Guidance which was officially launched by the Minister for the Environment on 14 October 1993.

The Forum sub-group on publicity was set up to see how the environmental message could be more easily spread into day-to-day local authority activity. A forum newsletter has been produced and a good practice guide on publicity to build on the public information chapter of the second edition of the Environmental Practice Guide is being prepared. The forum sub-group on the Local Government Charter was not such a successful process. Although the Charter has now been published by DoE, it received only grudging acceptance by the Local Authority Associations.

All in all, the Forum has proved to be extremely successful but it has two main drawbacks:

1. Although it is called the central and local government environment forum it is serviced by and attended by the Ministers for the Environment. Only on one fleeting occasion was the Department of Transport represented and on no occasion have the Local Authority Associations been able to discuss environmental issues with the Department of Trade and Industry, MAFF, the Department for Education, and in any meaningful way with the Energy Efficiency Office or the Department of Transport.

2. The three fora described above meet with the DoE
    separately. Only on one informal occasion have the
    business, voluntary and local authority sectors met together
    with the DoE. As we shall see later there is now world-wide
    recognition that cross sectoral participation is essential if the
    concept of sustainability is to gain any credence. This is a
    main message of the Local Agenda 21 process.

The buildup to UNCED

To understand the effectiveness of of the 1992 UNCED Conference
in Rio (often referred to as the 'Earth Summit'), it is necessary
to look at the process which led to it. The 1972 Stockholm
Conference and the Brundtland Report (World Commission on
Environment and Development 1987) introduced the concept of
sustainability to a wary public. The Rio Conference considered the
twin concepts of environment and development for the first time
and it brought together not just governments, but representatives
of thousands of non-governmental organisations and sectoral
interests, including what became known as the 'major groups' —
local government, business and industries, women, youth, trade
unions, indigenous peoples and so on. As it turned out, it was this
process of networking and integration which was as important as
the main outputs from the conference.

Before Rio, the international local authority organisations co-
ordinated action to produce a Common Declaration (IULA *et al.*
1992a) on behalf of world-wide local government which committed
itself to:

- promote the implementation by cities, metropolitan and
  local authorities, of measures needed to alleviate the
  impact of economic development on the environment and
  guarantee the protection of natural areas and the harmony
  of the urban setting; these should include measures to
  rationalise the use of natural resources and energy consumption, in particular through the control of production
  and storage of waste, on-site treatment of all pollution
  generated by urban activity and, more generally, the use
  of renewable resources;
- implement, in co-operation with their member authorities
  through action programmes, the recommendations which
  will be made by UNCED, as an essential complement to
  commitments which will be made by governments;

- develop, jointly with their member authorities, decentralised co-operation as an instrument of international policy for the environment, to show solidarity among local authorities and to enable them to take their rightful place in the action being undertaken through the United Nations.

It went on to recommend that:

- national governments recognise formally the autonomy of cities, metropolitan and local authorities so that they may acquire the powers and obtain the resources to implement sustainable development strategies in their areas and to take part in international co-operation agreements;
- support be given to international co-operation networks between local authorities to strengthen partnerships promoting the exchange of environmental expertise and solutions developed in the cities and countries in the southern as well as the northern hemisphere;
- machinery be established in the United Nations to involve representatives of the international associations of cities and local authorities to ensure that these principles, projects and actions are followed up.

In the week immediately before UNCED the leaders of world-wide local government met in Curitiba, Brazil to endorse the Common Declaration and produce further principles. These principles were embodied in the Curitiba Commitment (IULA *et al*. 1992b) which stated that local authorities should:

- as a first step, work to extend basic services to all citizens without additional environmental degradation;
- progressively increase energy efficiency;
- waste the minimum and economise the maximum;
- combat social and gender inequality and poverty;
- integrate environmental planning and economic development;
- increase involvement of all sectors of the community in environmental management;
- mobilise resources to increase co-operation among local authorities.

To fulfil the above commitments to sustainable development it was agreed that each local authority should develop an action plan — a Local Agenda 21 — which includes targets and timetables and incorporates measures such as the following:

- establish a community consultation process that brings together representatives of community organisations, industry and business, professional associations and trade unions, educational and cultural institutions, the media and government to create partnerships for sustainable development;
- set up an inter-departmental committee within the municipal government to co-ordinate planning, policy and development activities so that those activities result in environmentally sound land use, transportation, energy, construction, waste, and water management practices;
- perform regular environmental audits involving all sectors of the community and develop data banks on local environmental conditions;
- review and improve the collection of all existing fees, fines, and taxes collected by the municipality to (a) support sustainable behaviours and discourage non-sustainable activities, (b) charge the full environmental costs of a particular activity, and (c) increase revenues available for investment in local sustainable development projects;
- develop procurement guidelines that result in the purchasing of products and materials which are environmentally friendly;
- establish a sustainable development curriculum to be taught in schools or other institutions under municipal jurisdiction;
- create a forum for the further education of municipal and community leaders about environmental and sustainable development issues;
- join and participate in regional and international networks of local authorities to increase information sharing and technical assistance among municipalities; and to press national governments to support and fund their environment and development goals.

In the UK the build up to Rio for local government was orchestrated by the local authority associations and the LGMB. *A Statement to UNCED* (LGMB 1992a) was prepared, which attempted to set a framework for achieving sustainability at the local level. The statement set a challenge to the earth's peoples to secure the quality of life for future generations by:

- respecting environmental absolutes;
- recognising the need to develop within the carrying capacity of the planet;
- responding holistically to a multi-levelled problem;

- acknowledging the high risks arising from incomplete understanding of ecological processes;
- erring on the side of caution where there is doubt.

It discussed the goal of sustainable development that meets the needs of the present without compromising the ability of future generations to meet their own needs and pointed out that this is a necessity if life on this planet is to survive. To protect the planet's ability to support life, while enhancing the quality of that life, we must limit both our consumption of resources and our waste production to a level within the earth's carrying capacity. Industrialised countries will have to alter their way of living which has led to the current environmental crisis. A new partnership between north and south to ensure equitable and efficient distribution of limited resources is required.

Governments must recognise that undirected market forces alone cannot achieve the necessary changes but must be guided by government intervention to promote the conditions within which sustainability can be achieved. It is essential that all levels of government must be involved in partnership in this process.

In meeting the challenge of sustainable development the principle of subsidiarity must be followed, that is, the principle that policy formulation, decision making and administration should be carried out at the lowest or most local level possible.

As the elected governments of their communities and as significant resource users and employers, local authorities are the essential partners of national governments, non-governmental organisations and international institutions in implementing sustainable development in cities, towns, villages and rural areas.

Local government is the level of elected government closest to the citizen. This local democratic mandate enables local authorities to inform, mobilise and speak on behalf of their communities. They have direct powers and responsibilities in planning and land use, environmental health, highways and transport, waste disposal, housing, education, social services, leisure and recreation and economic development. They can use these powers both to enforce and to encourage good environmental practice.

The Statement also emphasised the potential of local government in applying the principle of subsidiarity which rests upon the following essential characteristics:

- closeness to the issue;
- a capacity for learning;
- local choice and local voice;

- local differences, local diversity, local innovation;
- the basis for citizen participation;
- an understanding of local interactions and impacts;
- the starting point for actions leading to sustainable development within the community;
- the ability to set conditions for local action;
- a partner for global action across districts, regions and countries and a key player in the local economy.

Outputs from Rio

The main outputs from Rio were:

- A convention on climate change.
- A convention on biodiversity.
- A statement on desertification.
- A statement on forest principles.
- The Rio Declaration.
- Agenda 21.

Agenda 21 is generally recognised as the most important document to come from Rio. It was signed by all attending governments and contains over 40 chapters and, depending on which version you read, runs to 500 or 700 pages. It is a tortuous and verbose document but several plain language versions are now available – the best one has been written by Michael Keating and published by the Centre for our Common Future (Keating 1993). The LGMB has also produced a guide to Agenda 21 specifically for local authorities in the UK (Levett 1993).

It has been suggested on many occasions that over two-thirds of Agenda 21 cannot be delivered without the commitment and involvement of local authorities and the communities they serve. One can argue about the figures but the message that local authorities are key players in delivering sustainability is plain and is now being recognised by the newly created Sustainable Development Commission (CSD).

It is all the more surprising therefore to recall that two years ago it looked as though there was not going to be a slot for local government at Rio. The concept of Local Agenda 21 did not exist and in the first three UNCED preparatory committees no recognition had been given to the role that cities, urban areas and local authorities should play in delivering the UNCED message. Before the 4th Preparatory Committee in New York in March/April 1992, Jeb Brugmann, the Secretary General of the International Council for Local Environmental

Initiatives (ICLEI), acting on behalf of the major international local government organisations, succeeded not only in persuading Maurice Strong and the UNCED Secretariat that there should be a separate section on local authorities in Agenda 21, but also that he should write it. Chapter 28 of Agenda 21 was therefore born and survived unscathed through the remainder of the UNCED process.

Local Agenda 21

By now the language of Chapter 28 as it relates to local government will be familiar. Essentially it recognises the vital role that local authorities play in educating, mobilising and responding to the public to promote sustainable development. It also encourages local authorities to establish comprehensive action strategies for sustainable development within a set timescale.

ICLEI, the international driving force behind Local Agenda 21, has suggested four basic elements:

- Firstly, a self-sustaining community consultation process which will ensure that all sectors are fully involved with and remain informed about plans and strategies. Ideally this should not be the 'normal' top down process whereby a local authority informs the community what it is going to do, but more of a bottom up community led initiative which allows all sectors and disciplines to define problems, develop solutions and implement strategies in a comprehensive manner. Consultation should also ensure that the action plan reflects the priorities of residents and local institutions, and in so doing gains their support.
- Secondly, sustainable development auditing — methods which allow more participants to assist local authorities in auditing current conditions. This base line information can be used to measure changes in conditions over time and to assess the success of actions taken.
- Thirdly, target setting — this is a crucial part of the Local Agenda 21 process. The agreement of short and long term targets by all sectors should be the backbone of any strategic action plan and provide the community, not just the local authority, with measures of whether it is reaching its goals.
- Finally, and perhaps the most interesting element, to develop and use indicators of sustainable development which should be clear, meaningful and achievable.

Based on these four elements ICLEI is inviting authorities from all over the world to participate in a model programme. It is seeking to work directly with 21 authorities to assist in the design and implementation of their campaigns.

Of course many local authorities are already engaged in some of these elements. Many are carrying out audits of their local environment, some have developed targets to measure their performance, a few have even started to look at local indicators. Many more might have entered into some form of consultation process with their local communities as part of the structure planning, local planning or UDP processes, but very few authorities are engaged with these four elements in a co-ordinated way. Very few have really involved all sectors of the community in preparing strategies and action plans which are based on sound principles of sustainable development. Even those authorities which are regarded as so-called leaders are surprising themselves by their non-performance when they compare their very sound environmental policies with where they spend and invest their money.

In the UK, the local authority associations, including the Council of Scottish Local Authorities (COSLA) and the Association of Local Authorities in Northern Ireland (ALANI), have recognised the importance of this part of the UNCED follow-up. In November 1992 at the Local Government and the Earth Summit Conference, Councillor John Harman, speaking on behalf of UK local government, launched the initiative in the UK and gave notice that from April 1993 the Associations will be actively involved in promoting the initiative, advising authorities on the basic elements of the campaign and carrying out a number of specific tasks to seek to achieve the objectives of Agenda 21 (LGMB 1992b)

Consequently the UK local authority associations, including COSLA and ALANI, have entrusted the task of advising UK local authorities on the implementation of Local Agenda 21 to The Local Government Management Board, under the direction of a Local Agenda 21 Steering Group. A Local Agenda 21 Project Officer was appointed at the end of April 1993. The Local Government International Bureau is also closely involved in the Steering Group's work. Chaired by Cllr John Harman, Vice Chair of the AMA and Leader of Kirklees Metropolitan Council, the Steering Group has high level representation from all the local authority associations, including colleagues from Scotland and Northern Ireland.

Given the emphasis that Agenda 21 places upon partnership in achieving sustainable development, the Steering Group has issued invitations to other organisations to participate as equal partners in the group and to join in the Local Agenda 21 work as follows:

- the Confederation of British Industry;
- the Advisory Committee for Business and the Environment;
- the Royal Society for Nature Conservation;
- the United Nations Environment and Development United Kingdom Committee;
- the National Council for Voluntary Organisations;
- the Committee of Vice Chancellors and Principals;
- the Council for Environmental Education.

Further places have been allocated to the TUC and to a national women's organisation.

The Steering Group's work programme for 1993/4 includes the following components:

- producing a summary of Agenda 21 which draws out the main implications for UK local government referred to above;
- developing indicators of sustainable development which can be built into existing local authority auditing and planning processes, and used by local communities to assess the state of the local environment;
- organising a series of round tables to look at particular aspects of sustainable development and to formulate simple, practical guidelines for all UK local authorities;
- collaborating with government on the input to the first national sustainable development strategy, and producing a statement on behalf of UK local government;
- further work on environmental auditing and environmental management;
- producing further publications on examples of good practice (continuing the work in the first two editions of the Guide to Environmental Practice in Local Government);
- studying the tensions between the economic development and environmental functions of local authorities;
- organising a number of awareness-raising conferences/ seminars for local authorities;
- developing training programmes for local authority staff, including the production of a video on sustainable development issues and how staff members acting individually, and corporately within a local authority, can help effect change.

On the international scene:

- promoting UK local authority participation in European and international environmental partnerships and networks;
- providing assistance with training and consultancy in Africa;
- providing encouragement and support for the Local Agenda 21 process in selected African countries.

In the improved spirit of partnership between central and local government on environmental matters, the DoE has publicly aired its support for the Local Agenda 21 initiative and has offered funding for some of the work outlined above.

As a result of Rio, the Government has prepared its first report to the Sustainable Development Commission. This is the Government's first strategy for sustainable development and builds on its earlier work, taking on board some new ideas generated by the Earth Summit. In particular, it looks further forward than the previous White Papers to the year 2012 — 20 years beyond the UNCED. The Government hopes that the strategy will provide an opportunity to involve all sectors of society in considering what sustainable development means for the UK. It is aimed at stimulating decision makers in the public and private sectors as well as individuals, to adopt a sustainable approach throughout all their activities.

Local government's response

UK local government reacted positively to the Government's intention to prepare a national Sustainable Development Strategy, and as part of the consultation process, produced an Initial Statement (CAG 1993) and a Declaration on Sustainable Development (LGMB 1993). The Initial Statement endorsed both the Brundtland Commission's definition of sustainable development cited in the previous chapter, and that of 'Caring for the Earth', the report of the World Conservation Union, UN Environment Programme and the World Wide Fund for Nature where sustainability is defined as:

> Improving the quality of life while living within the carrying capacity of supporting ecosystems (WWF *et al.* 1991).

The Initial Statement linked these two definitions with the concepts of quality of life and equity. Sustainable development is not the same thing as sustainable economic growth. The concept of 'quality of life' recognises that standards of living cannot be measured by purely economic indicators or delivered by a simple quantitative growth in income. Factors such as the quality of the environment and the overall health of the population — which are in themselves closely linked — must also be considered. Quality of life is difficult to measure, and its components will not always be agreed. But this demands further work on attempting to measure it and to gain consensus, rather than claiming that income growth is therefore the sole or best measure of development.

The importance of equity in sustainable development is widely recognised in relation to the developing countries of the south. However, questions of social equity and the distribution of both the benefits and the costs of development are intimately and inextricably bound up with the environmental aspects of sustainability in industrialised countries such as Britain too (Agyeman 1993).

As Agenda 21 argues, it will only be possible to reduce environmental impacts if poorer and other disadvantaged groups are given greater access to resources and to decision making, with both benefits and burdens shared more equally. In particular, as shown both in the developing world and in (say) energy consumption in Britain, poverty often forces people into unsustainable behaviour.

Sustainable development means more than just giving certain environmental factors more weight in decision making. It means accepting that there are limits to the capacity of the environment to support human activities. Beyond a certain point, natural systems such as the earth's atmosphere which provide the basis for human and other life begin to deteriorate. The life-support functions provided by the atmosphere cannot be 'substituted' by human-made technologies. Sustainable development involves a recognition that society has to live within these absolute limits.

Exactly where the environmental limits or 'thresholds' lie is still a matter of uncertainty, but this does not mean that such limits do not exist. Rather, it implies that we need to understand the biosphere better, and, more importantly, that we should act on the precautionary principle by which there is a presumption against actions whose environmental impact is uncertain.

Sustainable development therefore means that for certain activities with particular environmental impacts, the decision making process cannot involve, as it has done in the past, a process of 'trading off' costs and benefits. The costs of certain activities, in terms of environmental integrity and the effect on future generations, are simply too great. Society must impose constraints on its activities and find ways of living within these.

The Initial Statement builds on the Curitiba Commitment by implying that sustainable development means:

- consumption of natural resources, including energy, should be reduced;
- where possible, renewable resources should be substituted for non-renewable resources;
- fewer wastes should be produced;
- wastes should be re-used or recycled where possible;
- wastes which are produced should be assimilable by the environment with as little pollution as possible;
- biodiversity should be preserved and where possible enhanced;
- valuable natural and physical assets and other amenities should be preserved and managed for their long term protection.

These points lead to two basic principles of sustainable development policy making:

- activities and policies which are leading in the opposite directions should be stopped; and
- whenever possible, new activities and policies should be designed and implemented so that they lead in the same direction.

The Initial Statement defines the requirements of policy making for sustainable development and discusses principles and tools which are now central to future activity by local government and other sectors:

Partnership: Agenda 21 emphasises the need for all groups in society to be involved in the debate about and implementation of sustainable development. This requires public education and awareness raising; a round table approach, involving all sectors, to the design of targets, policies and instruments; and a participative approach to implementation which seeks to mobilise the skills and commitment of the community. These are the guiding principles of local government's Local Agenda 21 initiative.

Policy integration: Sustainable development requires that government policies are integrated between departments and across sectors. The environment cannot be the concern simply of one department, with the effects on the environment of other policy areas treated as subsidiary. Environmental objectives must be adopted, and environmental effects assessed, in all fields of government activity. The machinery of government — and its relations with other sectors such as local government and industry — must be designed to achieve such integration.

Appropriate scale and the 'partnership of responsibility': Policy towards the environment is most effective when it is handled at the scale of government most relevant to the incidence of particular environmental issues. This may be international, national, regional or local. Many issues have different effects at different scales, and these should all be recognised, giving a 'partnership of responsibility' for policy making at all levels. If issues are not being dealt with at the appropriate scale of government, other scales have the right and the responsibility to take action themselves: what might be called the principle of 'residuarity'.

Freedom of information and open government: It is particularly important that people have the right to know about issues affecting their health and quality of life. They must also have the opportunity to participate in the processes which will shape these things. Local government has a tradition of openness and of providing public access to environmental information which should also be adopted by government and by industry.

The precautionary principle: Sustainable development is concerned with protecting the life support functions which the natural environment provides. Damage to these can have very serious effects on the quality of life on present and future generations, and may be difficult, impossible or very slow to reverse. Where there is uncertainty about potential environmental impacts, it can be far riskier to make optimistic assumptions than pessimistic ones.

Demand management: Sustainable development requires that society lives within the boundaries of the environment's carrying capacity. This means that there are limits to the extent to which growing demand for environmental goods and services can be accommodated. Managing demand means assessing a range of alternative approaches to achieving objectives in the policy design process.

Continuous environmental improvement: Policies for sustainable development will not be achieved immediately. Targets must be realistic if they are to be effective. To maintain the momentum of policy it is therefore important for targets to be progressively increased over time.

The polluter pays: Environmental damage should be paid for by those who cause it. The principle must be applied in such a way as to discourage environmentally damaging behaviour rather than simply to raise revenue from it. (It is therefore a mistake to believe that the polluter pays principle favours financial incentives as instruments.) Regulations also require the polluter to pay by changing behaviour, and may be more effective: the wealthy can often afford to ignore financial incentives while the poor can often not afford to respond to them.

UK local government has also adopted the following managerial tools to improve environmental policy making and implementation:

State of the environment reporting, sustainability indicators and resource accounting: Policy making for sustainable development requires sound baseline information about trends in key environmental indicators and the pressure on key environmental domains. Local government has been in the forefront of information collection through local 'state of the environment' reports, and there is a need for standardisation of environmental indicators and a national framework for information collection, both in coverage and updating. Allied to the standardisation of environmental indicators is the need to integrate these into economic indicators and models.

Strategic environmental assessment: Environmental assessment of individual development projects is now well established. It is now important that assessment is extended to plans, policies and programmes before development takes place. SEA must be undertaken as part of the policy design process and requires that a variety of policy options are assessed. Local government is beginning to apply the principles of SEA, it needs to become standard practice in all departments of Government.

Environmental management systems: Particularly among larger firms, management systems such as BS7750 and the Eco-Management and Audit Scheme (EMAS) are expected to have a significant impact on environmental performance. Although focused on manufacturing industry, they are also relevant to the service, commercial and distribution sectors. Particular assistance is required to encourage take-up of these systems, almost certainly in a simplified form, in smaller and medium-sized enterprises. They also need to be applied to government auditing. Local government has adapted EMAS for its own use, and this is discussed in Chapter 5.

Investment appraisal: Standard accounting practice, which discounts future costs and benefits, is often a barrier to the introduction of sustainable policies. Public bodies have an advantage over the private sector in being able to plan longer-term and to take into account benefits and costs to third parties. Local government is often prevented from using longer payback periods for investment through accounting rules imposed upon it. Some authorities are now experimenting with 'whole life costing' of physical assets such as buildings, to take into account the full range of costs, including maintenance, over the asset's life.

Environmental information, education and training: Raising awareness about environmental issues is a prerequisite for improvement of policies and practices in all sectors. Local government has done much to promote environmental education as a cross-curricular theme in schools, and to raise awareness in local communities. A further need is to introduce environmental components into vocational, professional and management training, so that awareness is spread throughout the private and public sectors. More widely, if sustainable development is to be understood, governments at all levels will need to stimulate a public debate on future scenarios of environmental change and the options therefore facing society.

The Sustainable Development Commission

To complete the UNCED picture, it is necessary to look at the objectives and potential of the Sustainable Development Commission (CSD) which held its first meeting at the United Nations in New York between 14 and 25 June 1993. At Rio, Chapter 28 of Agenda 21 contained a resolution to set up a high level Commission to carry forward Agenda 21 matters. Subsequently 53 members of the UN, including the UK, were elected to the CSD and ambassador Razali Ismail of Malaysia was elected its first Chair. Mr Nitin Desai of India is the new UN Under Secretary General in charge of the CSD Secretariat at the UN.

In the first session a work programme until 1997 was agreed; it considered guidelines for national reports, looked at how the UN system and donors can assist those reports and how sustainability might be integrated into the UN system. It also considered the transfer of environmentally sound technology, financial commitments and new structures for decision making both within the UN and for national governments. It also met again in May/June 1994 to consider the first stage of its work programme. Before then it held inter-sessional meetings on finance and technology transfer while individual countries hosted working groups on fresh water, sustainable economics and toxic chemicals.

In each year between 1994 and 1997 the CSD will consider reports from governments on poverty, consumption patterns, population, finance, education and capacity building. It will also look in detail at how major groups including local government will fit into new decision making structures. In 1994 it will also consider national reports on health, human settlements, fresh water, toxic chemicals and hazardous wastes; in 1995 reports on land, desertification, forests and biodiversity; in 1996 atmosphere, oceans and seas, while in 1997 there will be an overall review of progress by governments in implementing Agenda 21.

Although not as well prepared as they were for UNCED the international local government organisations were able to present a statement to the CSD which emphasises the willingness of local government to work closely with the CSD to implement Agenda 21. It stresses the tremendous policy and technical expertise which exists in local government worldwide. It reminds the CSD that all the major associations of local government are encouraging their members to carry out Local Agenda 21s. It states that national reports to the CSD should contain regular inputs from local government.

The International Union of Local Authorities (IULA) is taking the lead in persuading national governments to include representatives of local government on their national delegations. The opportunities for local government, other major groups and non-governmental organisations (NGOs) to participate in the CSD process were greater than at Rio or in the preceding UNCED Preparatory Committees. There was an acceptance of the crucial role that local government and major groups can play and although no formal mechanism is yet in place for major groups to report formally to the CSD other than via national governments, they are now able to make interventions, statements, and comments in the main plenary sessions and working groups.

It is interesting to note that at the close of the CSD, Ministers from 53 member countries each made firm commitments to its work. In particular they welcomed the active participation and input from the major NGOs and their undertaking to work in partnership with governments in furthering the sustainable development process. They recognised the sense of urgency for promoting sound sustainable development through concrete actions by governments and reconfirmed their commitment to global partnership between nations and with local, national and regional parties.

They realised that progress since Rio had been limited and that further political impetus should be given to the work of the CSD. Financial resources remain a major restraint particularly in the developing countries. They underlined the important role of local authorities in national report and strategy formulation.

New structures for sustainability

At Rio governments were asked to set up national co-ordinating structures to follow up Agenda 21. These structures could vary from country to country. Options include a national sustainable development commission as in France, or a national co-ordinating committee. The way in which local governments, NGOs and major groups are involved could also vary. The CSD emphasised the importance of these mechanisms and the inclusion of local authorities, the private sector, NGOs and other major groups.

The UK Government is currently considering how best to carry these recommendations forward. The DoE favours a national co-ordinating committee or round table which would monitor progress, and this recommendation is contained in the National Sustainability Strategy.

Clearly the CSD has opened up real opportunities for the voice of local government to be heard on a global stage, but it is locally that the improvements have to be made. Work on indicators and targets is on hand both locally and nationally. The process of creating policy with other sectors by the round table process is being explored and experimented with by both central and local government, and despite the continuous assault by national government on the fabric of local authorities there remains a strong commitment to Local Agenda 21 and the move towards local sustainability.

The Earth Summit gave hope to many but money to few. Of course only time will tell if those two short weeks in June 1992 were fundamental in affecting the future of our planet. In the immediate post-Rio phase there were some real feelings of optimism. Those feelings are now dulled as world governments divert their attentions to the traumas of the world's crises and we watch government after government, including our own, indicate cuts or potential cuts in overseas aid budgets.

It is depressing that the basic message that economic strength depends on sound environmental performance is not yet understood. Achieving healthy economies and healthy environments are complimentary not contradictory objectives. How often have we heard the argument that we can have a healthy environment, or we can have a strong economy but we cannot have both? We must realise that this is a false choice.

Europe and the Fifth Action Programme

Up to now few EC documents have mentioned local authorities. After Maastricht this has changed as local authorities are recognised as a tier of government. We can assume therefore that as far as the EU is concerned the role of local authorities in implementing legislation and initiatives will be more clearly defined in the future. The Fifth Action Programme or 'Towards Sustainability' (EC 1992) is one of the first programmes to adopt this approach. Not only are local authorities recognised as major actors but many of the initiatives can only be implemented by local authorities.

There are other reasons why local authorities may not have understood the relevance of the Programme. Firstly, there has been little involvement of local authorities by government in the implementation of the earlier environmental action programmes. Secondly the scale of the Programme may seem to extend beyond the general remit of local authorities in the UK. This is because the Programme is directed towards all local authorities within the EU, where powers vary.

Much of the Programme has yet to be developed in detail but local authorities and their staff have a vital role in advising the Commission on the best ways to implement the initiatives. The Programme will be given legal force as and when new Directives or Regulations are adopted.

Within the EU, the approach taken to the development of policy on the environment differs from all other policy areas. Since the environment was introduced as a key feature of the EC's work in 1973, successive action programmes have been produced. Up to now, these programmes have been little more than lists of proposed legislation. This approach has been very successful, with over 200 pieces of environmental legislation already in place and these have found their way into UK domestic law, for example, in the Environment Protection Act 1990. The influence of the EU's environmental programme within the UK has also been seen through the DoE's publication of *This Common Inheritance* in 1990 and the subsequent annual reports.

The EU's Fifth Action Programme on the Environment has been prepared in two parts. The first provides a review of the State of the European Environment. The second part of the Programme, 'Towards Sustainability' sets the objectives, policy and implementation programmes for the environment for the period 1993–2000. The Programme identifies where new initiatives or instruments are needed and who is responsible for their implementation.

The State of the Environment Report presents an overview of environmental and natural resources in the Union, of the damage and pressures to which they are exposed and observed trends. The EU recognises that the data on which the review is based is fragmentary and one of the key tasks in the Programme is to remedy this problem. The review of environmental conditions comprises detailed consideration of a variety of issues, e.g. air, water, soil, waste, quality of life, high risk activities, biological diversity.

The Fifth Action Programme is also based on the principles of subsidiarity and shared responsibility. This runs through all levels, from the citizen to the Commission. It also recognises the EU's international obligations. The Programme recognises the differences in government arrangements in each of the member states but clearly specifies target dates for action and indicates the responsibilities for local and regional authorities which include:

- spatial planning;
- economic development;
- infrastructure development;
- control of industrial pollution;
- waste management;
- transport;
- public information, education and training;
- internal auditing.

The Programme also indicates that it will be imperative for local authorities to have the necessary resources to implement their responsibilities.

The EU, through the Fifth Action Programme clearly identifies local authorities as one of the key actors in implementation. Member state governments have an important role but as in Rio, it is recognised that it is at the local level that many of the important environmental decisions are taken. Many of these decisions are routine in nature, yet cumulatively they have considerable effects.

'Towards Sustainability' will have a major influence on the development and delivery of the new environmental agenda in Europe for the next decade. It will:

- provide the framework for legislation;
- introduce new controls;
- escalate fiscal measures in support of the environment;
- promote transparency;
- implement the 'polluter pays' principle.

Local authorities are responsible for implementing 40 per cent of this Programme. It is therefore important that they understand it, advise Government and the EU of the most appropriate means of implementation and ensure that they play a full part in promoting a sustainable future in Europe. A Guide to the Fifth Action Programme for local authorities has been published by the LGMB (Morphet 1993).

Conclusions

Local authorities have been at the forefront of environmental policy and strategy making for nearly ten years. Today, with myriad policy influences, from Rio to Maastricht, authorities continue to develop original and innovative policy approaches in the quest for sustainability. They have worked in partnership with local communities, Friends of the Earth, Central Government and the private sector, and are now embarking upon perhaps their most challenging and original project: Local Agenda 21. The development of Local Agenda 21 will require not only that new consultative structures are developed in order that as many community views, ideas and attitudes as possible are incorporated, but also that new ways of working are developed by local authorities in order that their organisational structures are as accessible, accountable and flexible as possible.

3 Environmental strategies

Philip Webber

'Environment' is without doubt the organisational buzzword of the 1990s, and many local authorities have been striving to polish up, create or re-cast their environmental credibility. One way of doing this is to have or to publish an environmental strategy. There has been and continues to be, some debate over what exactly constitutes an environmental strategy. This is an important debate because of the plethora of statements and documents emanating from various local authorities including charters, action programmes or plans and numerous leaflets and pamphlets. The uncertainty as to what constitutes an environmental strategy is perhaps less important than the mushrooming growth in environmental actions by an increasingly wide range of authorities across the British Isles. Practice is also evolving very quickly. The seemingly radical expectations of yesteryear are often quickly adopted by a new breed of local authority worker across the land: the Environmental Co-ordinator. Because of the very fast development of environmental thinking amongst the new co-ordinators there is a very great need to translate some of the perhaps unrealistically high expectations to mainstream service responsibilities and actions in a local authority.

An environmental strategy may be defined as 'a set of broad environmental priorities and principles which act as a framework for action and activity, together with a description of the resources needed to implement it'. A description of the mechanism and processes by which such action is to be implemented is vital, otherwise there is a danger that the strategy will remain just another document. This is particularly important where an authority may have numerous strategies within one service area. A strategy document should strive to stay strategic and thus should be relatively short and succinct. Supporting the strategy document, if the authority in question is really serious about taking action, there needs to be a comprehensive management system to develop, review and implement the strategy. The BS 7750 model specification for Environmental Management Systems, discussed in Chapter 5, is a useful one to use as a checklist. There is no doubt that the scope of environmental problems is huge, and reflecting this, local authority environmental policies and action statements address a very wide range of environmental issues and problems.

The most detailed policy statement many authorities are likely to have is their environmental charter or their environmental action programme which may contain anything between 100 to 1000 specific recommendations for action covering every aspect of how the authority operates and functions. Local authority environmental strategies address both global and local issues from promoting sustainable development in the developing world, to litter patrols in local streets. Many strategies link local and global issues or span the two, showing the interconnectedness of environmental action.

Why is an environmental strategy necesary?

The purpose of an environmental strategy is to set priorities for action based upon an authority's judgments about what is most important, achievable or newsworthy. The environment strategy, by setting priorities and defining broad objectives should enable this huge task to be tackled in the most efficient way. Without a strategy, progress is likely to be piecemeal and progress difficult to monitor. A strategy framework also enables an authority to monitor progress in policy priority terms rather than in terms of how many recommendations out of, say, 170 have been met. This facilitates the development and implementation of a management system. A really comprehensive environmental strategy may only be felt to be absolutely essential for authorities who are sufficiently committed to have a corporate approach spanning the activities of all services in the council. In other authorities, well defined but more limited targets have been achieved by small groups or individual services working within an authority and making changes within their areas of influence.

As the need for environmental action becomes more talked about by government and business, and with the arrival of BS 7750, any authority without at least a token commitment to strategic environmental action will seem more and more out of date. For instance, in the case of competitive tendering, large contractors may insist upon checking the 'green credentials' of local authorities bidding for business, for example through their direct labour organisations.

The broader context

The national and international context to environmental action is increasingly important and, following UNCED, increasingly recognised at all levels of debate. The rhetoric expressed in Rio has yet however to be matched by action at national level. The European Union has also had something of an environmental renaissance by means of its Fifth Action Plan: 'Towards Sustainability' and the associated financial instrument LIFE (L'Instrument Financier pour l'Environment). Again, the buzzword is 'sustainability' which some have dubbed the civil servants' dream, able to mean all things to all people. (For example, in the EU one senior official at least, interprets sustainability as meaning sustainable jobs, that is jobs which last for five years or more.) An alarming range of projects are running throughout Europe and in many academic institutions where the 'S' word keeps coming up, some in an effort to justify funding, others seeking to define what it is, how to measure it and how it relates to issues such as quality of life, and equity.

The definition of sustainability, and the debate which surrounds it is clearly very important, but a definition is emerging which interprets sustainability, at least in part, as 'limiting the effect of human activities to within the carrying capacity of ecological/environmental systems'. This type of definition ties the concept of sustainability closely with continued human survival. For the political acceptance of sustainability, or to put it another way, for it to be implemented, issues of equity both within and between generations need to be considered which in turn imply large shifts in existing patterns of consumption and the adoption of much less damaging lifestyles. However, there is a danger in somehow equating quality of life issues with sustainability because increases in QOL simply led by unrestrained or loosely regulated market forces mean decreases in sustainability as consumption levels rise.

In the UK, as in most of Europe, and indeed the world, most, if not all environmental actions are very far from sustainable. It is notable that UK local authorities have taken substantial strides towards reducing local environmental impacts and thus towards the goal of sustainability well before the concept was clearly upon the agenda. More recently, central government has made major changes commencing with the annual publication of the White Paper on the environment followed by annual progress reports. This has now been followed up by the *UK Strategy for Sustainability* (HMSO, 1994).

Certainly 'much remains to be done' as government ministers are fond of saying. In the UK, to put it mildly, pro-active local authorities are frustrated by what seem to be unnecessary obstacles to progress. Whilst local government has fairly wide environmental powers most of these powers are not embodied in statute, nor are they funded by government grant. The powers that do exist are somewhat fragmentary and often subject to over-ruling by government inspectors or ministers (for example in the land-use planning area). Local government has no statutory general power of competence in the environmental field. In the specific area of strategies and management systems there is no legislation requiring local authorities to have overall environmental strategies or policies. Nevertheless, local authorities in the UK have been amongst the most active agencies of government in taking action to protect the local and global environment, a role which is recognised by government.

There is an emerging international consensus towards defining both the role of local government in environmental action and the key issues to be addressed in environmental strategies. Various environmental competitions have for some time now stressed the importance of the concept of sustainability as the unifying principle behind environmental strategies. The UNCED process towards the Earth Summit centred upon sustainability as the focus for a new mode of governing at local, regional, national and international level. One idea floated is for a new mode of government based on a recognition that a multi-levelled system of government is needed to match the multi-levelled ecosystems linking the global environment to the local environment. This, to some extent, may be code for 'subsidiarity' — taking decisions at the level nearest to those affected.

The multi-levelled management model of the environment carries with it the implication that central government needs to give to local authorities the recognition of role, resources and powers to do the job effectively. In their turn local authorities will need to accept responsibility, environmental audits and new ways of delivering services. It is hoped that this role for local authorities will be increasingly acknowledged and local authorities be formally accepted as the local agencies for environmental monitoring and management.

The government White Papers on the environment, and the annual reviews, have provided a useful mechanism. Most recently the Government has moved towards a UK Strategy for Sustainable Development and has sought input from many quarters through a process of wide consultation. This is to be welcomed as a way forward. Local government is lobbying for a wide range of changes mostly to enable or to formally recognise local government's role. It is to be hoped that central government will make the changes necessary to enable local government to nurture the environment properly, since central government needs local government to enable national sustainability targets to be met. For example, to meet national CO_2 targets, a programme of local government CHP (combined heat and power) installation could reduce electricity consumption dramatically. The plants would even pay for themselves. To be able to do it all, Government needs to make provision for the specific increases in Capital Programme plus relatively minor loans for revenue costs during the first few years of running.

Evolving practice

Examining a representative range of fifteen local authorities at the leading edge of environmental action and awareness, there is a general consensus that an important part of the document supporting an environmental strategy consists of a policy statement, sometimes called a charter, together with an action programme. In some cases the action programme or 'green action' is a list of actions ongoing or already undertaken. In others it is a proposed plan of action or an implementation strategy. Charters range in size from a document of one or two pages to documents containing up to 500 specific recommendations together with an indication of who is responsible for specific actions and by when they are to be achieved. In the larger documents it is often hard to discern a clear set of priorities for action, whilst in the shorter documents it is not possible to see how the objectives are to be met.

Many strategies, charters and policy statements are at a very early stage, many in the public consultation phase. Only in a few instances are authorities able to state what action has been taken to date and how the recommendations for action are to be revised. There is quite a high degree of consensus between authorities on the range of topics that are priority areas for action. Many have been identified in numerous reports.

Sustainability

A clearly emerging unifying theme is sustainable (or more sustainable) development and sustainability. Precisely what sustainability means in detail at local level is gradually being worked out, but the goal of sustainability implies severe limitations on the consumption of non-renewable resources (most resources at present, particularly energy) and limits in the production of waste (both air pollution and solid wastes) to levels within the earth's carrying capacity. The pollution and waste carrying capacity is the volume of pollution that can be absorbed and processed by the environment without irreversible or catastrophic damage. There are also different emphases emerging within the concept of sustainability which need to be differentiated, in particular, the sustainable use of natural resources, sustainable economic development, and sustainable land use.

Several local authorities now put one sort or other of sustainability as the overall goal of their whole strategy and try to define priorities closely related to working towards it. These are:

- energy conservation (including renewable energy generation);
- transport (encouraging public transport and transport choice);
- raising awareness/environmental education (working towards longer term changes of attitude);
- recycling (sometimes included with energy or waste);
- waste management (and waste minimisation);
- health for all/public health (sometimes including pollution monitoring);
- purchasing and contracts/green workplace;
- pollution management and monitoring (including water, air etc.).

An emerging issue which rather neatly ties all these together in a holistic environmental approach is the identification of sustainability indicators (for example open land per head of population, or energy/waste consumption/production per head) and the subsequent setting of target levels for each indicator, and the measuring of performance against these targets.

About four local authorities are now working on various aspects of this problem, with the intention of 'nailing down' the concept of sustainability at a local level and translating national and global targets into actions at local levels. This cannot be the sole province of local government because target levels for many activities and products need to be negotiated by all the relevant actors and responsibilities assigned to each sector. This process of negotiation should properly be the province of national sustainability plans.

There are also several other issues which are somewhat less frequently referred to:

- natural environment (sometimes specifically referring to major local problems);
- built environment;
- wildlife;
- archaeology;
- dogs;
- noise;
- water;
- air;
- Europe (grants available for environmental work etc.).

This is rather more of a 'traditional' list, with the exception of 'Europe' picking up on State of the Environment report type headers. Of all the latter list there is at least some consensus that dog mess and litter are not sustainability issues and that energy, transport, waste and raising awareness, from the former list are priority areas. Noise is an increasingly important issue in urban areas and rural areas near roads.

Defining objectives and targets

Within the topic areas identified for environmental action authorities need to define clear targets. Targets for action are needed to convert the broad objectives contained in a charter or policy statement into specific defined activities by identified people with specific responsibilities for action. This does not mean that those identified have to actually do the work, but they do need to make sure that it happens by a combination of means — facilitating, enabling, co-ordinating and by their own specific direct actions. Probably the most important issue is not the 'what?' but the 'how?'. To achieve change there is a great need for raising awareness to a point where local people start to set their own agendas and to take a proper partnership role with local government as one of the local key players.

Priorities or lists?

There is a tendency among current environmental charters and strategies simply to list a comprehensive array of proposed action. As a result, they can be misleading to the public, implying that an authority will do all that it would like to do, and unhelpful to those within the authority charged with pursuing the authority's environmental objectives.

Some prioritisation of programmes is necessary as given limited, and most likely diminishing resources, an authority will need to select the areas in which it will take direct action first. An authority needs to give highest priority to those programmes it is best placed to pursue. In this way, it will avoid duplication of effort and make best use of its own resources.

The setting of priorities should be a result of assessing specific actions against:

- how effectively they move the authority towards one or more of its objectives (such as greater sustainability);
- their profile — good media coverage increases morale and supports other longer term objectives;
- the achievability of actions in the shorter term — useful to show that actions are really happening;
- how they relate to the authority's overall environmental objectives (for example, priority might be attached to programmes which prevent undesirable changes, with long-lasting or perhaps difficult-to-reverse implications);
- synergism — how groups of actions together can achieve a greater impact than the sum of the parts;
- moving towards longer-term desirable changes in practice.

Means and resources

It is important for the success of a strategy that it is properly resourced and financed. A common element of all good authorities' practice is the creation of at least one post or an environment unit, to consider and facilitate environmental action. The more comprehensive or ambitious a local authority environmental strategy is the more people are needed to make it happen. The numbers of people needed — either as separate identifiable staff or as proportions of existing staff time should not be underestimated. Implementing, as opposed to just writing, an environmental strategy is a major commitment; the equivalent of at least 10 officers is likely to be necessary in a larger authority, particularly in services such as planning, environmental health, education or chief executives' departments. Such staff resources are very difficult to find as local authority services face increasing pressures upon service delivery across the full range of their activities. If staff are to effectively contribute part of their time to managing or monitoring or implementing an environmental strategy it is vital that some of their work tasks are taken on by others.

Turning to financial resources, many local environmental actions cost money — particularly for publications, publicity materials and landscaping of work in the built environment. Many areas of work are, however, of zero or minimal cost, for example changes to transport allowance schemes.

Many other actions can in the longer term save an authority appreciable amounts of money, for example installation of CHP plant or energy monitoring and saving. In the longer term all environmental work should save money in real terms. The problem is that many of the benefits, for example in reduced pollution levels, improved public health, sustainable economic development, reduced traffic, and reduced waste, will benefit other agencies in monetary terms rather than the local authority. Until or unless an economic framework exists which enables a local authority to benefit directly from their actions for the environment, an authority is faced with the choice of spending time and resources somewhat altruistically, of limiting actions to direct savings (such as energy savings) or of severely limiting the scope of its activities. In any case it is important that the implementation programme for a strategy clearly states what financial resources are allocated and tries to define the amount of staff time needed.

The corporate approach

Where authorities have a strong commitment to environmental action the advantages of what is often loosely called a 'corporate approach' have become increasingly apparent. The 'corporate approach' means taking co-ordinated action with all the services within an authority. A quite successful model is the 'Green Team' or 'State of the Environment Working Party' where groups of members and officers from key service areas recommend the allocation of funds, act as a forum for debate, develop the strategy and monitor progress. The Green Working Party can also be used as a channel for receiving views from Environment Forums and passing recommendations on to the relevant committees.

A very powerful method for developing a corporate approach is to give the Working Party a budget and the power to recommend its allocation for innovative environmental work throughout the authority and, if desired, local voluntary groups. However, the danger of this is that so much time can be spent actually allocating money that little or no time is spent developing policy. Another problem is that in most authorities 'real' decisions are taken by very specific committees, such as Highways, Planning or Policy and Resources. Once 'big' issues such as sustainability potentially affecting all areas of the Council's operation are raised, there can be a very real power struggle between committees and officers serving those committees over who 'owns' the environment, and who is setting the agenda. It is asking a lot of members and officers on a working party to be astute enough and sufficiently well informed to influence decision making at a sufficiently early stage to have a real impact.

In most authorities, by the time a paper comes to committee, all the real decision making has already occurred and it is too late for a working party lower down in the committee pecking order to be able to do much to change anything. Another problem is that in many authorities the 'Environment' Committee is in reality the Environmental Health Committee and many decisions with large environmental implications are taken by other committees such as those mentioned above.

What to do if a corporate approach is not possible?

The answer might be to become a 'green guerrilla'. This could mean selecting just one area for action, say for example, office paper recycling, raising awareness or energy saving. Progress may then depend solely upon informal, but nevertheless, potentially powerful co-operation with like minded people in the organisation. A green activist could also usefully channel some unpalatable messages via a local environmental group thus helping create external political pressures towards the actions the activist desires. It is also important to remember that many very successful approaches have developed out of sheer opportunism or chance action by individuals. Only later is the credit taken by the authority.

Involving others

Environmental issues, perhaps more than any other concern of local government, cut across traditional service boundaries outside of the formal remit of much local authority work. A local authority can however become a catalyst of broader-based community action to protect and improve the environment, building on its strong links with the public in its area, particularly in its role as a local advocate and shaper of opinions. To achieve this a comprehensive and co-ordinated approach is needed, with each service area contributing, but led and managed within a corporate approach. Comprehensive development and implementation of a corporate strategy should involve the public, other (local and national) organisations, elected members and all staff. Such involvement is vital as a source of ideas, co-operation, resources, expertise, commitment, authority and credibility.

Involving others is particularly important because local authorities, like many other organisations, still have much to learn about the environment and about their current and potential impact on it. Both local groups (such as Wildlife Trusts) and national organisations (like Friends of the Earth) will have considerable expertise on which an authority should draw. The general public, businesses and other sections of the local community must be involved in both definition of problems and formulation and implementation of solutions.

A now generally accepted means for consultation and involving the public is to hold regular environment forums/public meetings, usually facilitated by a local authority, where specific issues may be discussed, awareness raised and feedback obtained. The amount of time and effort needed to work effectively with the public and outside organisations should not be underestimated. It is also often not clear how one can tell whether consultation has been effective or not, although the continued interest and participation of members of the public is usually a good sign. There are however, some key factors:

- An authority must put its own house in order. It will need to acknowledge its own shortcomings (in its purchasing practice and so on) and show a commitment to overcoming them.
- An authority must demonstrate a willingness to listen and to learn. In this field more than most, local authorities are only slowly acquiring expertise. The best way of doing this is to canvass the views and draw on the expertise of others to consult widely and welcome comment about its current performance and potential contribution.

- It is important to match words and deeds. The local authority may not succeed in achieving all of its environmental targets, but it must make a serious attempt to so do.
- Commitments need to be visible. Using news-sheets, departmental briefings, open meetings, the local media and other means, the authority must inform both its own staff and external audiences of its efforts.
- Policies must be understood. Complex environmental issues must be translated into objectives and measures that can be easily grasped by staff, other organisations and the general public.
- Authorities must seek to promote freedom of access to environment information on all matters relating to the local environment.
- They should also seek to promote an awareness and understanding of environmental issues throughout the local community.
- Finally, authorities should ensure equal opportunity and access, for all sections of the community, including disadvantaged groups, to a safe and pleasant environment.

Conflicts

Environmentalism and sustainable development are about issues which many people care and worry about. They imply changes in the way we do things, and potentially affect every area of personal life, and the means of government and management. Developing and implementing an environmental strategy will thus involve conflict, negotiation and frustration. There are clear potential and almost inevitable conflict areas between different and often competing local authority strategies. Perhaps more surprisingly, there are also likely to be conflicts within a strategy itself.

The classic perceived conflict is between the environment and jobs — the 'do we want the polluting factory and the jobs or do we say no?' question. Other conflicts are between the desire for many car parking places to encourage shoppers to use a new shopping centre versus the desire to limit traffic to a reasonable level. Recycled paper costs more than its non-recycled counterpart creating a conflict between savings and the environment. Government PPGs value high grade agricultural land more highly than lower grade land irrespective of the ecological value a steeply sloping wood may have. Green Belt land is also protected more strongly than urban open land, although the latter often has higher ecological and amenity value than expanses of Green Belt monoculture. Ecological planting in parks or near playing fields may conflict with public safety and crime prevention policy by supplying hiding places for muggers.

All these conflicts can be resolved within a new way of thinking that takes into account a multiplicity of factors in a fairly complex way, more in fact in the way which most people think when they are not artificially forced into 'either–or' thinking. For example, the jobs versus the environment conflict is a very real one. This however can be circumvented by strong environmental regulation which is uniformly applied across the country and Europe. It has also been shown that strong environmental regulation forces innovation which in itself creates new jobs. Also, there are many environmental activities which create jobs far more efficiently than less environmentally friendly alternatives: local energy insulation installers and co-operatives create jobs directly; also, by combating poverty due to excessive heating bills, they release capital into the market place thereby rejuvenating local shopping centres. Properties with excessive heating bills also usually have condensation problems with extremely high incidence of childhood respiratory complaints costing the health service in doctors' time and medicines which could be transferred to other health needs. The local authority benefits from lower rate arrears and lower maintenance costs of property which is now worth more. Local people benefit from participation and their sense of community and self-worth is greatly enhanced. Such a convergence of social, economic and environmental needs has been noted in several local energy insulation schemes.

The parking conflict can be resolved by the provision of an adequate public transport system or perhaps a strategy to regenerate the corner shop. In Germany some cities are now building car ownership-free zones where people can only live if they sign a legally binding agreement not to own a car. These zones are very popular. Car-free cities are also being planned in Europe. People actually find that they prefer being in a car-free or car reduced zone. They still have access to a car by means of a car pooling system in some cases for trips where a car is the only means of transport suitable.

These few examples show that, in addition to new ways of working, there is a need for a new way of thinking to be reflected both in local government, and more particularly, in central government official land-use guidance and allocation of resources such as grant aid for transport systems.

An example of a conflict that can emerge within an environmental strategy is that of cars and the effect that traffic calming can have upon air pollution levels at traffic junctions or on main roads. By taking traffic off the smaller roads network and because the actual overall volume of cars is not reduced, air pollution at key junctions can be much worse. This illustrates that one environmentally motivated intervention may not be sufficient or may cure one problem (child accidents and noise) by creating another (more concentrated pollution). The real answer may lie in addressing the real problem: too many cars. Traffic calming, unless it is combined with other measures does not usually reduce car traffic volume. A truly sustainable approach to this problem would be to look at the carrying capacity of the various roads in the network to avoid pollution targets being exceeded and then to operate some kind of quota system to limit the number of vehicles moving in a given zone at any one time perhaps in the same way that an automatic car park ticket machine restricts access when the park is full.

Another interesting conflict is between grasslands and tree-planting. Many local authorities have quite extensive tree planting plans or urban and community forestry schemes. Non-experts assume that tree cover is always better than open land, however some areas of grassland may have a great diversity of species which can only be determined by a survey before a tree planting schedule is drawn up.

Conclusions

For the future, it is vital for local authority strategies, and for the environmental movement in general, to find a broader constituency of support for environmental actions taken at all levels. The environment, whilst an important factor in political decision making still lags behind economic factors. Perhaps addressing peoples' fears about the damage being done to the environment is not the best approach. Perhaps there is a limit to the number of people sufficiently affluent to be able to worry about the ozone layer and greenhouse warming of tomorrow. The answer is at the heart of sustainable development, interpreted in local actions which make very good sense economically, socially and environmentally. A good example is local housing improvements which drastically improve people's living conditions whilst cutting their heating bills by retro-fitting redesigned environmentally sensitive solar passive heating and good insulation. Local work-sharing co-operatives may be another, by starting to create a local economy based upon local produce and work and which to some extent opts out of the environmentally unfriendly status quo. The Local Agenda 21 process should help to start to find such actions at local level by making the environment more accessible to the community, hopefully supported by enlightened local government and central government.

Convergences of environmental, economic and social objectives expressed in local actions can, and hopefully will, put the environment properly on the policy map in a new agenda for mainstream political parties in the UK. At the time of writing it is still too early to say what the likely consequences of Local Agenda 21 will be. It is to be hoped that they will be a necessary development of local accountability through the increasing transparency of local decision making and greater participation by people in local decisions. The European Fifth Action Programme and the Sixth Action Programme to come are also important influences. The Fifth Action Programme addresses environmental factors rather than people at the grass roots and should have an interesting impact upon Government as the implications of the Maastricht Treaty and local access to justice take effect. Increasingly, environmental policy making will be led from Europe with local government firmly recognised below central government with final recourse to the European Court.

It is to be hoped that all these welcome developments will for the first time start to properly empower local government to in turn empower ordinary people within a new, more relevant agenda for the environment.

4 Local authority investment and the environment

Anne Simpson

Local authorities are collectively responsible for one of the UK's largest pools of investment: the Local Government Superannuation Scheme whose combined assets approach £40 billion. Investment of these funds has placed local authorities in the position of being major shareholders. The majority of superannuation fund monies are invested in the shares of British companies, giving local authority pension funds new rights and responsibilities as owners of industry. However, a growing number do not see themselves in a passive role in relation to these investments, simply awaiting their stream of dividends to fund the pension fund's liabilities. Many take the view that their position as shareholders gives them the opportunity to have a positive impact upon corporate policy, to foster long term socially responsible growth to the mutual benefit of the company's shareholders, employees and other stakeholders. The environment is a central issue in this strategy, in which issues of long term financial success are bound up with corporate responsibility.

The realisation that environmental factors will increasingly determine financial returns has led a number of local authority investors to develop policies to 'green' their portfolios. The potential costs of funding environmental liabilities under new legislation, both UK and overseas, actual clean up costs, the impact of the 'green consumer' and new regulatory standards have all begun to change the terms of business. Environmental trends have posed both a threat and an opportunity to companies, in which shareholders can play an active role.

Environmental factors are now recognised as an important part of the investment process, and interest in the issue is reflected across the financial establishment. The City's leading analysts, James Capel, announced to clients that taking environmental matters seriously in investment was not a matter of sentiment, but of good business, announcing that their research would be focusing on the issue because they realised that 'companies which are in tune with the environment are on the way up' (Capel 1991).

However, if companies are going to deal positively with environmental challenges then they will need the support of their shareholders. Environmental responsibility does not always come cheap. Recycling and energy conservation measures may result in direct cost cutting for a company. Sprucing up their public image with promotional material may be good marketing. Developing products to capture the new markets that environmental trends are producing is simply good business. However, making provisions for liabilities on the balance sheet, employing consultants to advise and assess corporate progress on the environment and investing in new plant, equipment and training can be expensive.

During the early 1990s when interest rates were high and the economy is suffering its worst post war recession, environmental issues have been pushed down the agenda. Companies have felt under acute pressure to keep their share prices buoyant by paying out dividends even though their earnings fell during the period, in some cases even paying dividends to shareholders out of reserves or borrowings. Short term pressures are all too evident and shareholders are the culprits. However, many of them are in fact long term investors, like local authority pension funds who should be considering returns over a 25 to 30 year time horizon.

There appears to be a mismatch of expectations between companies and investors. A survey conducted by MORI Finance in 1992 indicated that a majority of investment managers considered companies to be making an inadequate response to environmental issues. In response to the assertion that 'British companies do not pay enough attention to their treatment of the environment' the majority of investment professionals, including researchers and financial journalists overwhelmingly agreed (MORI, 1992).

This seems to be borne out by research on corporate environmental policy. When the British Institute of Management surveyed its 3,000 members in 1991 more than half did not have a statement of their environmental policy. The then Secretary for the Environment Michael Heseltine responded to this news by calling on investors to do something about the situation.

The relatively low level of adoption of good practice as revealed in the surveys prompts me to put the question directly to you in the financial community.

Are you getting it right on the environment? Are you playing your full part? Are you putting Britain's managers under the right kind of pressures to improve their environmental performance. As I have said earlier, your fate is bound up with theirs. It is your assets that are at stake if companies fail to manage their environmental risks competently. It is your profits that will be lower if British companies fail to detect and exploit the burgeoning markets for environmental goods and services (DOE 1992b).

Many local authority pension funds did not need to be persuaded of this, having begun as early as 1989 to develop strategies for environmentally responsible investment. These local authority pension funds recognise that shareholders have an important role to play in leading business through the hazardous path of threats and opportunities which environmental trends have laid before them. They are in a unique position as democratically elected investment committees, for considering not only long term financial growth, but also the impact of corporate activity on the local community.

Convenor Anne Wallace argued in explaining Central Regional Council's approach to environmental issues and investment:

We want to take a corporate approach to major issues of policy. It is logical that our investment function should make an appropriate contribution to the council's environmental strategy, just as every other department does (Wallace 1993).

The local authority perspective

Local authorities are playing a leading role in green investment issues because of their overlapping interests on environmental issues — illustrated clearly in the waste industry. Local authorities span the breadth of the waste management industry via their multiple responsibilities. They have an interest in the waste sector for three main reasons: as regulators (via the Local Authority Regulatory Authorities set up under the Environmental Protection Act 1990) as operators (directly via the provision of cleansing and collection services and indirectly through the 'arms length' Local Authority Waste Disposal Companies) and as shareholders (via their superannuation fund investments in private sector waste companies listed on the British and overseas stock markets).

This position of overlapping functions was graphically illustrated by a local authority engaged in litigation with a waste company over the incineration of rubbish in the West Midlands area. Unbeknown to the councillors dealing with the complaints of local communities over emissions and taking forward prosecutions over emissions, one of the local authority pension funds in the region was a major shareholder in the company.

This position throws up new opportunities for negotiation, but also potential conflicts of interest. When another authority in Wales was commissioning studies to trace possible links between tests over toxic emissions and the health of its local community, it took the decision to sell its shares in the parent company in order to avoid any conflict of interest.

Developing strategies

In developing a strategy as investors on environmental issues, local authorities have to approach the situation carefully. There are three prime considerations. The first is the legal framework for investment. This provides the context within which local authority pension funds must operate. This requires that local authorities are clear about their legal duties as investors. The second is the impact that environmental trends are having on investments now and those predicted for the future. This requires research.

Thirdly, there is consideration of the policy options open to local authority investors. In this aspect of local authority activity, policy is no different to other departments. For an environmental investment strategy to be effective, there needs to be the development of clearly understood goals, practical methods of achieving stated objectives and a review mechanism for monitoring progress and revising aims and objectives. One approach to this issue is described below.

The legal framework

The investment of superannuation funds is governed by regulations set out in statute under the Local Government Superannuation Regulations, laid down in 1986 and most recently updated in 1992.

This makes local authority superannuation unique amongst pension fund investors in the UK. A national framework of legislation governs the administration of the schemes and provides a standard set of benefits, but it also allows for a devolved form of investment through 98 administering authorities who are responsible for the funds on behalf of contributing bodies. These administering authorities are the County Councils of England and Wales, the London Boroughs, the Scottish Regional Councils and the former Metropolitan Boroughs, whose funds have been passed to Districts in all cases bar one which was handed to a quango.

The investment of the superannuation fund is controlled by a committee or sub committee of the administering authority, usually with employee observers. A number of administering authorities employ their own officers to invest the funds, and others employ external managers who report to members on a quarterly basis (*Local Authority Pension Fund Yearbook* 1993).

The Local Government Superannuation Regulations governing the investment of these funds are simple and straightforward. In summary they provide that:

- investments must be appropriate;
- they must be diversified;
- advice must be taken at suitable intervals.

Further rules provide that regular reports must be received, place a 10 per cent limit on unquoted investments and allow for delegation of investment to external managers. In addition, it is generally considered that the principles of trust law apply as the money is held by the authority on behalf of others. The most important of these are that those acting in a capacity of trust over such funds have a duty of care to the beneficiaries and must act prudently (*Local Authority Pension Fund Yearbook* 1993).

The beneficiaries of the Local Government Superannuation Scheme are those members of the scheme who will draw a pension at a point in the future, and who make fixed contributions from their salaries. It also includes the local charge payers who make a contribution on behalf of the employer, and who also will be obliged to make up any shortfall in funds should that arise, as the levels of benefit are guaranteed under statute.

Both employees of the council and the local charge paying population have an interest in the investment of the funds. That interest has two dimensions. The primary interest is in the investment returns to the pension fund. The goal of the pension fund is to provide for its liabilities as and when they fall due. As local authorities will be paying pensions over a long time period, the investment horizons of these funds stretch up to 30 years into the future.

The local authority therefore needs to consider not just investment returns today to pay pensioners who have retired, but long term growth in the fund to pay the pension of those who have just joined the workforce but may not be retiring for 30 years in the future. Local authorities above all, are long term investors. This gives them a direct interest in environmental matters due to the long term nature of the liabilities they need to cover.

The interest of the local charge payers is also clearly financial. However, the charge payer has an interest not just in the returns to the fund but in other costs created by environmental impacts. For example, the local community wants to ensure that the investments in the pension fund are successful in order to minimise the contribution levied to keep pensions paid. They also want to minimise the costs of environmental damage, both financial and social. In the case of a company operating in the area the link is fairly immediate. The pension fund of the authority may benefit from higher profits if the company does not invest in equipment to reduce pollution.

However, the authority will bear the cost of that pollution in other ways, through clean up costs which may fall to it, through the loss of amenity, and potentially falling land values or reduction of business in the area. This link has been seen in recent years with the oil spill by Shell into the Mersey Estuary, the pollution of local beaches which are important to the tourist industry by water companies and pressures on ICI to clean up its waste before disposal to sea off the Humberside coast.

At a global level, the combined activities of companies in their use of natural resources, for example, through the use of tropical hardwood logged from rain forests which contribute to the stability of the global climate, through to the destruction of the ozone layer by chemicals produced and used by companies that are in many local authority pension fund portfolios. Here the environmental 'cost' to the authority cannot be quantified at local level, but it is clear that each community has a shared interest in the successful resolution of global environmental issues too.

The impact of environmental trends in investment

In recent years, environmental issues have come centre stage. It seems hard to imagine that any quarter of the business community is not actively aware of the need for change and therefore has not begun the long process of setting out detailed plans for the future.

The onset of legislation introducing higher standards and liabilities, the use of fiscal measures, changing consumer demands, green campaigners and even the interest of shareholders, should be leading to the greening of British board rooms. However, this is not necessarily the case and local authority investors stand to lose out, both financially in the returns to their portfolios and socially in the impact companies are having at local and international level. From this perspective it is clear that tackling environmental issues in investment falls within the general statutory framework and also within the principles of trust law. In order to be making 'suitable' investments and in order to be 'prudent', local authority investors need to have taken environmental factors into account.

The first initiative was taken by a group of local authority pension funds with combined assets of £15 billion, who were co-ordinating their activities as shareholders through Pensions Investment Research Consultants (PIRC). In 1989 they commissioned a research paper 'Towards a Green Portfolio' in which PIRC argued that local authorities could best develop environmental investment strategies through developing a co-ordinated and long term approach focusing on a policy statement, followed by a research programme and implementation through shareholder action. The issue was discussed at a conference held in 1990 'Green investment strategies: the role of local authority pension funds' addressed by local authority investors, city analysts and environmentalists. From this PIRC drew up a detailed strategy paper entitled 'Pension Fund Investment and the Environment' which set out a programme of policy, research and activity for local authority investors. The paper and its recommendations were reported on at quarterly meetings of the Local Authority Pension Fund Forum.

The UK Environmental Investor Code (see Figure 4.1) was the resulting policy statement developed in consultation with these funds, other investors and a range of environmental groups. The purpose was to establish a clear commitment to an active approach on the issue, and provide a public statement which would frame the approach to companies.

It was decided that the principles behind the statement should be simple and within the reach of most companies. It would also be a statement of policy which could be elaborated and extended in relation to particular companies and sectors. The principles it embraced should be applicable to all investments and have the result of improving shareholder value. At the heart of the code was a recognition that investors should make public their

Figure 4.1: **The UK Environmental Investor Code**

As investors, we recognise that corporate performance and the value of our investments are increasingly affected by environmental factors.

In pursuance of a prudent and environmentally responsible investment policy, we will encourage and support companies that demonstrate a positive response to environmental concerns.

We call on companies:

— to make a commitment to achieving environmental excellence;

— to institute regular monitoring of their environmental impacts;

— to establish procedures which will lead to incremental improvements in environmental performance;

— to comply with all environmental legislation and to seek to anticipate future legislative changes;

— to make available to shareholders regular and detailed reports of progress made towards attaining improved environmental standards.

support for environmental responsibility by the companies in their portfolio.

The supporters of the Code also took a decision to support similar initiatives overseas, such as the CERES principles in the United States which form a parallel shareholder initiative on the environment.

Environmental research

Having taken an 'in principle' decision on policy, investors need to know two things when considering the impact of environmental trends on their portfolio. First of all, in what way will companies' operations be affected by environmental issues over the long term. Secondly, are the management aware of this and are they making plans to deal effectively with change?

Establishing an answer to these two questions has led a group of local authority pension funds to engage in some detailed research through surveying the leading companies in their portfolios. This focused on those aspects of environmental policy which were common to all companies. The questions included:

- Had they established a policy on the environment?
- At what level was responsibility for implementation held?
- Is the policy group wide, or does it only apply to UK operations?
- Does the company adhere to standards such as those issued by the BSI, International Chamber of Commerce or Business in the Environment?
- Had targets been set and was there a review mechanism for improving on these (for example, an energy or waste audit, a compliance assessment, liability provision, environmental management assessments)?
- Were reviews carried out in-house or by independent bodies?
- Was staff training on the issue established?
- Was there provision in the accounts for potential liabilities?

The survey also asked the companies to identify the source of pressure for environmental changes. How sensitive did they consider their operations were to legal developments, consumer or supplier views, and of course, whether shareholders could or should be playing a more constructive role.

Linked to this analysis which compares policy between companies, the local authority pension fund clients of PIRC have commissioned further research looking in detail at the practices on particular sectors. The first sector analysed has been the waste management industry. This is due to the particular importance of the sector to local authorities who are active as waste authorities, regulators and investors in private sector firms.

The report produced has been commissioned from the perspective of long term shareholders. It provides an overview of the industrial trends in the waste management business, considers the impact of environmental standards (both set down in legislation and the emergence of new issues led by environmental campaigners) and finally it provides a detailed assessment of the individual waste companies quoted on the UK stock market in terms of their environmental practices. This report sets out recommendations for shareholders which centre on the need for liabilities to be assessed and provided for and pressure for improved environmental management standards in a number of companies.

The programme of research also identified a number of environmental issues of wider importance where shareholders could have a role to play. The local authorities commissioned a detailed report on the issue of ozone depletion. The focus of the report was the role of companies in their portfolio which were either producing or using chemicals that were causing damage to the ozone layer, and which would be phased out by the 1989 Montreal Protocol.

The report considered the operations of ICI as the largest European producer of CFCs which was developing a range of substitute products. Again the focus was on a critical but constructive role for shareholders in ensuring that ICI was aware that its investors supported the capital expenditure on the new chemicals, and saw the commercial as well as environmental benefits to developing ozone benign alternatives. When PIRC staff visited the company's production plant, ICI representatives informed us that no other shareholder had expressed an interest in visiting the project, even though it represented one of their largest developments.

This programme of research will continue over the next phase as the results of each stage feed into the policy considerations of the local authorities participating in the project.

Shareholder action

Having assessed the degree to which companies within a portfolio are affected by and respond to environmental trends, via this combination of general and specific research projects, local authority investors have a number of policy options before them. In simple terms, they are as follows:

1   Sell shares in companies which are unsatisfactory in terms of their environmental performance, on the grounds that this represents a risk to the investor.
2   Buy shares in companies which are considered to be satisfactory in their approach to environmental issues, on the view that this will lead to better performance in the long term.
3   Hold on to existing shares and develop an active share-holder approach which is aimed at bringing about positive change in the policy of companies within the portfolio on the grounds that this will reduce risk and improve value over the long term.

These policies are not mutually exclusive, and each has played their part in the development of an overall environmental strategy by local authority investors.

Selling out

The first option, however, is not as simple as it seems. The investor in a company has presumably bought shares in the first place because an opportunity for long term growth existed. The assumption must be that the company is essentially sound, and the shares well priced, otherwise the investment would not have been made. The question then is, at what point do environmental factors override the other judgements which have been made about the company's prospects?

Taking the waste sector as an example, a local authority investor could assess the available evidence on the operations of the different companies in the industry and come to the conclusion that a particular firm was not up to scratch on environmental policy. More seriously, the investor may consider that the company has potential liabilities due to the nature of the waste disposal activities it was involved with which posed unacceptable risks. A policy can be developed, but liabilities cannot be simply removed. They can only be provided for, at a cost to the shareholders.

Should the investor sell? The investor's duty to consider the interests of the beneficiaries requires that the local authority consider the financial consequences. If a loss is not made on the sale, and an alternative investment is available then the investor simply has to consider the costs of the transaction. However, selling the shares does not actually solve the environmental problem. The investor sells the shares to another institution, who may or may not share the concern for environmental issues.

Also, the research which is emerging suggests that it is the majority rather than the minority of British companies which need to put their house in order on environmental issues. Selling shares in companies that are not up to scratch could result in a somewhat depleted portfolio.

It would inevitably mean that the investor would have to be selective about which environmental issues were considered. This is clear in the range of unit trusts which have been launched in the UK which claim to avoid investment in environmentally 'unfriendly' companies. The diverse nature of corporate activities means that a rather loose net has been provided in which certain environmental issues inevitably fall through.

For example, those 'green' unit trusts which claim to avoid tropical hardwood importers do so in order to satisfy the investor's concern about climate change via the preservation of tropical concern about climate change via the preservation of tropical rain forests. The contribution of mainstream British companies to global warming through their use of energy is not factored in because it would exclude too many potential investments and make the unit trust unviable. However, energy saving measures that reduced the consumption of electricity by companies would have a marked effect on emissions of carbon dioxide and hence on climate change.

Buying in

Buying shares in 'environmentally friendly' companies includes some of the same difficulties as a policy. It is clear that there are certain companies and industries that are set to benefit from environmental trends. For example, the market for catalytic converters has boosted the platinum based company Johnson Matthey. However, the smelting of metal is an environmentally unfriendly activity in itself. Likewise, how would investors judge the activities of companies involved in a number of businesses? ICI has developed a biodegradable plastic. However, it is also a major producer of toxic waste.

In recent years, those companies which have successfully marketed their 'green' credentials have seen their share price rise. This has not always been matched by the rise in profits, making them expensive stocks to buy. This means they do not necessarily represent good value for money. This factor has been seen with retailers such as the Body Shop and certain companies in the waste sector like Caird whose shares were overrated and then more recently have fallen back.

The volatility of the share price in such companies has dogged the performance of some of the 'green' unit trusts. There is clearly a point at which environmental factors introduce a risk or an opportunity which justifies trading shares. More research and analysis, even from mainstream fund managers and brokers is geared towards identifying these situations. However, such trading will usually be at the margins. The great swathe of British companies that form the majority of a local authority investment portfolio will fall somewhere in between the balance of risk and opportunity on environmental issues.

It is here that the third policy option of pursuing an active shareholder strategy can produce benefits.

The active shareholder

Traditionally, investors have seen their role as the buying and selling of shares. Indeed, the trading of shares has grown in volume in recent years. During the 1960s pension funds held their shares in a company for an average of 15 years. In the 1990s the period has fallen to less than 5 years. Such trends have led to criticisms about 'short termism' and the need for a new relationship between investors and companies so that long term growth can be fostered.

Local authority investors have been at the forefront of developing strategies as active shareholders who aim to focus on the long term, and take up their responsibilities as owners of companies, rather than as traders of shares. However, this strategy is itself long term and requires detailed research and co-ordination between investors. Generally, any individual local authority investor will only hold a small proportion of the shares in a company. This means that although it is in a position to ask questions and to exercise its votes as it sees fit, it is not in a position of decisive influence. Local authority pension funds have therefore come together in the establishment of PIRC, which was formed in 1986 to provide independent investment advice, research and co-ordination of shareholder action. PIRC now works for local authority pension funds with combined assets of £15 billion, representing an influential body of shareholders.

This has provided a basis for co-ordinating shareholder strategies on a range of environmental issues. To date, PIRC has represented these funds to a range of companies. Over a period of three years PIRC worked with a number of environmental groups in negotiating with Fisons over the digging up of peat from Sites of Special Scientific Interest. The initiative was led by South Yorkshire Pensions Authority, which has a number of rare bogs in its region, notably Thorne and Hatfield moors. Also, the pension fund was an important shareholder in the company. Environmental groups supported by the Prince of Wales launched a boycott of Fisons' products in order to pressure the company to stop digging peat. Local authority shareholders saw a potentially damaging boycott launched, and intransigence from the company which initially refused to reconsider its management of the bogs. Environmentalists considered that the company was engaged in the destruction of a rare habitat for short term commercial gain, which was triggering an extensive consumer boycott of the company's products both by 'green' retailers such as B&Q and the environmental groups.

On behalf of the local authority investors PIRC had meetings with senior executives, drafted a resolution for consideration by shareholders at the Annual General Meeting and liaised with other institutional investors in the company. The issue received extensive media attention, both in the UK and in the USA. Feature articles appeared in the New Yorker and Gentlemen's Quarterly highlighting the value of Britain's 'rain forest bogs' and the work of local authority investors in calling for an end to their destruction.

In 1992 the company agreed to hand over the freehold of the sites to English Nature and a compromise was reached over the extraction of peat which included the development of alternative products to peat and a halt to digging in certain areas.

Similar projects have been undertaken with ICI over its development of substitutes for chemicals causing ozone depletion, and local authority pension funds were the first shareholders to send a representative to meet with the company on the issue and to visit the new site in Runcorn. Local authority pension funds have also had discussions with British Gas and its oil exploration on indigenous peoples' land in Ecuador, and with the regional electricity companies and generators over their investments in renewable energy sources. Extensive meetings have been held with representatives of the waste sector companies to establish the level of environmental management standards and provision for liabilities in their accounts.

Central Regional Council's involvement in these projects provides an example of how one authority came to develop an investment strategy on environmental issues. The starting point was Central Region's development of an Environmental Charter which sets out overall goals and underlying principles for the whole authority. The Charter identifies eight major policy areas where the council considered it had the opportunity to make a significant impact on local environmental standards through its functions.

An action programme to implement the aims of the Charter was established for each department, setting practical targets and goals appropriate to the particular function of the authority. The action programme has since been revised to allow for updating and the incorporation of ideas and input generated from the council's practical experience, and the views of local people.

Central Region's overall strategy includes a broad based employee communications programme to educate and motivate staff and to inform the local community about the council's priorities and seek their involvement. The authority has also developed an environmentally sensitive purchasing policy and initiated a review of transport policy and land management.

Within this approach, Central Region focused on the particular issues facing the finance department on environmental questions. The statement in the Charter was straightforward, that the council would 'develop an environmentally sound investment policy'.

The council at this point was running one of the country's best performing local authority pension funds and also one of its most innovative environmental programmes. The intention was to integrate the council's environmental concerns into its investment process, in a way which supported its outstanding financial success.

Originally, the council considered an approach in which it would, where possible, avoid investment in companies which were damaging the environment. This threw up a number of difficulties, not least the problem of identifying companies which should be considered 'damaging to the environment' at a time when most British companies needed to improve their performance. Inevitably, the definition of environmental damage will vary depending upon the sector and the company concerned. There was also the consideration that avoiding companies would restrict the portfolio's ability to invest widely, and that may ultimately have been detrimental to the returns to the fund. The third consideration was effectiveness. Simply not holding shares in a company would not result in any change in policy.

Central Regional Council took on PIRC as a new adviser in 1991 to develop a socially responsible investment strategy for its £225 million superannuation fund. Environmental issues were central to the new approach. Following detailed consultation with environmental groups, investment managers and local authorities, PIRC set out a strategy paper for Central Region and its other pension fund clients in a paper 'Environmental Investment: A Strategy for Local Authority Pension Funds'. This set out a medium term plan of action for long term responsible shareholders which involved commissioning detailed research on corporate environmental policy, identification of immediate priorities in the form of ozone depletion and waste disposal and a general statement by shareholders to highlight pension fund concerns with companies in the UK Environmental Investor Code (see Figure 4.1).

Central Region supported the UK Environmental Investor Code which sets out basic targets for companies in its portfolios: the development of an environmental policy, institution of sound environmental management practices, compliance with the law and anticipation of new standards, plus regular reporting to shareholders.

The purpose was to allow Central Region to use its influence as a shareholder with companies in raising environmental standards. Through PIRC, Central Regional Council Superannuation Fund has also jointly commissioned detailed research on the environmental policy and practice of the leading 600 companies in the UK which will allow it to focus attention on those where change is most needed.

Through linking with other local authority pension funds, Central Region contributed to an effective shareholder strategy which pooled the influence and experience of investment funds with others. This approach takes as its starting point the view that good environmental performance will underpin the continuing financial success of the superannuation fund's investments.

Conclusions

Local authority investors have proven themselves to be innovative in many areas and the environment is but one example. They are developing a progressive strategy which has been shaped by best advice and experience. The approach they have taken is long term, and that is appropriate given the nature of their investments and the complexity of the issues at hand.

Their approach has been threefold: to develop a formal policy statement, to carry out detailed research and to act collectively in working for change as shareholders. This has proved effective with a number of companies on specific issues and proved an efficient approach for each fund individually. Ultimately, they have been able to share the benefits, pooling experience in working together on policy, sharing the costs of commissioning research and benefiting from exerting combined influence with companies. Where the authorities have held shares in the same companies they have been able to develop a common approach which is anchored on their legal responsibilities for prudent long term investment, whilst allowing them to play a constructive role in environmental improvement in the companies in which they invest.

The impact of their activity in recent years is already being seen. According to research conducted by PIRC in 1993 on behalf of local authority pension fund shareholders, companies are increasingly aware of pressure from investors to tackle environmental issues positively. 42 per cent of 120 leading companies with an established environmental policy responding to the survey identified shareholders as a constituent which had put pressure on them about their environmental performance.

This compared with 6 per cent who identified environmental organisations as a source of concern. Shareholders are in a position to play a decisive role in the greening of British industry, and local authority pension funds have been at the forefront, willing and able to take responsibility as owners for corporate environmental improvement.

5 Environmental management and audit

Denise Hill and Trevor Smith

The pace of change in the field of environmental auditing is accelerating. Auditing in local authority practice is dealt with in some detail in the Local Government Management Board publication *Environmental Practice in Local Government* first published in 1991 and reviewed in 1992 (LGMB *et al.* 1992c). A section dealing with auditing describes the European Commission's Eco-Audit Regulation, now the Eco-Management and Audit Regulation (CEC 1992b) and the British Standard 7750 *Specification for Environmental Management Systems* (BSI 1992a). It considers a number of case studies where auditing has been used in practice and identifies a number of possible key issues that are problematic. It concludes that in future publications auditing might not warrant a chapter of its own but will form part of a wider section dealing with corporate environmental management systems. This is the general thrust of the Eco-Management and Audit and the British Standard — that auditing is not an end in itself but a vital part, but only a part, of an iterative process that reflects an integrated approach to environmental management.

This chapter seeks to examine auditing more closely in the context of the processes advocated in the Eco-Management and Audit and the British Standard. It looks at the origins of auditing, some strategic and managerial dimensions including agreed standards, environmental liability and the economic and social costs of service impacts. It considers the boundaries for appropriate environmental auditing and management and the organisational structures that might deliver sustainability and finally, it offers some comment on alternative futures and policy options, drawing upon a range of examples, most particularly experience at Brighton Borough Council.

Wedged in between the sea and the South Downs there is considerable pressure for change at Brighton and the Council has developed a strong tradition of environmental assessment and analysis to assist in dealing with the town's problems. As a former County Borough it promulgated a method of landscape analysis that identified areas to be protected and that served as a model countrywide for some time (Fines 1968). More recently, it was amongst the first Councils to produce a Local Environment Charter that is still used as the basis for the Authority's annual environment position statement. It has a specialist environmental policy officer and a local community forum currently engaged in establishing the town's Local Agenda 21. In addition, it has completed a major customer oriented change in the structure of the Council which brought together all the environment and development control functions so as to achieve a more integrated approach to environmental management.

This chapter suggests that environmental auditing is an aid to decision taking but to be effective in improving environmental performance it is only part of a wider process of environmental management. However, before environmental auditing and management becomes a new paradigm for local government, there are some unresolved issues that must be addressed in order to prevent local authorities from wasting slender resources.

The origins of auditing

If we turn to auditing in the dictionary it is described as 'an official examination of the accounts' or, perhaps more appropriately in our present context and in relation to the environment, 'Day of Judgement'. It is a straightforward management device to assess whether the books balance — that what we have spent matches what we have produced, hopefully in a legitimate way and giving rise to a legitimate profit.

Auditing methods were first applied, beyond straightforward financial matters, to social indicator research. This has a long history but gained credence in the United States during the middle years of the 1960s and early 1970s when public agency programmes were under scrutiny and having to account for their costs and benefits. The search began for systematic accounting techniques. The application of auditing methods proved difficult given that the measure was quality of life rather than dollars and the legitimate profit added value. These data defied adequate analysis and results were criticised as misleading because they suggested a precision in the measurement of intangible and elusive factors such as satisfaction with housing, jobs and recreation (Campbell, Converse and Rogers 1976). It is important to remind ourselves that the measure was our personal benefit in relation to the service provided and based on utility in relation to our needs — rather than a systematic evaluation of environmental resources consumed.

At the same time that social auditing was being applied to public programmes, it was also proving attractive to business. In some cases, large companies were sufficiently community minded to wish to demonstrate that their output had some desirable wider benefits beyond the profit to shareholders, and others were having to defend themselves against increasing litigation. Claims of liability through negligence necessitated the systematic analysis of environmental effects and one of the first companies to undertake an audit of its environmental performance was Allied Chemical in 1975. It subsequently resolved to keep itself informed upon environmental performance on a continuing basis.

Thus in the USA audits were perceived as a mechanism for self-enforcement of environmental regulations against a background of an increasingly complicated regulatory framework. Whilst environmental auditing is not mandatory at Federal level in the USA, from the 1980s onwards the Environmental Protection Agency encouraged and promoted it and the standard government text, *Environmental Audits* is still to be recommended. (Thompson and Therivel 1991).

The international framework — UNCED and Local Agenda 21

In 1987 the World Commission on Environment and Development (Brundtland Commission) published *Our Common Future* (WCED 1987), and proposed that global economic development, in order to be sustainable, should be sufficient to meet current needs while allowing future generations to meet their own needs. This definition still offers a view based upon personal utility and can be criticised for this reason. Nonetheless it represented a significant step away from conventional economic theory that has consistently set environmental effects outside the development equation (O'Laoire 1993).

Agenda 21 was established in June 1992 by the United Nations Conference on Environment and Development and represents the United Nations Sustainable Development Action Plan for the 21st Century and includes support for local authorities in the development of Local Agenda 21s. The aim of a Local Agenda 21 is to establish a process for sustainable development in a community that is based upon development that achieves basic environmental, social and economic services to all people within a community without threat to the viability of the natural, built and social systems upon which the delivery of the service relies (UNCED 1992). The process is to include community consultation, sustainable development auditing, target setting (the Local Agenda 21) and the development and use of indicators to measure progress.

The Local Government Management Board has produced a guide to Agenda 21 for local authorities (Levett 1993) and the local authority associations have set up a steering group with a work programme addressing models of community participation; examples of good practice in achieving sustainability and ways of building upon recent practice to create a national framework for environmental auditing. The strengths of Local Agenda 21 lie in the broad framework of issues covered, the weight given to the involvement, particularly of women, youth and indigenous people and the challenge to conventional processes of policy making. However, it has some weaknesses, most seriously that it is not legally binding and it sets no targets for environmental capacity (McClaren 1993). Nevertheless the rich and the poor nations have agreed for the first time on what is necessary for human beings to adjust their requirements and numbers to protect the earth (Piel 1992).

Europe and the Fifth Environmental Action Programme 1992

Since 1973 The European Community has adopted consecutive Action Programmes for the Environment. The first programmes established a number of underlying principles that all subsequent programmes, legislation and advice have followed: that pollution should be eliminated or reduced at source and that the polluter should pay the cost of prevention, disposal or elimination measures. The Fifth Action Programme 'Towards Sustainability' runs from 1993–2000. The basic strategy of the Programme is proactive dealing with the root causes of environmental degradation rather than waiting to remedy matters after problems occur. To achieve this, the Programme is committed to the introduction of new instruments and to involving all sectors of society. Amongst other things, local authorities are identified as having a particular role in environmental auditing and reporting. Steps under the Action Programme that relate directly to environmental auditing include the assessment of environmental effects, eco labelling and auditing.

Taking Environmental Assessment first, the requirement for the assessment of development projects and their impacts prior to the grant of planning permission was introduced by way of a Directive in 1985 (85/337) (CEC 1985) and was transposed into UK Law in 1988 under the Town and Country Planning Regulations (HMSO 1988). The Commission has argued that the UK Legislation is defective in implementing the terms of the Directive and any approved review is likely to recommend a number of substantial changes. Added to this it is the Commission's view that, to achieve sustainable development, it is necessary to apply an assessment of the environmental implications of all relevant policies, plans and programmes (CEC 1991b).

In this context a number of local authorities, including Lancashire County Council, in reviewing their structure and local plans, are carrying out assessments of land use policy. Lancashire devised a matrix comprising environmental indicators and allocated to each policy a sustainability score in relation to the indicators. Results at Lancashire led to the modification of policy (LCC 1992b). Elsewhere Strategic Assessment is already being applied in a diversity of programmes (Lee and Walsh 1992, Therivel *et al*. 1992).

EC Regulation 880/92 (CEC 1992c) was adopted in December 1991 setting down the criteria for the award of a European Eco-label to provide consumers and suppliers with a rational basis for the selection of green products clearly identified by a standard symbol. The standards require a 'cradle to grave' evaluation of environmental impact and the scheme therefore favours products of the highest 'total environmental quality' at all stages of the product's life-cycle. The implications for local government lie in the assessment of environmental effects of products, development policies and action over time. Product life-cycle analysis was originally a popular management technique for portfolio management but was discredited as too narrow an analysis upon which to base strategic planning and investment decisions (Twiss 1974). Nevertheless, as a model for assessing the impacts of a product, policy or activity over time it is of renewed importance.

The Eco-labelling Regulation was followed by the Eco-Management and Audit Regulation (CEC 1992b) which allows for voluntary participation in an eco-audit scheme. This was considerably watered down during the original drafting stage but complements the Eco-label scheme by suggesting a process for environmental management that goes beyond the product to the management of inputs and outputs in such a way as to minimise their environmental impacts. The main elements of the scheme allow companies to develop an environmental policy, set objectives for environmental performance and devise management systems to achieve these goals. The scheme includes commitment to an externally validated self-assessment of progress and the provision of information to the public. Auditing is a fundamental part of this process.

UK national policy

National environmental policy is embodied in the Government's White Paper on the Environment, *This Common Inheritance* (DOE 1990) which supports the practice of auditing by recommending that local authorities monitor and review their performance. The Government subsequently has endorsed Local Agenda 21 and has vouchsafed support for the European Eco-label and Eco-Management and Audit schemes. This interest is paralleled in demands from central government in a plethora of White Papers for increased quality, efficiency and accountability in the delivery of local services and local decision making. All support the use of proper standards, targets and indicators to monitor performance.

In particular the *Competing for Quality* initiative (DOE 1991c) sets explicit targets to measure environmental performance in the public sector and paves the way for an extension of Compulsory Competitive Tendering to a wider range of public services. In addition, despite opposition to a European Directive requiring Strategic Environmental Assessment (SEA) to be applied to policies, plans and programmes, the Government has published a guide to assist policy makers in government departments with the evaluation of environmental effects, *Policy Appraisal and the Environment* (DOE 1991b).

Definitions of environmental auditing

The evolution of environmental auditing in local authorities derives from the definition of auditing offered by Friends of the Earth, and practice has been influenced by its 'Environmental Charter for Local Government' that was published in 1989. This was to be a guide for local authorities to change practice to achieve more sustainable ways of working and more sustainable development decisions.

> An environmental audit is designed to assess the current state of the local environment, the factors affecting it, and the environmental impacts of local authority policies. It is to be used as a baseline against which to assess the progress and impact of local environmental policies and practices (FOE 1989, p. 7).

The Local Government Management Board has identified two specific types of audit: state of the environment reports comprising a comprehensive appraisal of an area's environmental condition, including a database that can be updated as monitoring occurs and used to compare performance with local, national and international indicators of environmental performance, and internal audits that comprise a systematic and objective evaluation of an authority's policies and practices. These are the models that many local authorities have sought to follow to varying degrees so that over fifty state of the environment reports have now been commissioned or undertaken and many more authorities have undertaken internal or management audits together with policy impact appraisals often resulting in explicit environmental statements or green charters.

In contrast the European Commission has defined environmental auditing as:

> a management tool comprising a systematic, documented, periodic and objective evaluation of how well environmental organisation, management and equipment are performing with the aim of contributing to safeguard the environment by facilitating management control of environmental practices and assessing compliance with company policies, which would include meeting regulatory requirements and standards applicable (CEC 1991b, p. 44).

This also closely follows the definition proffered by the International Chamber of Commerce (ICC 1991) and it is in this context that the British Standards Institute developed the two standards BS5750 dealing with quality and BS7750 dealing with environmental management systems. The former allows for the award of a certificate that guarantees that a business's quality performance is properly organised. In a four stage procedure a quality manual is prepared that sets out the policy and procedures on quality assurance using standards of performance that the company may produce for itself.

This is followed by a visit from an assessor who will check that the procedures are in place. A certificate is then issued which can be shown on letterheads and the final stage comprises continuing assessment including periodic visits from the certifying authority. BS7750 comprises a set of procedures for managing environmental performance and is designed as a companion to BS5750. It is intended to be suitable for all organisations not just those in the manufacturing industry. It is not based upon a quality standard for a product but upon a specific process.

The process recommended comprises a rational analytical model for environmental management, with twelve prescribed and progressive stages of: commitment; initial review; policy formulation; staff training; registration and evaluation; objectives and targets; management programming; the formulation of a management manual; control; explicit records; auditing and review. It is suggested that reviews or audits will not be effective unless placed within the context of a structured management system that is integrated with overall management activity and addresses all aspects of environmental performance.

Before examining the processes advocated in both the Eco-Management and Audit Regulation and the British Standard in some further detail it might be useful to consider one or two wider strategic issues that the processes raise.

Agreed standards and environmental liability

The Eco-label and Eco-Management scheme and BS5750 and BS7750 are intended to make environmental quality a new market barrier to commerce, industry and services, theoretically eliminating those who fail to meet the standards. This raises the first fundamental question about the processes that are being urged upon us — they assume that the market is the proper place to regulate our actions to achieve sustainable performance and development.

This in turn relies upon appropriate standards being agreed and set and not left to the discretion of individual concerns who prescribe their own standards and by complying with them gain a market advantage. It also depends upon the dissemination of full information in relation to sustainable objectives and appropriate standards, otherwise customers in the marketplace will not be able to judge adequately sustainable performance but could be seduced by marketing hype.

This is a grave problem for beleaguered local authorities whose own performance has never before come under such public scrutiny and who are tempted to rush pell mell into the processes advocated as a new paradigm for local government without proper standards having been set. In this context local authorities may undertake and publish superficial audits that only deceive themselves and their customers. Apart from the moral dilemma that this might raise, it also raises issues regarding environmental liability. Hitherto the public sector has acted in the public interest and has been protected to a large extent from direct liability because of the difficulty in proving a duty to care in respect of individuals. Where explicit standards are set and performance falls short of these standards there is an increasing likelihood of successful individual challenge in respect of local authority negligence. This of course raises one of the fundamental debates about the differences between the public sector and private sectors and the applicability of private sector management methods and techniques.

Service impacts and social and economic criteria

In contrast to industry, where environmental effects arise through the process of industrial production, in a local authority they will arise not only through such processes, such as how much paper it uses or waste it generates, but also through service impacts. In commercial organisations the principal value on which management is focused is return on investment. It is being suggested that this focus needs adjusting to take account of environmental effects and, although in the short term this might lead to a reduction in profits, in the longer term it will yield a competitive edge in the market place to any company that undertakes proper auditing and can demonstrate that its product has benefitted as a consequence.

Aside from the effect of shifting the burden of environmental responsibility to the consumer, the difficulty in applying this principle to local authorities lies first in the fact that the value of local authority services is not only in the commercial formulation of means and ends but also in achieving social results — better housing, a healthier community, better educated children. These services can of course be subject to rigorous scrutiny for their environmental effects but this is quite likely to lead to painful choices about protecting threatened flora or fauna or allowing the construction of housing to meet an identified need.

Take a simple example from Brighton, a Council that is firmly committed to the principles of achieving sustainable development. The authority has acknowledged that traffic in the centre of town is causing unacceptable levels of visual and atmospheric pollution. In order to discourage use of the private car it supported a policy of higher car parking charges in the town centre and sought to establish a ring of park and ride facilities on the outskirts of town. Soon town centre retail operators were complaining that their business was suffering unacceptably and, as the recession continued, this was manifest in a rising number of vacant premises bringing pressure to lower the charges again.

In these circumstances environmental auditing may lead to better informed decisions but does not eliminate the need for painful choices to be made when social or economic criteria are also applied. The County Planning Officers Society has highlighted this problem in its report *Planning for Sustainable Development* in which it points out that policies for sustainable development are not necessarily complementary and that:

> the most ardent commitment to the cause will not obviate the need for difficult judgements (CPOS 1993, p. 37).

The most fundamental point raised here relates back to the definition of sustainability. Other chapters deal with this concept but some local authorities already take the view that the Brundtland definition is too strong — despite the fact that in global terms it is regarded by many as too human oriented — and are suggesting that a more appropriate way forward might be to seek to reduce unsustainability.

Whatever definition is chosen it will clearly represent one value of the organisation that will require incorporation within a sound agreed strategy and strategic framework, and perhaps this is the next hurdle for the implementation of environmental auditing — that there must first be strategic commitment to its implementation and this must be integrated across appropriate functional lines. This leads to two further considerations:

Firstly local government re-organisation. The organisation of local government is under review and the criteria for the determination of appropriate boundaries are concerned with financial and social or community issues and do not include explicit reference to effective environmental management. This has a bearing on the amount of work that existing local authorities are likely to be able or willing to undertake to provide the baseline information for environmental management whilst the outcome of local government re-organisation is unknown. In addition, it raises questions relating to what are appropriate boundaries for environmental management and, in the absence of agreed standards, what might be the arrangements necessary for inter-authority collaboration on trans boundary issues. These uncertainties place great emphasis upon the need for shared information regarding best practice.

Secondly formulating effective strategy. The point to be considered is the process for effective strategy making within local authorities, that is the setting of broad organisational objectives to provide a framework for decisions about what services will be offered and how and to whom they will be delivered. There are two principal approaches that have been identified over time: corporate planning and logical incrementalism. In practice they are seldom discrete but they have individual shortcomings that have been well documented. Reference is made to them because it appears that the systematic processes recommended in Eco-Management and Audit and BS7750 borrows from the corporate planning model for strategic management, whilst, logical incrementalism is the model that many local authorities adopted when corporate planning became discredited. The current management climate embodied in Eco-Management and Audit and BS7750 appears to represent a return to the pursuit of ever more rational models of decision taking.

Taking the corporate planning model first, this is a formal and analytically oriented process that evolved during the 1960s. It proceeds through a number of separate activities which should be undertaken in the sequence specified in the model. The stages correspond to those advocated in BS7750; goal setting, analysis, evaluation. The problems with this model that have been identified include several matters that have a bearing on the adoption of sustainability as an organisational value and its implementation through an 'environmental management system':

- Public relations — where a strategic approach is intended to impress or satisfy outsiders. Here the focus can shift to producing an impressive document rather than developing a useful strategy. This was common criticism of corporate planning in local authorities during the 1970s where vast corporate plans were produced, only to become out of date as soon as they were committed to paper because of the dynamics and pace of change (Langley 1988). This might be a problem encountered by those authorities that have embarked upon or commissioned or undertaken State of the Environment Reports.
- Information — here the process is used to provide information for strategic visions. However, it has been observed that senior managers develop strategic visions before all the information is available. Further studies have found that decision makers are not capable of comprehending more than a very few interrelated variables (Bowman and Asch 1987). Again this might suggest that managers in local authorities may not be assisted by the volume of information likely to be gathered under the stages recommended in Eco-Management Audit and BS7750.
- Paralysis by analysis — systematic formal planning activities can stifle creative solutions, can breed increasing irrelevance and the development of ponderous apparatus.
- Ownership — where the plan is drawn up centrally by a few specialists, the process can be seen as an unbearable annual ritual; 'Thank God its over, now lets get back to work' (Lenz and Lyles 1989, p. 58).

The second approach has been described as logical incrementalism, and here policy is not made once and for all but is a process of successive approximation to some desired objectives in which what is desired itself continues to change under reconsideration (Lindblom 1959). The problems most associated with logical incrementalism have been identified as:

- Dubious causality — that the outcomes of strategic management undertaken in this way cannot necessarily be attributed to the undefined process.
- Strategic shift — that without express objectives and in the context of an implicit commitment to perceived desirable outcomes there will be a drift away from what are the real desirable outcomes (Quinn 1980).

If strategy is to be managed effectively, it must overcome the problems of ownership identified in the rational model and the problems of drift in the incremental model.

Organisational structure

The allocation of responsibilities, their grouping, decision taking, co-ordination and control are all fundamental to the operation of an organisation and in particular to organisations that are genuinely committed to achieving sustainable development and to changing practice in significant ways.

For some local authorities the 1980s represented a decade of restructuring to allow for cuts to be made, to provide a more customer oriented service, to become more efficient, to rationalise the use of space and so on. Nevertheless many local authorities are still organised along traditional professional lines with services managed by a lead professional qualified in the core discipline of the department. This organisational structure may give rise to a fundamental contradiction of values and objectives between 'professionals' who see their prime duty to aspects of the 'environment' and others whose concern is the effectiveness of the whole service. Although there are some advantages to this model it has several disadvantages that are likely to militate against achieving sustainability and its implementation through environmental auditing and management.

Firstly, it is often the case that top management in local authorities has difficulty in integrating services across departmental lines. Professional departments often funnel issues up to the top of the organisation, with good working links between professionals in the same department assisting this process but creating barriers to effective communication between different groups of people in different departments.

Secondly, in local authorities, professional values have occasionally filled the gap left by inadequately articulated political values and this creates a problem of legitimacy between departments, between staff and elected members and between the electorate and the politicians. Thirdly, to the public the professional model often appears inconsistent and impenetrable, with different departments speaking different languages and with different values. Finally, as different areas of concern are added to the local authority agenda, these are grafted on to an existing professional domain, resting there sometimes more or less appropriately. So far as environmental auditing is concerned, the least painful way in which authorities might grasp the nettle is by simply placing the responsibility for such auditing with one profession — where it might rest undisturbed and unacknowledged — a huge amount of data collected, owned and understood by a few people.

The prospect of new organisational structures and new ways of working to deliver sustainability may seem absurd, but if it is necessary to deliver it through an integrated environmental management model then it must be recognised that there are factors described above in the traditional structures of local government that are likely to militate against its successful implementation. More appropriate structures are likely to be organised in such a way that sustainability is not the exclusive responsibility of any single cognitive competence (Evans 1993) but is part of the common purpose of the council articulated through management structures that reflect a multi-disciplinary approach to environmental matters (Parston 1991).

Implementing an 'environmental management system'

Both the Eco-Management and Audit Regulation and the British Standard set out a process for environmental management incorporating environmental auditing. The main difference between the two is that the former requires an externally validated statement. CAG Consultants have summarised the main components of both systems and have compared the stages set with what has generally occurred in local authority practice (Jacobs 1993). This summary is illustrated in Table 5.1 and has been slightly modified to reflect more recent developments.

From this it can be seen that the Eco-Management and Audit and BS7750 are broadly similar, use similar and familiar terms and identify a sequence of events that are on-going and iterative. The main difference with what appears to have occurred in local authority practice is in the explicit and systematic setting up of a framework for environmental management.

BS7750 — The case of Brighton

Figure 5.1 outlines the stages of the British Standard prescribed management system BS7750 and the place of auditing within it,

Table 5.1 Eco-Management Audit, BS7750 and local authority practice (adapted from Jacobs 1993)

Activity	System	Approach advocated or adopted
explicit environmental strategy	Eco-Audit BS7750 *LA practice*	No explicit statement specified Explicit commitment required *Incorporated in Council's Mission Statement*
examine how current activities affect the environment	Eco-Audit BS7750 *LA practice*	Environmental Review Preparatory or Initial Review *Internal Audit/State of the Environment Report*
set overall aims and priorities	Eco-Audit BS7750 *LA practice*	Environmental Policy Environmental Policy *Green Charter*
policy implementation	Eco-Audit BS7750 *LA practice*	Environmental Programme Environmental Management Programme *Action Plan*
allocate responsibilities	Eco-Audit BS7750 *LA practice*	Environmental Management System Organisation Personnel/ Operational Control *Appoint co-ordinator/muddle through*
document intended procedures	Eco-Audit BS7750 *LA practice*	Environmental Management Manual Environmental Management Manual/Documentation *Policy/position statements/files*
records	Eco-Audit BS7750 *LA practice*	Environmental Management System Environmental Management System/Records *Records/establish database/do nothing*
assess and monitor progress	Eco-Audit BS7750 *LA practice*	Environmental Audit Environmental Management Audit *Performance Review*
publish information	Eco-Audit BS7750 *LA practice*	Environmental Statement not required *Annual Environmental Report*

and we now examine this process in the context of practice and experience at Brighton Borough Council.

1.   Commitment to an 'environmental management system and initial review'

In a local authority this has to mean political commitment as well as management commitment. In the present economic climate the first question asked by elected members is how much is this going to cost? At some levels, amending practice does not necessarily cost and sustainability can be achieved by using existing resources in a different way. However, the implementation of the thoroughgoing process recommended here, can only come from a council's administration adopting sustainability and integrated environmental management as one of its values, one of its essential priorities, for the whole organisation and for that to be translated into a programme or, series of programmes, through the chief executive and the chief officers. As already discussed, for a council the action is doubly complex — not only as an organisation itself wasting paper and consuming energy, but also as an enabler in and controller of the wider environment. Whilst the former may be relatively straightforward to deal with, the latter will highlight profound policy conflicts.

2.   The definition and documentation of an 'environmental policy'

The British Standard explains that this is to act as a base encompassing all relevant regulatory and legislative requirements, including health and safety. It should also seek to develop standards in some or all sections of an organisation's activities. Policy commitments may state, for example:

- reduce waste and consumption of resources;
- re-design products and practices to reduce their environmental effects in production, use and disposal;
- re-evaluate purchasing policies to minimise environmental impact.

Local authorities should be better off than most organisations to undertake this stage. Statutory land use plans, policy documents, committee resolutions provide a rich vein of existing policy to

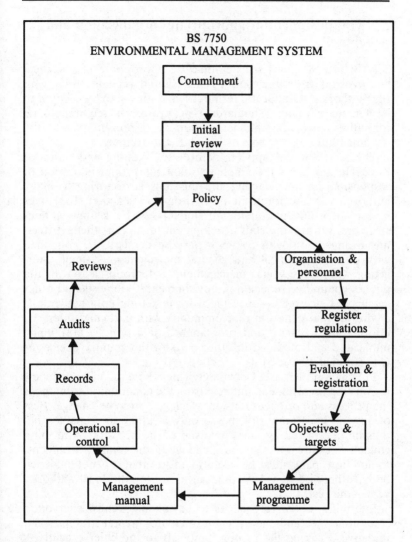

Figure 5.1

act as a base. A variety of vehicles can be used to bring this work together. In Brighton the approach to a Green Charter was modified to provide a review of existing policy (including some explicit targets) that is still reviewed each year to identify progress, changes and refinements in the form of an environmental position statement.

3.   Establishment of appropriate 'organisation and personnel'

The British Standard stresses that the appropriate people must be involved from the outset. This should include those with the authority to allocate resources and the staff necessary to implement particular standards. The process is required to be formalised involving the designation of responsibility and the documentation of the role of key staff and training.

The fact that this appears before any auditing and action in the cycle illustrates the emphasis upon the proper allocation of responsibilities and training and this now is occurring to many authorities in the forefront of environmental action. Initiatives in the environmental field are unlikely to be lasting without structural reform and staff development to support them. Effecting arrangements with common purpose needs to be combined with effective political and general management systems interacting with professional management and groups and with the public, commerce, education, environmental lobbyists and other agencies. Leicester's pioneering work in setting up a network of environmental panels in the community with particular interests, information to share and programmes of action, is now being duplicated and modified in other parts of the country (Leicester City Council 1990a, b).

In Brighton there is a Community Environment Panel. Openness in enlisting involvement and help from the community strengthens the process and provides tension which can promote change. Best of all, the local authority should only facilitate and enable, and thus be one of the agencies involved in the network. After all a council can only effect so much change in the total environment. In addition, pains must be taken to ensure that it is not a council body, otherwise it will become an arena for the local authority versus the rest.

Internally, equal care needs to be taken to enlist everyone's commitment to and endorsement of environmental strategies and initiatives. Taking the responsibility off to the chief executive's department does not work, in our experience, or that of large authorities with central policy units — everyone else feels excluded. Chief executives should show essential leadership by seconding a policy officer to themselves for a fixed period to promote and set up the corporate processes, but use a network of liaison officers throughout the organisation to plant and germinate ideas and action. This network can be given further status by including a member of the chief officer's group in its number.

These people must then work with existing departmental policy officers, particularly in the environmental service groupings, to review policy and practice and develop initiatives. Without them involved, change will be illusory. The officer network has a further purpose. In informing itself about environmental issues, its members become a valuable training resource for others, adding to the more formal training opportunities that conferences, seminars and courses provide. Additionally, in some authorities like Brighton, organisational values (which include environmental issues) are re-enforced in management development programmes.

4. Registration and evaluation of 'environmental effects'

The standard specifies that these should include: atmospheric emissions; discharges to water; waste management; use of natural resources; noise dust and other relevant issues; the potential consequences of abnormal operations, incidents and disasters. Anyone who has examined a State of the Environment report will know that the scope of a local authority's interests are more complex and extensive than the list described above. Therefore, for many councils the prospect of resourcing reports like those of Kirklees, Oxford and Lancashire are daunting (the latter cost £200,000), particularly as they may only produce a snapshot, can have lengthy gestation periods and can lead to confrontation and defensiveness between the agencies that are responsible for the general environment. More feasible perhaps for the small and medium sized authority is to take this stage in steps, concentrating on a particular area, be it air pollution, or a further subset, traffic generation, and undertaking the next stages in the environmental management system just for that area of concern. This of course raises problems with regard to the inter-relationships between activities, effects and impacts and can lead to duplication as future subjects of analysis and action are reached; but it does make a start and it is probably the case that something is better than nothing.

The other issue here, that has already been touched upon, is the environmentally arbitrary nature of local authority boundaries. Nowhere perhaps is there more occasion for collaborative working between authorities than in the preparation of work under this section. As well as producing more relevant groupings of land areas, it may lead to economies of scale and reduce duplication in research.

In addition, one of the aspects of the environmental assessments of projects and one of the likely recommendations for change to the statutory procedures is that the scope of assessments should be pre-determined with the authority that will judge the assessment and in consultation with the public. The scoping stage in auditing might also be the most appropriate stage to begin community consultation, particularly where there are choices to be made about the environmental issues to be covered.

If the foregoing steps are right then steps 5–9 should be easier:

5. Setting of explicit 'environmental objectives and targets'

6. Preparation of an 'environmental management programme'

7. Preparation of an 'environmental management manual and appropriate documentation'

8. Institution of 'operational control and verification' procedures

9. Maintenance of appropriate 'environmental management records'

Whilst changes to a council's internal processes, such as purchasing and waste management, are one matter, and relatively straight-forward, setting objectives and targets and preparing the action programme for the community have to have broad based agreement. Town planners working in policy and plan making know what that entails — a lengthy and largely iterative process of internal and external, community and political, resident and business debate, compromise and endorsement. However, without discussion, a co-operative and therefore genuinely effective strategy will not be implemented. A local authority working alone cannot affect enough. Proper consultation and participation is time consuming, it must involve elected representatives as well as the community, it will prove difficult and more or less confrontational; but there is no substitute. However, with endorsement in place, specialists in the community will be more willing to assist with operational control and verification procedures and with record keeping; reducing the burden on the local authority.

The last two stages raise questions about who audits the auditors?

10.   Operation of 'environmental management audits'

These are defined as mechanisms to assess both the effectiveness of the management system and the achievement of environmental objectives.

11.   Implementation and programming of 'environmental management reviews'

In contrast to the audit the review checks the relevance of policy, up-dates evaluation of environmental effects and checks upon the efficacy of audits and follow up action.

Part of a council's deal with its community in enlisting its endorsement of the council's objectives, targets and strategy, might be that experts in the community would form independent assessors of practice and success. If this feels uncomfortable, then of course that is intended — creative tension again — however, if it feels too uncomfortable, too out of control, it can be demotivating and therefore something more creative should be followed. Employing consultants to do the auditing is a good fall back, but may be costly; perhaps even better, another local authority may collaborate in the review. This happens in other agency fields, Health Authorities and Police Services, and it should prove to be cheaper; particularly so if a group of authorities network to provide specialists for each other (much fairer than a simple reciprocal arrangement). The management review stage however, should be undertaken by management itself as a precursor to starting the cyclical model again. If the officer network including its chief officer link, is working well, it will be best placed to help with this task and provide assessments for an authority's senior managers and members to commit any necessary changes to policy and process.

Conclusions

Environmental auditing is a powerful tool if incorporated within an effective environmental management system. It can be used to measure the extent to which management systems are performing, it can assist in verifying compliance with local, national and European environmental legislation and in the development of internal procedures to ensure improved environmental performance. It is an aid to decision taking — to pollute or not to pollute, to pay or ameliorate, or change current practice. It may be offered in support at inquiry of policies, plans, programmes and development decisions. It is an explicit statement and is therefore open and accountable and it may highlight gaps, inefficiencies and inequalities in policy and practice. Set in the context of a formal environmental management programme, it may allow for an integrated approach towards achieving more sustainable ways of working and sustainable development decisions.

Environmental auditing and management represents a challenge to conventional processes of policy making, however, before it becomes a new paradigm for local government, there are unresolved problems that should not be overlooked:

- The first must relate to the definition of sustainability to which we are working, a proper analysis and understanding of the trade-offs involved in development decisions and whether the market can or will bear the costs.
- Second are agreed standards for achieving sustainability. These cannot be left to individual organisations to determine and then confirm that they have met.
- This in turn leads to considerations regarding the appropriate agencies, boundaries, structures, technology and skills for the delivery of integrated environmental management and the development of appropriate techniques for auditing and assessment. This will only be achieved if old professional allegiances and barriers are dismantled in favour of more co-operative ways of working.
- Finally, genuine commitment to environmental management will require proper support from government and resources, perhaps most particularly for research, staff participation, development and training.

6 Empowerment and decentralisation

Albert Golding

In the 'big bang' approach to policy development in local government in Britain it could be argued that while 'decentralisation' was the talk of the 1980s, environmental policy is the preoccupation of the 1990s. How interesting it would be however to fuse these important urban policy agendas into one, coupled with the political imperative of making empowerment an everyday activity rather than an obsession of academics and Government officials.

In the increasing global debate on environmental policy, including Local Agenda 21, it is essential, in the drive for more corporate strategic frameworks, not to forget the customer. Of the many fundamental declarations made by government ministers and municipal leaders at, and following, the Rio Summit, the need to engage the citizen and other non-governnmental organisations in the environmental debate was probably the most important radical proposal announced to enable a truly new approach to solving the world's environment problems. Clearly environmental policies must not be developed and delivered in a theoretical straight-jacket, however well intentioned.

The method of implementation of policy and indeed the determination of local environmental policy to meet local needs must be constructed in a pragmatic political and administrative environment. The involvement of the consumers of environmental policies, including residents and businesses, must be effectively engaged and they must also be empowered if they are really to be given the opportunity to influence decision making in these critically important areas of policy which will determine the shape and quality of life for both urban and rural areas in Britain.

If Local Agenda 21 is really to provide a framework for change it is one whose parameters must be imposed upwards. Subsidiarity must be embodied in an international–national–local–neighbourhood framework with clear linkages, a coherent set of strategic and local policy programmes involving practical enhancements to environmental policy. While this may be theoretically accepted, the implementation of such an important and radical policy agenda requires corresponding radical approaches to political and organisational management. If Local Agenda 21 is to be successful it will require radical organisational change based on empowerment.

To believe in the principles of empowerment in local government means that radical decisions need to be taken about organisational structures and the traditional methods of officer to officer and officer to member relationships. Equally important is the need to genuinely involve local residents, businesses and other community and voluntary sector agencies in the determination of policy and the process of 'government'. The 'Common Declaration on Behalf of Cities and Local Authorities' is clear: 'any sustainable development strategy requires increased local autonomy and democracy as well as an extension of decentralisation process and the possibility of establishing inter-authority co-operation where environmental issues transcend municipal boundaries' (IULA et al. 1992a).

There have been several exciting decentralisation experiments over the last decade but seldom has a radical political conviction been combined with executive support through officers to break the mould of traditional thinking and establish new political and administrative models of government which truly empower the citizen.

In the London Borough of Tower Hamlets, a radical approach to decentralisation has been developed since 1986 which has involved the complete reorganisation of the political and administrative structures based on a genuine commitment to empowerment. It is a demonstration of a 'bottom up' approach to corporate policy making and organisational management which could well provide a transferable model to promote the principles of Rio. Indeed the various governmental statements following Rio imply that a prerequisite for practical development and application of environmental policy is a decentralised approach. In this sense, Tower Hamlets' decentralised structure provides a practical working model which embodies the main principles of Agenda 21

While a radical restructuring of the Local Authority has occurred, East London has also been subjected to some of the largest construction projects in Europe which has necessitated the Authority developing a strategic view on environmental issues which are very much part of the Agenda 21 debate. However the fusion of clear strategic policy development has also been combined with the need to tackle environmental issues from the grass roots. Such pragmatic local agendas gain strength from the decentralised approach to decision making and enable strategic policy to have substance rather than being a top down imposed framework.

Before expanding on the local developments in empowerment illustrated in Tower Hamlets, some commentary is required on current decentralisation thinking to show the variety of models and possible opportunities to both develop and implement strategic environmental policy.

Environmental policy in a decentralised authority — the case of Tower Hamlets

Political and organisational structures

The development of local environmental policy in Tower Hamlets has always had a dual purpose: to improve the quality of life in a rapidly changing urban environment, and to enable residents to gain control over policy and processes which ensure that they are able to drive, rather than be driven by, policy development.

Decentralisation was introduced in Tower Hamlets in 1986 because the new Liberal administration perceived the existing structure to be monolithic, bureaucratic and a completely enclosed organisation where both politicians and professionals showed an unwillingness to be open or to be accountable. The breakdown in the insularity of the Authority was immediate and is best illustrated by the radical political restructuring of the Authority with the creation of seven autonomous Neighbourhood Committees with their own political structures and policy development programmes. This fundamental political change was followed by administrative organisational change which substantially altered the professional relationships of officers with a move towards generic officer working and the disappearance of static, rigid departmental structures. This change which was almost entirely internal had a fundamental effect on officer to officer and officer to member relationships, empowering both to develop environmental policies which had their roots in a community driven agenda and the opportunity to think freely and laterally outside the traditional constraints of local authorities. The concept of the 'enclosed organisation', a theme which Clarke and Stewart have identified as being one in which the citizen can feel powerless, was tackled early in Tower Hamlets enabling new models of resident involvement to be developed (Clarke and Stewart 1992).

Following the establishment of the new internal structures, recent consideration has been given to the application of empowerment principles in partnership discussions with external agencies, particularly the private sector, to ensure that the citizen can influence all institutions which can both promote, and prejudice, the quality of life. The 'export' of these important guiding principles into our contact with external agencies ensures that our approach to partnership is guided by a strong empowerment theme not only to improve policy but to change the method of implementation. These principles, which were firmly established by 1990 and enabled the Authority to react swiftly and successfully to the City Challenge opportunity enabling further advances in decentralised organisational thinking about urban policy and initiative, are discussed later in this chapter.

Resident forums/resident election

One of the most obvious principles of British local politics is that the 'public is empowered through the electoral process'. This may be a convenient truism for politicians who are content with the status quo but usually such traditional views are accompanied by depressingly low turnouts in local elections. In Tower Hamlets for example voter turnout in 1978, 1982 and 1986 averaged 33 per cent.

Clearly, to truly develop the principles of empowerment, particularly in the local environmental policy context where the interaction between the community and local authority are so close, it is essential to consider other forms of participatory democracy which enable real empowerment. In an attempt to address 'the politics of place . . . where local environmental concerns . . . grow' (LGMB et al. 1992c) new models of local empowerment were considered by the Council after 1986.

As part of the radical organisational change introduced following 1986, with decentralisation becoming the guiding force in the development of local policy, new forms of resident involvement were attempted. Several Neighbourhoods experimented with resident election to Neighbourhood Forums which would become Advisory Bodies to guide the Neighbourhood Committee.

In Globe Town Neighbourhood, for example, Tenants' Associations have representation on Estate-based Committees and together with the elected representatives of the Tenants' Forum, play an advisory role in the ultimate decision making body, which is the Standing Neighbourhood Committee. Through this process it is possible for any resident to exercise his/her influence on the decisions made by the elected members of the Council. In Bow Neighbourhood, there are sixteen elected area representatives, who form the Residents' Forum, which has a direct input to the Standing Neighbourhood Committee. The residents, also have a line of communication to the Standing Neighbourhood Committee, via 'ad hoc' interest groups, set up for particular issues.

Poplar Neighbourhood has established twelve Community Forums feeding back via elected members to the Neighbourhood Committee. Bethnal Green Neighbourhood devolved internal management and resident involvement to three ward based structures. An important common characteristic of each approach to further decentralisation of power through these models is that these bodies are given some responsibility in deciding how money is spent.

These four examples demonstrate that decentralisation has, most certainly, empowered the residents, who now possess a far greater awareness of the activities and issues surrounding them, due to improved communication and a higher level of personal involvement. This has enhanced their quality of life and instilled a level of self confidence in them, to be in control of their own destiny. It is the practical application of the essence of decentralisation as defined by Hambleton that 'it involves the service organisation getting closer to the public and it often involves an attempt to shift the balance of power in favour of those the organisation is intended to serve' (Hambleton 1992).

The result of this greater devolution of decision making has been an increasing emphasis on local environmental policy issues which ensure an immediate and direct link between policy and implementation with the Neighbourhood Committees, and their associated Advisory Forums, having important community based environmental responsibilities for noise pollution, health and safety, food hygiene and communicable diseases, etc. In parallel with this community based devolution has been the development of coherent corporate environmental policy programmes which has enabled the Authority to break new ground in tackling urban policy and environmental protection matters.

Environmental policy achievements

The green agenda with a special emphasis on environmental protection has always been one of the key objectives of the Council. Environmental concerns permeate all areas of the Neighbourhoods' and Central Departments' service provision. Strategic policy and Neighbourhood implementation are inter-linked to provide a coherent programme while allowing Neighbourhoods to develop their own programmes to meet local needs. It is important that environmental issues are not tackled as discrete areas of professional concern with little interconnection.

As a result of the major construction projects in East London, particularly Canary Wharf, the Docklands Light Railway and the Docklands Link Road, the Council has developed a broad range of Environmental Protection Strategies based on real achievement. In response to the construction of the Docklands Light Railway the Council was successful in pursuing the first rail noise policy in the country which imposes noise restriction levels on the construction process which if not adhered to would trigger noise insulation glazing for adjacent residential properties. It took, however, a petition to the House of Lords to achieve this national breakthrough in policy making. The Council is actively seeking the support of other organisations in plugging the gaps in the field of environmental protection, including the interesting areas of dust and TV interference which demonstrates the capacity of a decentralised Authority to combine major national policy agendas with the needs of the local citizen through the Neighbourhood structure.

Indeed, as was argued earlier, the necessity to fuse this extremely important local agenda with regional and international environmental policy issues can perhaps only be satisfactorily developed in a decentralised structure. Clearly this is a theme to which local authorities will return as they prepare their own Local Agenda 21 statements in due course.

The major corporate environmental policy initiatives have their root in the community which involves a real engagement of local residents and community groups. Apart from the Neighbourhood structure there is also the need to ensure that non-government agencies such as tenants associations, campaign groups, voluntary sector organisations and local businesses are a real part of the development of environmental policy and most importantly its application.

In recent years environment-based action groups have sprung up, arguably empowered by the Council's decentralised structure but also because of success in establishing major policy changes, which now provide the framework for a looser confederation approach to decision making. The promotion of such groups requires a proactive approach to capacity building and a genuine desire to share power. Of the programmes that have developed in recent years, there have been many single issue campaigns such as opposing the damaging effects of major rail construction projects such as Crossrail in an urban environment, and more generic issues such as the protection of the residential environment from rat-running commuter traffic.

The most significant of these campaigns in Tower Hamlets, because of its size and task, is that conducted by SPLASH (South Poplar Limehouse Action for Secure Housing). This consortium of tenants associations formed to tackle perceived unfairness as a result of the construction of the LDDC's roads proposals and the Docklands Light Railway, is perhaps a case study in empowerment. Originally campaigning on a single issue agenda of seeking compensation for noise and environmental pollution, it has grown, with the support of the Council and other organisations, into a compact body which, while still seeking to redress compensation issues is also trying to develop as a community based forum in order to take on the additional challenges of improving the urban environment and seeking to enhance the education and economic well being of the area. SPLASH were closely involved in the Council's unsuccessful South Poplar City Challenge submission in 1992 but are now supporting the largest civil action against an environmental pollution issue in the country. A true example of an empowerment based community campaign and perhaps the sort of example that Local Agenda 21 is seeking to promote.

A coherent strategy of environmental policies in waste management, energy management and purchasing has also been adopted by the Council setting the framework for Neighbourhood implementation and initiatives which include a Considerate Contractor scheme on the Isle of Dogs; the adoption of a Green Policy Strategy in Globe Town; the adoption of the Friends of the Earth Strategy in Poplar and an Environmental Week in Wapping.

Models of decentralisation

Decentralisation and empowerment in local government has been approached from a variety of different angles and political agendas in recent years. Some local authorities during the 1980s saw decentralisation as a radical way of taking services closer to residents. This consumer orientated approach had also been heavily influenced by central government policy with the devolution of power in education and health to improve service delivery and introduce internal markets. The Education Reform Act (1988) is probably the best example, with the programmed introduction of local management of schools.

Other local authorities have approached decentralisation from a community based perspective, the agenda of which is primarily political — to break down traditional monolithic political and administrative structures to ensure greater involvement and empowerment of local residents, politicians and indeed management. Hambleton (1992) describes the different approaches: 'The consumerist approach is essentially concerned with the reform of local government considered as an administrative system, whereas the community based approach seeks to reform local government considered as a political system'.

It is not clear that either of these two approaches corresponds to the experience of those radical local authorities that are driving the decentralised model forward. Certainly as far as the London Borough of Tower Hamlets is concerned it is impossible to separate the objective of radically improving service delivery through a devolved management structure with the equally important political task of changing the face of local government, enabling residents to have a real voice in decision making and indeed, alone among local authorities in the country, giving the political opposition control.

Perhaps of most interest to those agencies determined to develop environmental policy is Tower Hamlets' approach to empowerment which ensures that the citizen has a real role in decision making. It is where the citizen, rather than the citizen as consumer, comes first that Local Agenda 21 has its best opportunity for innovative practical application.

In determining the extent to which decentralisation and empowerment are key tools in local environmental policy it is important to retain a semblance of balance. As the Local Government Management Board has recently commented: 'Devolution and decentralisation does not mean autonomy. They will normally take place within a framework set by the Authority' (LGMB et al. 1992b). Tower Hamlets' Corporate Environmental Strategy provides the coherence for a decentralised Authority to concentrate on practical targeted local implementation to meet defined needs as expressed and influenced by the citizen.

However, it would be naive to suggest that the theoretical framework and practical implementation of decentralisation does not contain some fault lines. It has proved to be a difficult balancing act in some policy areas, most notably housing, to ensure that the Authority has, and just as importantly is perceived to have, a coherent framework within which Neighbourhood autonomy can develop and flourish. Occasionally the local autonomy of Neighbourhoods has deflected a clear strategic view, with the result that initiatives have been delayed although not negated. The issue is one of putting the local issue first and the corporate second. While this is perfectly laudable in respect of service provision on front-line services, it can clearly become problematic if the Authority negates its corporate role and is seen as an unco-ordinated federation of unconnected autonomous entities. Clearly, such a perception will not gain favour with government departments and indeed external investors who require a clear corporate focus.

The difficult, but extremely interesting task in any decentralised model is to establish a balanced and coherent set of rules which ensure maximum benefit for Neighbourhood autonomy while retaining and indeed strengthening, the corporate body. More interestingly, when one transcends the local authority structure and looks at regional and national structures in the context of subsidiarity and empowerment, the balancing of corporate indentity and local autonomy becomes even more important. At an international level, particularly in the sphere of environmental policy, the necessity of developing community empowerment will present an interesting but complex challenge to political leaders.

City Challenge

During the formative stage of creating the 'Pacemaker' City Challenge projects, different organisational models were developed to adhere to the basic principles of local authority leadership, but not control, the implementation process. While some Authorities developed structures that were strongly tied to the Local Authority, primarily through the Council's decision making process, Tower Hamlets decided to build on its experience of decentralised organisation and developed an implementation process which most closely matched the empowerment intentions of the Council which were also those of the original principles of City Challenge 'government'.

In developing this approach it was decided to tackle directly one of the main assumptions of established organisation and management which is that accountability to the public is achieved through the hierarchy of an elected Council rather than directly to the users of the service.

It was clear from the outset that if the strategies and programmes were to have a long lasting benefit for the area then they had to be driven from the community and implemented by a truly collaborative partnership model. Long before the Action Plan was finally approved in March 1992 the Council had instituted a Shadow City Challenge Board which was always intended to be independent of the Council yet representative of residents, businesses and local organisations of the area. Of the original sixteen members only three were to be from the Local Authority the others coming from resident representatives from the local estates, other community representatives, partners from the private sector and representatives of other statutory sector bodies. The tenants' representatives were elected through a panel of chairs and vice-chairs of the respective estates and represent the collective view of approximately 6500 people.

This formative board was eventually constituted into a public limited company with its articles and memorandum of association, company directors and a formal legal contract with the Council to deliver the City Challenge programme on its behalf. It is a model which has been singled out by the Department of the Environment for special attention since it embodies the principles of empowerment intended in the early thinking of City Challenge. This approach to City Challenge clearly has its foundation in decentralisation philosophy and accords with the principles embodied by Clarke and Stewart (1992) that 'to give the public a choice means that the Authority alone does not choose'.

Of the many interacting programmes of the Bethnal Green City Challenge, environmental policy remains a critical theme. Interestingly however when this subject is determined by the citizens it most affects it takes on a direct, broader approach than the environmental strategies of 'intent' included in many 'green' approaches and formally produced by national and local government agencies.

The much acclaimed Local Government Management Board publication *Environmental Practice in Local Government* while documenting very well intentional local authority strategies and audit systems lacks a consumer or citizens' perspective which leads to a single question: Are corporate policy statements, however well supported by public consultation, really tackling the issues that dominate the citizens' agenda or does an empowerment based approach to the definition of the environmental agenda, particularly when coupled with a delivery vehicle that can yield practical and positive results offer a more realistic opportunity of taking forward the post-Rio debate?

The environmental issues that have been identified through the City Challenge approach are not fundamentally different from issues identified elsewhere. Parking, pollution and the quality of the urban environment remain key items in the City Challenge programme. However what gives added value to the debate taking place within the City Challenge arena is that environmental policy is seen as part of a much wider urban policy agenda including the need for capacity building in the local community to allow the disempowered to take control of their own destiny by becoming partners in the implementation of policy through effective programmes.

It is clear from both the practical fusion of environmental policy considerations in the City Challenge programmes as well as the linked connection of themes and issues which form the Earth Summit Agreements post-Rio, that a much broader based definition of 'environmental' issues is being formed. This is becoming much closer to a quality of life agenda.

At the same time through the active involvement of individuals and organisations that are normally outside the decision making arena of local and national government the debate has become much more 'generic' tackling both strategic policy matters and detailed concerns at the same time. It is common therefore that while pursuing a particular aspect of local environmental policy the discussion will centre on the way in which 'greening' the environment relates to the need, in the case of Bethnal Green, to integrate with a Language Development Programme to enhance the skills of the local population (over 80 per cent of which is Bangladeshi) to provide a coherent strategy for the general improvement of quality of life and advanced aspirations.

The separation of the environmental agenda from other important policy issues can lead to a segmented approach which could miss the real needs of those that such corporate policies are meant to serve. An integrated empowerment based approach, such as the one embodied in the Bethnal Green City Challenge programme, while being more difficult to conceive and implement does get to the heart of the subject with positive achievements being the result. It is still too early to evaluate the real benefit of the City Challenge programme to assess the importance that empowerment has had in creating a more coherent approach to environmental policy. However what is clear is that it has provided a real partnership mechanism including the true empowerment of all individuals and organisations associated with it, including the local authorities. The environmental policies that are being produced are those that are owned and relevant to those people that they affect most.

Can City Challenge be enhanced to give an even greater ownership of the programmes by the community it is to serve? The answer must be 'yes' but this will require a more radical approach to empowerment than perhaps many authorities and other organisations would be prepared to consider. By forming a private limited company clearly there is the opportunity of having shareholders. By issuing a share citizens would have a financial and formal link to the programmes and actions of the City Challenge Board. It would put the City Challenge programme funding into the hands of the shareholders rather than the organisations, however democratically accountable, and would be the principle element of the empowerment debate as far as local environmental urban policy is concerned. It would, in effect, increase the power of the public, over public, voluntary and private sector activities. Community ownership par excellence!

While this idea has been discussed informally it has not been taken forward by any of the City Challenge programmes. A radical step forward or a natural development of the principles of empowerment? Others can answer that question as the evaluation of the City Challenge is undertaken by a variety of academic organisations.

Partnership

A central theme emanating from Rio was the obvious need for a collaborative approach to solving global environmental issues. The requirement to include non-government organisations in the policy and decision making process is obviously a necessity if a broad consensus is the intention of a partnership approach.

Future consideration of the environmental agenda from a local authority perspective will need to give much greater consideration to the importance of partnership. The fragmentation of service delivery recently through special purpose agencies such as training enterprise councils, urban development corporations, housing action trusts along with urban policy initiatives such as City Challenge necessitate a different approach in tackling this agenda.

This new form of governance marks a shift in traditional local government perception and could be understood as a threat to those authorities which remain insular and closed. Those authorities which have a decentralised structure and are supportive of the principles of empowerment will be more able to engage with this new approach than those which retain the traditional control of all activities within the municipal realm. The important, conceptual leap required to engage serious and long lasting partnership arrangements can only be really achieved where all partners are confident of giving a little to gain a lot. This involves risk consideration which is easier to develop in a decentralised ethos than in one where traditional forms of rigid control, either political or managerial, remain the dominant culture.

There remains a key role that local authorities can play in promoting the environmental debate both locally and globally. As the elected representatives of local communities, that are closest to the new environmental agenda, they are best able to network and bring different agencies and individuals together. It could be argued that the politicians' mandate is made even stronger when their respective authorities are committed to the principles of empowerment that can be enhanced through a decentralised management structure. Others have stated that adopting such a strategic role is the kernel of being an enabling authority and, indeed, of empowering community and citizens.

In the changing role of local authorities, combining a reduction in powers by central government and a new emphasis on the enabling role via the purchaser/contractor split, there exists an opportunity for local authorities to reassert strategic leadership by concentrating on the overall policy direction of the authority and relying more heavily on the community based structure of devolved management and initiatives. It is through such a combination of roles, strategic and local, through a coherent decentralised structure that the benefits of true strategic partnership combining the global environmental agenda with the needs of the local community can best be achieved.

Partnership can only truly be established when there is a focused agenda with all members of the partnership clearly undertaking, and accepting, the framework of decision making. Local authorities as democratically elected institutions obviously have a key responsibility not only in developing the new environmental agenda but through radical empowerment based models of organisation ensuring that environmental policy becomes the catalyst of action and change. While the Earth Summit Agreements provide an international basis for change, real and long-lasting environmental enhancement will only be achieved if there are real and clear benefits to the community.

Most commentators would acknowledge that there exists a much greater opportunity in the 1990s to establish serious environmental partnerships which accord with Local Agenda 21. However all partnerships must have a lead agency — local authorities for the obvious truism that they are local and *have* local *authority*. They also remain the obvious agencies to ensure that Rio is not a grand ideal but a practical reality.

To convert well intentioned global environmental policy into practical local improvements requires a participative mechanism. Decentralisation provides that mechanism and furthermore Tower Hamlets provides a working model. However, whatever model is chosen, decentralisation based on true empowerment principles is surely the only way to achieve radical progress in this most important global agenda.

7 Environmental planning

Helmut Lusser

This chapter will briefly consider some of the major environmental issues now facing us, all of which require some form of precipitative action. It will then examine how the current planning systems, including the Town and Country Planning system is equipped to deal with those challenges and to see what other mechanisms are being tried and how some local authorities set about that task. The chapter will conclude with a reflection on decision making, exploring at what level decisions need to be made to achieve solutions to the massive environmental problems facing us.

> WE CANNOT AFFORD TO WAIT . . . AND BE WRONG
> (cri de coeur: end of Fifth Action Programme
> Commission of the European Communities 1992)

It has became common to recite the catalogue of major environmental problems and disasters looming if action is not taken. Most of the major problems cited have in common the concern that we are exceeding the carrying capacity of the local environment and ultimately the planet in a number of ways. Emission of gases, fuelled by increases in energy use and dramatic increases in road traffic, threaten global temperature increases, climate changes, desertification and rising sea levels. A seemingly uncontrollable flood of waste pours over Europe, leaving legacies of pollution for generations to come. The land take required for settlements, roads and other infrastructure year by year consumes vast acreages of open land and irreplaceable natural habitats.

Some disquieting trends

Any report on the state of the environment would clearly indicate
trends which, if not satisfactorily contained, could have significant
negative consequences for the quality of the environment as a
whole. For example:

- Energy: a 25 per cent increase in usage by 2010 if there
  is no change in current energy growth rates, resulting, in
  turn, in a 20 per cent increase in EC carbon emissions
  (reference year 1987);

- Transport: a 25 per cent increase in car ownership and a
  17 per cent increase in mileage by 2000 (reference year
  1990);

- Agriculture: a 63 per cent increase in fertilizer use between
  1970 and 1988;

- Waste: a 13 per cent increase in municipal waste over the
  last 5 years, despite increased recycling of paper, glass and
  plastics;

- Water: a 35 per cent increase in the Community's average
  water withdrawal rate between 1970 and 1985;

- Tourism: a 60 per cent increase in Mediterranean tourism
  projected by 2000 (reference year 1990).

(Commission of the European Communities 1992, p. 23)

Without a concerted effort underpinned by a will to make the
necessary changes, these problems will not be resolved. The tasks
are enormous and will require concentrated efforts at many levels
of government and industry, and will affect many interacting
sectors, all of which will need to work together rather than
against each other. Most important of all, consumer behaviour
and attitudes will need to change. After all, the problems which
have been have identified are a result of the cumulative impact of
excessive exploitation of the earth's resources ultimately caused by
individual behaviour.

It is therefore of great interest to note the emphasis given in
the EU Fifth Action Programme to the need to change behaviour
— driver behaviour and use of the motor car as well as the
behaviour of tourists are specifically mentioned — and there is
a recognition that similar behavioural changes will be necessary
if waste reduction and minimisation plans are to succeed.

The nature of environmental problems

In the recent Town and Country Planning Association report on planning for a sustainable environment (Blowers 1993), the chair of the group seeks to summarise the nature of environmental problems to provide an impression of how to deal with them. Not surprisingly, nature knows no administrative boundaries, ministerial portfolios or bureaucratic divisions of labour. The report observes the following four characteristics of environmental issues (pp. 14,15):

- They are transmedia in nature: pollution can pass through the different media — air, water or soil. By careless management a problem can easily be shifted from one media to another.
- They are trans-sectoral in that environmental issues cross traditional policy boundaries. Thus for example, to plan for a more energy efficient future will require interrelated responses to transport policies, land-use policies and arrangements, and standards for new buildings, as well as programmes of behavioural change across a number of areas.
- They are trans-boundary, in that environmental problems do not recognise administrative boundaries. Gone are the days when higher chimneys and longer outfall sewers were going to solve environmental problems. Still with us is the erroneous feeling that once our waste can be shifted two counties away, the problem will have disappeared.
- Finally environmental problems involve all levels of government, from the parish council to Brussels. No level can deal with the problems facing us alone: they all need to interact with decisions made at the appropriate level.

To achieve environmental objectives these characteristics need to be recognised. Solutions need a planning system which has an overview of environmental problems, which can set targets and objectives at different levels of government and which is holistic enough to deal with the complexity of the problems in hand.

Planning for a better environment

Two examples may help to illustrate the nature of the task ahead. Firstly there is the question of the flood of waste, and the seeming inability of Europe to stem the tide, in spite of massive efforts across the community. The EU Fifth Action Programme neatly summarises the position in pointing out that there has been 'a 13 per cent increase in municipal waste over the last 5 years, despite increased recycling of paper, glass, plastics'. Let us secondly look at the growth in car traffic and the measures mooted to deal with it (CEC 1992).

Waste

It is now recognised that decisive steps will be necessary to reduce the waste mountain. Officials of the Commission of the European Communities speak about targets for individual waste streams, where efforts to avoid the use of a material in the first instance is matched by concerted efforts to recycle the material. In these circumstances, only a small fraction should at the end need to be disposed of (say 10–15 per cent). This vision is substantially ahead of current UK thinking and waste reduction targets (25 per cent of all household waste), and would lead inevitably to a fundamental reorientation in production processes, materials chosen, consumer behaviour, recycling processes. The logical conclusion will be for each material and each product to be subject to a life cycle analysis, for each product to have a dismantling as well as an assembly line — a vision we can term the 'Recycling Society'.

What then is needed to achieve such a vision? The outcome will require a mesh of regulatory and enabling powers, of target setting for both private and public sector activities, of incentives and penalties for the individual citizen. To achieve this will require plans which are monitored and performance published widely. We will discuss such plans later in this chapter but here it will suffice to highlight some of the aspects which will need to be pursued:

- Mechanisms which reward the avoidance of using resources in the first instance need to be put in place: reduced packaging; returnable and reuseable packaging; less weight and material used for new products etc.
- Markets for recycled materials and products need to be created since these are critical to any successful recycling economy. Whilst there is scope for considerable imagination at local level it is unlikely that the necessary stimuli will happen without regulation. Demands for post-consumer waste in the production of recycled goods, be it plastic or paper products, will create a market for difficult to sell salvaged materials. The prospects of glass mountains of one colour (green) whilst more and more quarrying is

proceeding to extract the raw material for glass production for another colour (white) is one of the absurdities of a materials stream where there is no regulation but consumer preference.

- Mechanisms which carry financial rewards as well as penalties. Participating in resource recovery will need to cease to be a peripheral process, with niches for particularly profitable materials. It will need to become a mainstream activity. Incentives at local levels (no collection fee for recyclable materials) need to be coupled with charges for collection of any material not prepared for salvage such as unsorted household refuse. Disposal to landfill of salvageable material may need to be charged at even higher rates to discourage such practices. All materials which can already profitably be recycled should be dealt with in this fashion, for example road aggregate, builders rubble etc.

The planning processes which need to be established include a regulations timetable; national targets for individual waste streams; national, regional and local plans to put in place systems, infrastructure, charging mechanisms etc. We will examine below how far such systems are in place in the UK to meet this challenge.

The growth in road traffic

This is one of the key challenges Europe-wide and is discussed fully in Chapter 9. Projections for increases in car-borne traffic point to gridlock at the turn of the century. Two-hundred kilometre queues were recorded for the first time in Germany during the summer holiday period of 1992 according to Der Spiegel. The emissions from car borne traffic are now one of the greatest pollution threats in Western Europe in spite of catalytic converters.

The challenge is primarily twofold: emissions need to be brought under control by technology through smaller engines, different fuels and so on, and more fundamentally by achieving a shift away from private motoring. As the Fifth Action Programme states:

> . . because of the projected increases in the volume of cars used, the mileage driven and increases of road freight traffic, the transport sector's share in overall emissions will increase from 22 to 24 per cent of CO_2, from 4 to 12 of SO_2 and from 58 to 59 per cent of NO_x and thereby will offset any potential reductions attributable to the introduction of the new emissions standards (CEC 1992, para. 34).

The arguments why this is necessary are well known and yet it is an extraordinarily difficult issue to tackle. Each small progression made is instantaneously wiped out by a further increase in the number of motor cars. Whenever there is a reduction in car production, arguably a most welcome environmental development, then enormous pressure builds up to increase production to previous record levels. Transport infrastructure decisions are made with little reference to broader environmental issues. The current debate on railway privatisation, whilst continuous funding on major road schemes is promoted, demonstrates how far removed environmental needs are from current political willingness to deal with them.

What then would be needed to tackle the environmental fall-out from growth in car traffic? There are many menus on offer, all with similar components. Representative of all these is the challenge of the Commission of the European Communities. The EU Fifth Action Programme focuses on three types of measures:

- infrastructure, which includes land use, infrastructure investments in urban transport and a range of charging measures;
- fuels and vehicles, which include improvements to vehicles, including their ability to be recycled, as well as the composition and consumption of fuels;
- user behaviour, which aims to secure a more rational use of the car, improved public transport, restraint measures to discourage road traffic in inner cities and development of inter-active communication structures which avoid trips in the first instance.

To achieve the changes proposed in the Fifth Action Programme is going to require an extraordinary amount of energy and political determination. At a national level changes will be required to the costs of motoring. Toll roads now seem a likelihood in several more European countries since both Germany and the UK are actively discussing such measures (albeit from a need to raise additional income rather than from an environmental argument aimed to reduce trips). Nevertheless the German debate assumes that the income generated through tolls can be redirected to finance the rail deficit, whilst the UK proposals seem to intend to simply raise resources for the road building programme. If tolls result in a redistribution of resources from individual to collective transport then this would be an important cornerstone in achieving the aims of the Fifth Action Programme.

Similarly at a local level road pricing in urban areas could allow shifts of resources into better networks of more reliable urban collective transport systems. It would be necessary to create incentives to achieve such shifts, for example by allowing municipalities to raise and retain any resources created through local road pricing.

The most complex task, politically, psychologically and for any other reason imaginable, relates to the need to achieve behavioural changes. Observations from throughout Europe suggest that people will only leave their motor vehicles when the penalties, in terms of lost time, inconvenience or cost are quite substantial. Such an observation leads to the conclusion that collective transport systems need to be substantially enhanced, whilst individual road users must be actively discouraged. There is an argument for influencing attitudes towards the car as a tool which has its undoubted uses, but if used in excess adds substantial environmental costs to the environment, which no amount of catalytic converters or other technical improvements will wholly eradicate. A parallel to the anti-smoking campaign is relevant. To achieve anything in this field will require a sustained campaign at both national and local levels.

These two environmental problem areas, waste and the growth in car traffic, demonstrate the comprehensive policy approach required when planning for environmental solutions. A broad approach ranging from legislation and regulation at international and national level down to specific targets at local level will be needed if any discernible progress is going to be made. Before we look at the individual aspects of such environmental planning we should briefly examine how the Town and Country Planning system is able to cope with the challenge of the new environmental agenda.

The ability of the current UK planning system to deal with environmental problems

Let us examine the current ability of the Town and Country Planning system to deal with the type of environmental issues described in the Fifth Action Programme, accepting that it was not designed to take on board the complexity of environmental issues now facing us. The system was set up with the best of intentions in 1947. Thus the TCPA report claims:

> In practice it has been an effective instrument for achieving the policy objectives of the 1940s, particularly the demarcation

of built-up areas from the countryside and the designation
and protection of national parks, landscape areas, and nature
reserves (Blowers 1993, p. 20).

However, the report continues, the system has been much less
successful when responding to 'the new kinds of environmental
concern'. Thus little scope was given to the new land use planning
system to trespass on the preserve of agricultural policy. So the
town and country planning system has protected rural land
resources from building development but not from some of the
uglier side-effect of agribusiness. Similarly the planning system
made little use of the potential to control industrial pollution,
and had little success in achieving an integration of transport and
land-use planning issues.

Recently considerable emphasis is being placed by the DoE on
issues of sustainable development in a range of policy planning
guidance. Thus Planning Policy Guidance 12 (DoE 1992a)
suggests for example, that local authorities build in considerations
of energy use in local plan policies. At the same time however
local authorities are constantly reminded about the need to allow
development to proceed retaining a general presumption in favour
of development.

> The government has made clear its intention to work towards
> ensuring that development and growth are sustainable. It
> will continue to develop policies consistent with the concept
> of sustainable development. The planning system, and the
> preparation of development plans in particular, can contribute
> to the objectives of ensuring that development and growth are
> sustainable. The sum total of decisions in the planning field,
> as elsewhere, should not deny future generations the best
> of today's environment. This should be expressed through
> the policies in development planning (PPG12, DoE 1992a,
> para 1.8).

Indeed the entire current Town and Country Planning system is
heavily focused on planning for uses of land and the various
considerations to be brought into play when determining new
development. Little room for manoeuvre is left to 'non-land use
policies', although the management of existing resources within
existing settlements and infrastructure including traffic flows will
be of critical importance if any real progress is going to be made
towards the new environmental agenda.

Given these limitations, what is the ability of the TCP system
to bring into play a range of environmental considerations when
preparing plans and ultimately judge new developments against
it (the current system requires a reactive rather than proactive

language). A few examples from the world of practice may serve to illustrate the issues.

The out-of town superstore

This has been one of the big growth sectors in the last ten years. Free-standing large stores are erected to attract car borne customers in the main, and 500–600 car parking spaces per store are quite common. In many battles with local authorities the same arguments have been rehearsed again and again, principally the impact of such developments upon existing centres and the withdrawal of purchasing power from these established and often more widely accessible locations. A large number of appeals have been decided in favour of the proposed developments, fuelling the trend to out of centre locations.

If such developments were to be judged on more environmentally based criteria, questions such as the following would need to be asked. How much additional travel does such a development generate? How does this translate into additional emissions? If the emissions are greater than those created for the equivalent shopping trips today, then what alternatives are there to large out of centre stores? It may be argued that a network of smaller stores down to village store level, served by large central warehousing and providing door-step delivery in electric vans may be a much better environmental solution, which will help to retain settlements intact and will allow non-motorised modes of transport such as walking and cycling to be employed for the shopping trips. It may be a critical element in succeeding to achieve some of the transport aims as set out in the Fifth Action Programme.

These types of arguments have as yet not been tested seriously at appeal and would be furiously resisted. It is questionable whether a genuinely environmentally based solution could succeed unless very strong Government guidance was forthcoming which discouraged any potential disjointed settlement pattern promoted by many out of centre stores. A system of environmental impact analysis would need to guide the environmental impact of any such development.

The waste disposal site

Within every municipality large quantities of waste are constantly being generated as discussed in Chapter 8. The heritage handed down from previous generations in terms of inadequately treated dumps, ensure ground water and other pollution will become of increasing concern. New materials now being buried in the ground are more long-lived than those of previous generations — plastics are an obvious example. Moreover there has been the tendency to freely dispose of toxics such as batteries with the excuse that as long as it is 'diluted' by other waste it won't harm. The responsibility for the handling of waste has not been helped by the fact that most is buried far away and is thus out of sight. Whilst modern disposal techniques are much more sophisticated than those of previous generations, a healthy scepticism needs to remain as to the ability of new technologies to adequately contain materials and protect ground water from pollution not just for the next 10 years but for the next 500 or more.

Thus, faced with planning applications for a waste disposal site, an environmentally aware planning process would need to seek to minimise any dangers through the treatment of the waste to be deposited in terms of extracting any materials that can be reused, perhaps only receiving pre-sorted material; spending effort on composting putrescables in a controlled manner; and aiming to re-use the resulting compost and extracting any methane (a potent greenhouse gas). Perhaps each municipality would have to treat the local waste arising within their boundaries and would only be given a certain tonnage target each year which they could export elsewhere. Any local authority trying such a comprehensive approach today which would entail dealing with and minimising the waste before a residue is buried would find little help from the established Town and Country Planning system.

The protection of natural habitats

The presumption in favour of development, one of the cornerstones of the current British planning system does not halt before the need to protect sites with valuable natural habitats. Presumptions against development are discouraged in local development plans. Moreover the current Town and Country Planning system has no mechanisms to protect anything but trees; neither shrubs, ground cover nor grassland are protected. (Albeit some protection can now be afforded to hedgerows.) Whilst much political capital is made of the loss of rainforests in other parts of the world, no effective protection is given to SSSIs, to local nature reserves or other areas of nature interest. A recent survey of threatened SSSIs (*Observer* 14.2.1993) expressed the suspicion that natural sites, whatever their value are targeted for road programmes as their land value is lower than surrounding non-green sites. For the planning system to gain any credibility as an agent for implementing the new environmental agenda firm and long-term habitat protection must come within its remit.

From these examples it can be seen that much is left to be desired of the current Town and Country Planning system. In its present form it is not fully equipped to deal with the fundamental issues of the new environmental agenda nor was it ever intended to do so. Perhaps the main criticism is its current inability to be sufficiently pro-active to deal with pressing environmental issues. Neither is it sufficently absolute, within its present day restrictions, to protect our civilisation from destroying essential parts of our habitat. In an institutionalised desire to balance protection against development, whilst safeguarding the rights of the individual landowner, objectives of long term protection are bound to suffer. Are there then other mechanisms by which the new environmental agenda can be implemented?

Green plans

Many local authorities in the UK now seek to provide a planning framework for their own activities through the means of environmental charters and programmes, all of which seek to put their organisation as a whole and their output onto a green course. There are parallels in the private sector where many private businesses now seek to green up their organisations through environmental audits, action programmes and management systems. Much effort is spent on convincing members of the public and customers, such as potential developers, of the advantage of adopting green practice.

The recent guide, *Environmental Practice in Local Government* (LGMB *et al.* 1992c) gives a large number of case studies in 14 topic areas. In the chapter on Design, Construction and Maintenance, several guides for new development are referred to which have been produced because of the limitations of the statutory planning system to take fully into account the new environmental agenda. The Green Development Guide for New Housing (Stockport Metropolitan Borough Council) and Environmental Awareness and Building (London Borough of Sutton) seek to take the environmental debate substantially further than the current statutory framework.

It has to be recognised that such approaches are based on advice rather than regulation, which can easily be ignored by prospective developers. This is not to belittle the non-statutory approach as these experiments are needed to spearhead more formally recognised planning processes which should have the full weight of the law behind them and be recognised as a link in national and local environmental planning.

Some of the best established local environmental planning processes have been operating since the mid-to-late 1980s. *Environmental Practice in Local Government* cites seven case studies which demonstrate the effort and imagination which now is devoted to broadening environmental considerations and planning for the environment at a local level:

- Charter for the Environment — Colchester Borough Council
- Environmental Statement — London Borough of Sutton
- Environmental Initiative — Kirklees Metropolitan Council
- Environment City — Leicester Environment City
- UK Second Environment City — Middlesbrough Borough Council
- Environmental Strategy — Leicester County Council
- Environmental Management System and Audit — Hereford City Council

(LGMB *et al.* 1992c)

The most important green plan in Europe today must be the European Commission's Fifth Action Programme 'Towards Sustainability' referred to frequently in this chapter. It demonstrates the breadth of intervention needed across sectors, boundaries and levels of government to achieve environmental changes. The action catalogue in the Fifth Action Programme is not dissimilar from those of many local level green plans in terms of its approach, although of course, it is that much more far reaching and visionary with its emphasis on the need for new instruments and regulations. To deal with the issues outlined competently and speedily is going to require a much more structured and rigorous planning process than that currently available in the UK.

How do we plan for the new environmental agenda?

We can see that current procedures and systems are not geared up to deal vigorously with the big environmental tasks ahead. Making a success of the tasks set by programmes such as the EU Fifth Action Programme will require a determined shift in favour of environmental thinking, and this is bound to require deep changes to the existing planning system or entirely new procedures. The

Town and Country Planning Asociation in their report on planning for a sustainable development (Blowers 1993) terms the planning process required 'Environmental Planning'. Such a system can either be a radically adapted Town and Country Planning system or a new construction altogether.

Several fundamental principles will need to be built in in order to create a system able to cope with the nature of environmental problems as described earlier in this chapter.

- The system will need to be pro-active. There is a job to be done in using our resources more carefully (energy, water, soil, minerals, biomass), producing less waste and pollution both in relation to new development and existing structures and settlements.

- The system will also need to be a rock of protection for existing habitats and resources. The fundamentals of sustainability demand a radically different approach to our relationship with nature.

- The system will require a cascade of plans where targets and ways of achieving them are set at each level of government (the TCPA suggests national, regional and local levels) and for private sector industries and products.

- Information about the state of the environment needs to be publicly available, achievements at all levels regularly published and open to scrutiny. Non-achievements of targets need to be explained.

- The system will need integral resource allocation procedures which are the subject of environmental assessments. This should ensure debates and more informed decisions about the environmental value of expenditure.

- The plans will need to recognise the nature of the processes we are seeking to control and the need for long-term planning. Programmes to reduce CO_2 emission need a persistent effort over 10–20 years and programmes to change transport infrastructure and attitudes require similar time-spans.

- The plans need to be underwritten by an adequate financial base. Thus income generated through applying 'the polluter pays' principle for example, through the means of a carbon tax, could be redirected to fund the implementation of an environmental action programme. In their report the TCPA firmly recommends that a betterment tax on the unearned increments of land values forms part of any such tax mechanism.

It is obvious that the current statutory planning process in the UK which primarily focuses on the use of land, would need to be drastically expanded in scope and powers to deal with these tasks.

Environmental planning and subsidiarity

How would environmental planning function in reality? How would the various levels of government interact to achieve the tasks set? Let us explore this question in relation to one of the examples we used from the Fifth Action Programme, namely waste.

The biggest task ahead is to bring the waste stream under control. At the highest level, national targets would need to be set. They would need to be mandatory, their achievement linked to funding mechanisms for the various executive bodies. Taking the municipal waste stream, the Fifth Action Programme sets specific targets:

- Stabilisation of waste quantities at no more than 300 kg per person per year;
- Recycling/reuse of paper, glass and plastics of at least 50 per cent;
- 90 per cent reduction in dioxine emission (from 1985 levels by 2005).

Moreover it sets out the need for a community wide infrastructure for safe collection, separation and disposal as well as the creation of markets for recycled materials.

The Programme will require government intervention to create markets and encourage industrial infrastructure able to deal with the reusable and recyclable waste and particularly priority waste streams (defined in the Fifth Action Programme as used tyres, halogenated substances, used cars, demolition waste, hospital waste and municipal waste).

It will require targets for each successive governmental level, substantially more stringent than those currently set in the UK (25 per cent of household waste by 2000). The targets will divide into those requiring regulation and control, where the ultimate action is that of a third party, and those which require direct action by national or a subsidiary level of government. For example at national level the demand for recyclable products will need to be decidedly influenced, for instance, by specifying the proportion of recycled components in new products. Costs of new products may include the costs of ultimate disposal.

This in turn will require local authorities and industry to generate investment in resource recovery plants, and general salvage infrastructure. It will require particular care when permitting new development, the handling of wastes in future as well as the wastes generated by new development. Ultimately and at the lowest level of government, it will require awareness campaigns, as well as systems in place to allow people to realise their own ambitions in this field, for example by easy access to salvage facilities. These targets can only be achieved if they are consciously planned for and accounted for at every level.

Clearly, a hierarchy of plans throws up the spectre of a rigorous and unified dictatorial planning system with no sense of discretion at any level. This would be not only be undesirable but unworkable. An important key to achievement in the environmental field is the willingness of individual people to co-operate and to change behaviour and attitudes — this may indeed require different approaches from area to area, with differing emphases depending on local circumstances. At its simplest, people in a low density rural area may find it most effective to control their waste by very localised composting and controlled burning of waste for heating. Materials such as glass may be crushed locally as an additive to road and building materials or may be gathered for collection at relatively long intervals. Paper may effectively be turned into animal bedding and then composted after use. In a more densely populated area, larger infrastructure will be cost-effective both in terms of bring and collect schemes and at highest densities the introduction of Combined Heat and Power, using residual waste to generate electricity and heat may well be an option.

All these situations would have in common the fact that they respond to given targets and need to find locally suitable solutions to achieve them. How each level of government then carries out its duties within the parameters of the environmental framework set is up to that level. Subsidiarity, not one of the most attractive examples of Eurospeak, expects the lowest possible appropriate political level to take decisions and carry them out. Where the village pump is the right level, this should be accepted and not interfered with.

This is not to deny that the new environmental agenda is demanding a mighty shift of attitudes and practises, with a number of holy cows having to be sacrificed. The most unpleasant political decisions which will arise from, for example, discouraging road traffic in cities, may lead many politicians to just wait until the build up of traffic achieves just that. When the situation becomes unbearable, when the pollution effects are more visible, when sufficient numbers of people become fearful of their safety and health and traffic grinds to a halt, then it will be more acceptable to constrain the motor car and individual motorist.

Environmental planning at its various levels must not encourage an avoidance of action. Subsidiarity in this context does not stretch to ignoring a problem but dealing with it, albeit in a customised fashion.

Targets and time-scales

Targets will need to cover the spectrum of the environmental media (soil, water, air, minerals, living matter) and will relate to the consumption and use of energy and resources as well as the generation of wastes and emissions. With the targets set at each level of the administrative hierarchy, plans for new development be it at national level, say transport infrastructure, or at the local level, say a new housing development, will be required to complement the environmental targets set and not, for instance, cause additional emissions.

One of the most profound effects of an environmental planning system would be its different time-scales. Each plan may be considered as a contract with the future (and future generations). This of course places in perspective the current 4 to 5 year terms of office of parliamentarians and local government administrations. The principle of more long-termism will by necessity constrain the freedom to act of any one administration, however inclined they may be to distance themselves from long term objectives to be able to deal with short term problems. No doubt this will be the subject of vigourous debate once the concept of a more sustainable future becomes common currency.

Conclusions

Currently the European Commission is showing the way with their Fifth Action Programme: a comprehensive first plan towards a more sustainable future. The plan demonstrates the importance of a broad approach to solving environmental problems, involving many levels of government, and many sectors of industry as well as individuals. The plan raises questions about the ability to deliver unless formal procedures and accountability for achieving its objectives are put in place. The plan is the big brother of many 'green plans' which have been produced in the UK recently outside any statutory framework, but all with a desire to make their contribution to the new environmental agenda. Regrettably one of the earliest and much respected environmental planning systems in Europe, namely the UK Town and Country Planning system, has over the years failed to adapt to the new environmental challenges by becoming a reactive tool and now lacks the power of proactiveness and innovation to deal with the challenge ahead. Although there is some indication that a broader scope will be given to this system it is questionable whether the system with all its appendages and limitations can be sufficiently reformed to make significant contributions in helping to implement wider visions such as those of the European Commission. If not then the call by the Town and Country Planning Association for a system of Environmental Planning is wholly justified.

8 Waste reduction and disposal

Jeff Cooper

For many environmentalists, the problem of waste reduction and disposal provides an excellent springboard for the exploration of a multiplicity of environmental issues. Everyone creates waste but, within limits also has choices with regard to the types of product and packaging which they purchase. In turn this will partly determine the options which people have with regard to the use of resources and their methods of waste reclamation and disposal.

Questions concerning the depletion of resources will become increasingly important, not only for non-renewable but also for renewable resources, such as managed forests in temperate areas. To what extent can newsprint, tissues and writing papers that are consumed be substituted by reclaiming and recycling paper from homes and workplaces? More generally, can local communities develop strategies which minimise resource usage and maximise the recycling of materials?

The location of waste management facilities, from the street corner recycling centre through to the proposed development of a million-tonne-a-year energy recovery incinerator, all cause concern for local people. Equally, the environmental effects of landfill, from the potential to pollute water resources, migration of explosive landfill gas and the generation of heavy goods traffic place a heavy burden on those communites currently receiving the waste which is generated.

Increasingly, the principle of sustainability will be invoked to justify society's action over waste management. Establishing suitable mechanisms so that political decisions over waste management can be taken within a sound environmental policy framework will be the main challenge for local authorities.

The legislative framework

The removal of waste, mainly to control nuisances and health problems, was one of the first responsibilities which local authorities acquired when the British local government system was formally established in the nineteenth century. Surprisingly, therefore, it was only with the introduction of the Collection and Disposal of Waste Regulations 1988 that for the first time every district council was under a duty to collect household waste in its area.

Local authorities now have a wide range of roles with respect to solid waste management, mainly performed under the auspices of the Environmental Protection Act 1990. The lower tier district, borough and city authorities are waste collection authorities (WCAs) and therefore responsible for the collection of household waste. In addition WCAs also collect commercial waste from shops, offices and other premises, although private companies also collect such waste. Due to government legislation WCAs are required to tender for the provision of their waste collection services, including street cleansing, and as a result of CCT (compulsory competitive tendering) around 25 per cent of local authority waste collection services are provided by private companies. WCAs also have to produce a recycling plan.

County councils in England and district councils in Wales and Scotland, as waste disposal authorities (WDAs), have an administrative responsibilty for the disposal of waste collected by their constituent WCAs. Also these councils as waste regulation authorities (WRAs) have responsibility for the regulation of all controlled waste, until such time as the proposed Environmental Agency takes over this role. Within the metropolitan areas in England there is a mix of waste disposal and regulation arrangements following the abolition of the GLC and Metropolitan County Councils in 1986.

Just as the WCAs have had to tender for their services so WDAs which previously had operational control over waste disposal (although in many instances the landfilling of waste was contracted to the private sector), now have to tender for all waste disposal operations. Many of the local authorities have established a LAWDC (local authority waste disposal company) which has taken over assets such as landfill sites, waste transfer stations and other plant and equipment, to be operated as a private company.

Waste generation

At present, controlled waste comprises household, commercial and industrial waste but the list could be extended by the Secretary of State for the Environment, most probably as a result of regulatory changes brought about by the EU. It is estimated that controlled waste accounts for about 25 per cent of the total 500m tonnes of waste which is generated in the UK each year, roughly equal to the amount of mining and quarrying waste and considerably less than agricultural waste (40 per cent).

Of the approximately 120m tpa of controlled waste only about 20m tpa is generated by households, up to 16m tpa through people's dustbins and other waste receptacles and around 4m tpa of mainly bulky and garden wastes through civic amenity (CA) or household waste disposal sites. Higher figures, of up to 28m tpa which are often quoted as representing the amounts of waste handled by the public sector, include the commercial waste collected by local authorities and their contractors and commercial and industrial waste delivered to CA sites for payment for disposal.

Unfortunately, due to a variety of circumstances including the fact that until 1990 less than half the household waste in the UK was weighed, it is very difficult to determine waste generation and disposal trends. Often commercial waste is collected at the same time as household waste, especially in rural areas and from smaller shopping and office facilities.

One trend which has developed over time is the tendency for a higher proportion of household waste to be delivered to CA sites possibly as a result of increasing car ownership. Associated with this is the reduction in the use of garden bonfires, and perhaps composting especially in newer houses with smaller gardens, so that large quantities of garden waste are going to CA sites.

With regard to the politically and environmentally vexed issue of packaging waste opinions vary. The packaging industry argues that it has enormous incentives to reduce the amounts of materials used through lightweighting and the substitution of lighter new materials, often plastics and composites. Therefore, despite the increased demand for goods more packaging is being produced from the same amount of material. In addition the enhanced preparation of food means that the waste is generated at one central facility which may mean that it can be processed for re-use rather than being deposited in a large number of individual dustbins where the potential for re-use is limited.

Against that there are fears that the main re-usable packaging product, the milk bottle, will soon disappear from many places as competitive pressures from supermarket chains capture too many of the dairies' customers to retain a sufficient consumer base for rounds to continue. This could lead to further disadvantage to those lacking mobility to go to out of town superstores, especially in rural areas where many village stores have closed down.

It has to be recognised that in order to develop a coherent strategy for the minimisation of waste, concentration on the final producer of waste may not provide the optimum utilisation of resouces. Therefore many producers of packaging products in particular have tried to prove the overall environmental soundness of their products by using life cycle analysis. Unfortunately the different bases on which these analyses are undertaken does not permit comparison between products (Guinee *et al.* 1993). Nevertheless they do provide indicators as to ways in which environmental impacts can be minimised, and help to develop strategies for the least damaging overall exploitation of resources rather than merely concentrating on the 'waste of waste'.

Waste reduction

It is generally agreed that the following hierachy applies with respect to waste:

1   waste prevention;
2   waste re-use and recycling (including energy recovery);
3   safe disposal of non-recoverable residues.
(SEC 1989)

This is often referred to as the waste management hierachy, adopting the perfectly reasonable assumption that it is best to avoid the generation of waste if possible, by the adoption of clean(er) technology, for example. However, if waste is generated then measures should be taken in order that as much waste is re-used or recycled prior to any consideration of disposal.

This presumption in favour of waste avoidance and re-utilisation is often reinforced by emotive statements with regard to waste management. Unfortunately some bear little relation to scientific theory. For example:

> 'Waste' is an abuse of natural resources, some of which may be scarce, others irreplaceable (SERPLAN 1992).

However waste generation and wasting are natural processes without which there could be no life on Earth. Therefore, with regard to waste which is generated while technically every molecule could be utilised, and indeed in physical terms will be utilised, there are strict limits to the extent to which in environmental terms, let alone economics, waste reduction and recycling ought to be pursued in attempting to re-utilise waste materials to satisfy human needs. This can be most easily appreciated in that if reclamation and recycling uses more energy than the exploitation of virgin raw materials then there has to be some overwhelming reason to prefer the use of secondary materials given their greater potential contribution to climatic change in these cicumstances.

At present the vast majority, over 90 per cent, of controlled waste in the UK is disposed of through landfill, with materials recovery of household waste accounting for 4.5 per cent, composting less than 1 per cent and the remainder being incinerated in capacity terms (incineration is split equally between energy recovery facilities and those merely burning the waste). In the UK there are several difficulties in trying to promote the reduction of waste, including the fact that while the Government has set a target for reycling it applies only to household waste and there is no target for the reduction of waste.

The recovery of household waste

Any examination of the composition of household waste usually starts with the statistics published in *Waste Management Paper 28* (WMP 28) provided by Warren Spring Laboratory (WSL) (DoE 1991a). What needs to be considered is that these statistics are derived from a number of waste analyses which have been conducted over several years and that the current national average dustbin content will be slightly different to that presented in WMP 28. In Table 8.1 both the original and the more recent statistics have been shown.

Perhaps not surprisingly, the most dramatic increase over time has been in the amount of plastics arising, currently around 12 per cent of the total, while the other categories have remained remarkably stable. Indeed the point which has to be made is that while the changes in the 'national dustbin' occur quite slowly over time there can be considerable local variation in household waste content and this could be critical in developing a recycling scheme. Seasonal variation tends to be more pronounced for the civic amenity component of household waste than for 'dustbin' waste (WMP 28, p. 27).

Table 8.1 Composition of UK 'dustbin' waste by weight (average percentage)

	WMP 28	1992
Paper/card	33	33.7
Rigid plastic	7	5.9
Plastic film		5.7
Glass	10	9.2
Ferrous metal	8	5.8
Non-ferrous metal		1.4
Textiles	4	2.2
Miscellaneous combustibles	8	8.5
Miscellaneous non-combustibles		1.5
Putrescibles	20	20.1
Fines (dust etc.)	10	6.0

Source: Warren Spring Laboratory 1992

Of the materials listed in Table 8.1, a considerable fraction could be recycled in one form or another, from recovery of the materials themselves through to composting or anaerobic digestion to energy recovery. Concentrating on materials recovery, estimates from WSL 'based on practical results from separation schemes' estimates that 40 per cent of household waste could be recovered (WMP 28, table 4.1). In addition WMP 28 suggests that a further 10 per cent is compostable, giving a total of 50 per cent. The Government's target is to recycle (by materials recovery and composting only) half this amount by the year 2000, approximately 25 per cent of the total.

The 50 per cent limit on the proportion of materials potentially available for materials recovery occurs for a number of reasons, mainly contamination or combinations of materials which would be technically difficult to separate. In many cases even these, however, would be potential candidates for energy recovery.

That the figure is not higher is a reflection of the fact that in addition to a number of technical difficulties there are also market barriers which limit the amounts which could be reclaimed. However, even if adequate markets were available there may also be psychological limits to people's participation in waste reclamation initiatives.

Technically, therefore, while glass can be recycled 100 per cent, there are container glass products which are outside the normal colour range of clear, green and amber, such as black, blue or white, for example. It would not be worthwhile separating these odd colours out in order to put them into a furnace when that colour is going to be made, which may in any case be in a foreign country.

Even if 90 per cent or more is potentially available, is that figure likely to be achieved even with the most sensitive and all-embracing curbside collection scheme? It would require almost complete participation by the community and the placing of almost every glass container in their blue box, wheeled bin, green bag or equivalent. In reality there will always be a small minority who will not participate and of those that do some will think that small jars are not required or not worth the trouble.

There is some useful data on this point from the WSL assessment of the Adur blue box scheme. Both blue box and dustbin contents of 504 households were examined at the same time on one day in February 1992. This produced a capture rate of 71 per cent for glass (up from 56 per cent in July 1991) and rates of 67 per cent (71 per cent) for paper, 60 per cent (52 per cent) for plastic and 54 per cent (43 per cent) for metal cans (IDG 1992). Therefore even when providing what most commentators would regard as the ideal system to encourage maximum participation in reclamation of household waste, a high proportion of materials were still going through the normal waste collection/disposal system.

Markets for household waste materials

For household waste materials a detailed assessment of the 'Market Barriers to Materials Reclamation and Recycling' was published by WSL in 1991 (Bardos et al. 1991). This showed in detail which materials were unable to be recycled because market capacity would be exceeded.

For the largest tonnage material, paper and board, while it was possible to push up the overall recycled fibre usage from the then 57 per cent, the scope for a dramatic improvement was limited. At that time and through to the present the UK benefits from the net export of waste paper and board so that already there is an excess of supply compared to available markets. Therefore, the only ways in which the potential supplies of waste paper can be absorbed are through further exports, which are unlikely due to the intense international market pressures especially from the USA and Germany, or from increasing the capacity of the UK's paper manufacturing base which at present is capable of providing only half the total requirements of the home market. In contrast both France and Germany, and indeed most of the smaller EC countries have a production to supply balance, at least in tonnage terms, even if not for the full range of products.

In 1993 the final Board approval for building the proposed £265m newsprint mill at Aylesford, Kent continued to be deferred even with the inducement of £20m Government funding because of a 1 million tonne world surplus of newsprint production capacity.

For glass, again the poor match of available glass supplies and the potential market is such that the WSL report suggests that the UK saturation level will be achieved when 39 per cent of glass is being reclaimed through the bottle bank scheme, a level comparable to the average for European countries and much below the 60 per cent levels achieved in The Netherlands, Germany, Austria and Switzerland. On this occasion it is the difficulty of matching the colour of glass production (68 per cent clear) to the bottle bank supply (>50 per cent green).

Thus in the UK the two main household waste sources most amenable to recovery as materials both have severe limitations. For other materials the problems may not be as great. British Steel has committed itself to accepting up to 100,000 tonnes of incinerated scrap metal and detinning facilities could be expanded to cope with any surplus in excess of that presented to the existing plants in Hartlepool and Llanelli. The main problem with steel is the low price offered while with aluminium it is the very limited supply available in household waste, less than 1 per cent, with some types, such as foil often heavily contaminated.

For plastics the problem is rather different. Because of the number of polymer types, their low weight to volume ratio and their overall low proportion (by weight) in the waste stream there are major difficulties in providing an economic load. The costs of collection and processing of household waste plastics will generally exceed the value of the reclaimed material and the markets for recycled plastics are underdeveloped.

Thus, establishing a viable material recovery system is difficult. Recent research from PIFA, the Packaging Industry Films Association (PIFA 1993) clearly demonstrates that while the materials recovery of industrial/commercial film will be viable the processing of household plastic films will provide negative benefits. This is primarily due to their thinness, extensive printing and contamination with other materials so that more energy is used in reclaiming them than would be used in producing them from virgin material.

It is evident from this analysis that there will have to be a considerable amount of adjustment to the market in order to accommodate the reclaimed materials which could be provided even from an intensification of existing bank/bring systems. In 1991 ERL were appointed by the DTI and DoE to examine a range of ways in which markets for reclaimed materials could be improved. Their report, *Economic Instruments and Recovery of Resources from Waste* was published in December 1992 (DoE/DTI 1992).

Economic instruments can be introduced to try to reduce the waste stream by changing the incentives offered to the major participants involved in the generation, reclamation and disposal of waste. Such changes can affect the management of waste through a number of mechanisms:

- by encouraging the setting up of, or higher participation in, recycling schemes;
- by encouraging minimisation of waste going to final disposal through consumption of lower waste products or by encouraging households, businesses or waste authorities to divert waste from final disposal to composting and energy recovery;
- by increasing the use of secondary materials;
- by increasing the use of re-usable packaging and containers;
- by raising revenue for recycling or waste management schemes.

The ERL report considered 13 economic instruments with the potential to stimulate the recycling of materials from waste, namely:

- product charges levied on products made from non-recycled materials;
- raw materials charges levied on raw materials in those cases where recycled substitutes are available in order to encourage their use;
- deposit refund schemes on potentially recyclable products, such as batteries and drinks containers;
- waste collection charges levied on households for collection and disposal of waste;
- waste disposal charges levied on all household and packaging waste at the point of final disposal;
- transferable recycling targets for industry and waste collection authorities;
- changing responsibilities/property rights by imposing responsibilities for packaging waste collection and recycling;
- direct subsidies to WCAs to invest in recycling facilities;

also

- tax concessions, accelerated depreciation etc. to increase tax allowances for recycled materials;
- VAT differentiation through exemptions or reductions for goods containing recycled inputs;
- market support schemes to overcome market barriers by price stabilisation or other price support systems;
- preferential purchase by public sector to discriminate in favour of goods with recycled inputs or which are recyclable;
- removal of tax allowances by changing allowances such as the removal of waste disposal costs from tax relief.

Of the options examined by ERL the last five listed showed less potential to stimulate recycling.

As ERL dismissed the potential for bank systems for reclaiming 25 per cent of the household waste stream, any combination of the economic instruments adopted would have to bridge the gap between the cost of kerbside collection and the cost of landfill, £200 and £40 respectively.

In February 1993 a report produced by Coopers and Lybrand for the DoE (DoE 1993c) examined the possible changes in waste disposal methods if a landfill levy were to be introduced. This meant that of the 13 economic instruments examined by ERL, waste disposal charges, specifically a levy on landfill, became the favoured option by virtue of the extra research undertaken.

That the Government should examine the potential of a disposal levy is not surprising in that several European countries and a number of States in the USA have adopted this policy. That there is a need for more than just a landfill levy has also become increasingly apparent. Although both studies use different cost structures for the collection and processing of household waste they show that the Government's recycling target cannot be achieved except through the development of markets.

Their analysis showed that there would be a move away from landfill but mainly to incineration with energy recovery rather than to recycling. This was due to the large gap between the costs of recycling household waste compared to the lower costs of incineration and landfill. This would indicate that in order to achieve the Government's household waste recycling target, more of the economomic instruments examined by ERL would have to be used.

The Coopers and Lybrand study revealed that even with a levy set at £20 per tonne only 12 per cent of household waste would be recycled, with more going to incineration with energy recovery as a cheaper option than recycling for household waste.

While beyond the terms of reference of the C&L study there is a need to carefully examine the the way in which any landfill levy may be structured. The C&L study came down in favour of a tonnage rather than an *ad valorem* levy, despite the operational difficulties posed by less than half of all landfill sites having a weighbridge. Also, given that charges for landfill are broadly related to the potential environmental impact of the disposal of the waste, then an *ad valorem* levy would push waste producers into reducing the amounts of their most difficult wastes, to undertake pre-treatment of waste and other measures to limit landfill levies.

In Denmark these charges are on all forms of destructive disposal, including incineration even with energy recovery, so that encouragement for recycling is greater than that proposed under the C&L study. Energy from waste initiatives are already supported through the non-fossil fuel obligation payments so it might be argued that this imbalance against materials recovery should be addressed. This could be resolved by setting differential levy charges for a range of destructive disposal methods. This type of regime is being established in Belgium.

There is also a further concern with regard to the landfill levy. Will it be subsumed as a component of general taxation or used to stimulate the infrastructure for recycling? Such hypothecation will probably require legislative provision. Although, perhaps unjustly singled out for special attention, it is likely that economic instruments and/or regulation will have to be applied to packaging waste under the proposed EU Directive on Packaging and Packaging Waste in order to meet its objectives.

Nevertheless, without some efforts to enhance markets by using some of the options which ERL stated 'showed less potential to stimulate recycling' such as tax concessions, VAT differentiation and preferential purchase efforts to stimulate behavioural changes will be directed only to the waste generation system.

Recycling plans

While the Government has belatedly tried to determine policies which would help it to fulfil its target of recycling 25 per cent of household waste by the Year 2000, local authorities have been forced to examine the potential for developing recycling locally through each WCA producing a recycling plan. In July 1991 the then Secretary of State for the Environment, Michael Heseltine, requested that all recycling plans should be submitted to the DoE by 1 August 1992.

For the present, given limited and poor market prospects for the materials reclaimed from household waste, most WCAs in their recycling plans have opted for the following strategy:

- expansion of bank facilities, both increasing the density of existing facilities and providing for new materials;
- development of composting schemes, initially through the promotion of home composting and then by the establishment of centralised processing facilities should those prove viable;
- establishing door to door collections should market conditions permit.

The main exceptions are those few authorities, less than 40 in early 1993, which have established trial kerbside source separation schemes. It has proven extremely difficult to establish the real costs and benefits of these schemes partly because several have benefited from the provision of private capital and equipment and a lack of common accounting systems. The main conclusion is that the most effective systems are those which are most closely integrated into the waste management system.

One of the main difficulties which local authorities face is how to achieve such integration when many of the services which have to be provided are subject to compulsory competitive tendering (CCT) procedures. In such circumstances, the renegotiating of a contract could be time consuming and expensive. Exceptionally, Leeds City Council were allowed by the DoE to keep a quarter of their refuse collection contract out of the CCT process in order to develop their twin-bin recycling scheme.

But it also has to be recognised that a uniform approach to the collection and processing of recyclable materials may not be appropriate anyway. Partly this is due to the intrinsic characteristics of the different materials, but also to the fact that the various reclamation industries vary in their requirements. Thus, the UK newsprint mills have preferred to become directly involved in the reclamation of materials from the provison of paper banks through to transport and processing. On the other hand, the glass industry has chosen to build the cullet processing facilities and until late 1993 provided a stable price for the glass and help with promotion, but left the collection, storage and transport of the glass to the local authorites and their contractors.

Local authorities therefore have to mesh their role in waste collection and reclamation into a wider industry context. It is important that all those with managerial responsibilities understand each other's perspective in order to promote the effective recovery of materials from household waste.

Composting

The most significant of the recent initiatives to set up centralised composting systems is the experimental scheme introduced by the North London Waste Authority (NLWA) at its Edmonton site in 1991. During early 1992 over 500 tonnes a week of growing media, including those refined through its extensive wormery, were being produced.

In the UK, following the example of North America and Germany, composting is being concentrated on green wastes and selected commercial and industrial wastes rather than household refuse. Thus the NLWA composting facility has taken both green wastes from civic amenity sites and from the parks departments in its constituent boroughs and wastes from a wide range of sources including coffee grounds, orange peel, manure, feathers and even old shredded banknotes to convert into a wide range of growing media.

In other cases where composting facilities have been established the councils have been turning their green wastes into growing media, mulches and wood chips. Most of these developments are of small capacity.

As an alternative to the establishment of centralised composting systems, especially when dealing with kitchen and garden wastes, several authorities have sought to encourage a greater number of their residents to compost at home. One of the main difficulties is determining how many people at the present time undertake home composting to establish a base line for waste reduction through this means, prior to the establishment of any initiative to promote home composting.

One of the most ambitious schemes to determine the potential of home composting as a waste reduction measure is that established by the London Borough of Sutton in May 1992. Using a £16,000 Supplementary Credit Approval provided by the DoE, Sutton chose an area in Carshalton of 7000 households which was serviced by one refuse collection crew. Given that figures on the tonnage of waste collected were available for the area for the previous few years it would be possible to calculate what the effect would be of providing people with home composters, at least to the extent that more people would be undertaking composting at home.

Nevertheless even with the inducement of one of three types of waste reduction unit: a wormery, a Green Cone or a Rotol composter at a heavily subsidised cost, less than 10 per cent of the households participated in the scheme. This may be due to the fact that a high proportion of households were already participating in home composting and that acquiring a further composting unit for £3.50 or £7.00 was irrelevant or that some would not wish to participate in composting at home. From the work undertaken by Sutton, which included sending someone to each household to discuss the initiative, it would appear that there was already a high proportion of people undertaking some home composting but perhaps not to the fullest possible extent.

One composting process which was reintroduced to the UK in October 1992 was the co-composting of household waste and sewage sludge (COWS). The scheme has been established by South West Water and Devon County Council at a cost of £1.3m, of which £400,000 was paid under the DTI's DEMOS initiative. At present mixed household refuse is screened prior to windrowing under cover with around 20 per cent of sewage sludge added. The product from this process will initially be used for landfill cover and the restoration of mineral workings. Experience in Northern Europe has shown that there are few market outlets for compost derived from mixed household waste.

A further option which can potentially provide either a growing medium or a source of energy or both is the anaerobic digestion of waste. Anaerobic digestion has been in use for the treatment of sewage sludge for a considerable period of time but its use for refuse also has a lengthy history.

Anaerobic digestion

As long ago as 1938 London had an experimental anaerobic digestion facility for refuse, in Kensington (Messent and Wilkinson 1938). The technique was proposed at that time as an alternative to incineration because with the adoption of new heating systems: gas, electricity and central heating, the wet putrescible component was threatening to become so great that supplementary fuel would be needed for incineration. Therefore it was proposed that the increasingly large putrescible fraction could be anaerobically digested for a period and then subsequently the digestate could be aerobically composted. While this experimental plant was certainly in operation both immediately prior to and after the second world war to date it has not proved possible to obtain performance data.

This itself, however, is indicative that the system was not providing an adequate means of waste treatment and/or a saleable/useable product. Subsequently while there has been some development work on the technique (WARM 1992) the use of anaerobic digestion in the UK has been confined to the treatment of sewage and a selection of other wastes in specific locations (dairy waste in South Wales and animal manures in Ireland). In some mainland continental countries the technique has been used for the treatment of household wastes with varying levels of success.

In France the Valorga facility at Amiens has not proved successful to the extent the original operators of the plant had hoped and they sold their interest for a nominal sum to Gaz de France. In Denmark a plant in Elsinore using German technology has also had considerable teething problems but the system has only been in operation since mid-1991. By the end of 1992 it had processed only 4000 tonnes of selected putrescible materials, of which disposable nappies comprised 20 per cent.

Incineration

Only 5 of the 30 incinerators in Britain in 1993 had energy recovery facilities, for either district heating or electricity generation. Because of the tight controls over the emissions of municipal waste incinerators under EU legislation almost all the existing incinerators will have to be closed down by December 1996. It is likely that the only facilities which it will be economic to retrofit with gas cleaning equipment will be those which recover energy.

For the last 20 years London has had only one municipal waste incinerator. Built by the GLC and commissioned in 1971, the Edmonton incinerator is an electricity generating power station, with a throughput of over 400,000 tpa of waste. As it approaches the end of its design life, there are proposals to re-build the plant on the same site, with about double the existing design capacity.

The Edmonton Incinerator was planned to be the first of three or four municipal incinerators within London, and suitable sites were earmarked at an early date, taking into consideration catchment areas of waste arisings. Edmonton was built during the late 1960s and early 1970s and due to its high costs together with protracted 'teething' troubles and the availability of lower cost landfill, no other incinerators were built.

A new combined heat and power waste to energy incinerator is currently under construction in South East London, although due to the fact that premium prices are available for its electricity for several years it will be generating only electricity. Situated in the Borough of Lewisham it also has a design capacity of just over 400,000 tpa and is due to be commissioned in 1994.

To an extent incineration is also a waste reduction measure in that a 90 per cent volume and 65 per cent weight reduction is made through incineration. However, even if ferrous metals are extracted, the residual ash normally goes to landfill.

Landfill

This system of waste disposal, as previously stated, is the preferred option at present for the majority of wastes. For the huge volumes of demolition and construction waste generated in the UK it will remain the only option when all waste reduction and re-use opportunities have been explored. At present some 25–35m tpa of demolition and construction wastes are sent to landfill, although even there some of it has a value either for the construction of roadways or as daily cover to prevent pests getting into putrescible wastes and for controlling odours.

Landfill does also provide an opportunity to reclaim land damaged by mineral exploitation and thereby to re-use the land or at least to restore the landscape to approximately its original contours. Nevertheless there are an increasing number of alternative options for the productive use of mineral sites, including their use for development and increasingly wildlife and leisure purposes, particularly for water filled sites.

With the filling of landfills closest to urban areas and increasing difficulty in gaining planning permission for the establishment of new landfill sites there is a move to extend landfilling to above ground by landforming. This is usually achieved by extending landfilling to above the original contours, to 60m in one case in the Midlands, or by utilising low grade agricultural land.

Landfill sites are one of the main sources of methane in the UK, around two billion cubic metres a year, with a greenhouse potency some 28 times greater than carbon dioxide. Controlling these emissions should be one of the main priorities of landfill operators and increasingly tight controls are being introduced to ensure that these emissions do not cause danger either to nearby residents and their property or to the environment. Therefore gas monitoring is being undertaken at all sites which are susceptible to landfill gas generation and, where the gas is being produced in sufficient quantity, it is being utilised for a variety of purposes, predominantly for the generation of electricity. There were over forty such schemes which had been developed in the UK by 1993.

A further potential impact of landfill is the leachate which is produced from every site which accepts putrescible waste. In the past many sites were based on the dilute and disperse principle whereby the effects of any leachate from a site were assumed to be attenuated as it became more and more diluted through mixing with increasing volumes of surface or groundwater. While this has worked quite successfully in the past it could not be relied on for the future as more persistent chemicals which do not degrade could enter the aquatic environment from landfill sites, and a wide variety of other sources. In order to ensure that the quality of the UK's groundwater is not adversely affected by landfill operations, the National Rivers Authority is introducing groundwater protection zones to prohibit landfill in certain areas and in others to demand the use of artificial and/or clay liners for landfills (NRA 1992).

All these additional controls will increase the operational costs of landfill but even so, given the large number of existing landfills, 4000 in the UK in early 1993, and the fact that geologically much of the country has a clay substructure it is probable that without additional incentives landfill will remain the most cost effective option for the disposal of the majority of wastes in most of the country.

Beyond integrated waste management

As may be readily appreciated, in an ideal world where waste is generated it should be dealt with using the principle of the best practicable environmental option. Thus there ought to be a finely balanced comprehensive range of reclamation, treatment and disposal facilities available to every waste authority. While much can be done within existing resource constraints the provision of, for example, an incinerator with energy recovery facilities is currently estimated to require a throughput of around 400,000 tpa of waste. Therefore there would be several parts of the UK in which the provision of such a facility would not be sustainable, to the extent that moving the waste to the facility may use more energy than could be reclaimed from the waste carried.

Recycling, energy recovery and composting are all key components of the highly desirable concept of integrated waste management. However, with the commitments made at the United Nations Conference on Environment and Development (UNCED) in Rio de Janeiro in June 1992 still to be brought into fruition, the focus should be shifting towards the development of a comprehensive resource management strategy. This perspective lies at the heart of the European Union's Fifth Action Programme on the Environment, 'Towards Sustainability'.

It will take time and effort to move the UK away from its overwhelming dependence on landfill disposal systems but political and public pressures are pushing in the direction of further development of recycling and this presumption in favour of that option can be used to promote waste reduction and re-use, not only in the home but in the work environment as well (Open University 1993). Defining the limits for a sustainable integrated waste management for the coming millenium will be a major task for local authorities in the next few years.

9 Transport

John Carr

Sustainability and transport

Sustainability is a concept that poses many difficult questions for an affluent, consumer orientated society and nowhere is this more so than for transport, which exists only to serve other economic and social activities. Often the extent to which modern society depends on transport is overlooked, for example:

- manufacturers using 'Just In Time' principles bring together components from a variety of suppliers to assembly plants using goods transport (usually lorries) virtually as part of their production lines;
- modern retail complexes, like shopping malls, depend on easy access for goods, staff and customers and demand large areas of land for car parking;
- community facilities and services, like hospitals, schools and leisure centres can take advantage of economies of scale over more local facilities by virtue of their dependence on transport;
- mass tourism is an industry created almost entirely because of the availability of plentiful, low-priced transport;
- the location and form of cities and towns has been, and is being shaped by transport needed to support their industrial, commercial and social functions.

Thus transport is an integral feature of modern life, taken for granted to the extent that it often does not cause comment unless major failures or accidents happen or congestion regularly occurs because capacity is no longer adequate to meet demand. In terms of sustainability, transport is *prima facie* a profligate consumer

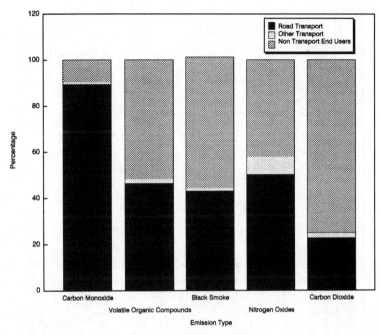

Figure 9.1. Emissions of Some Major Pollutants by Sector 1991

of scarce resources — land, primary materials and energy — which produces large quantities of pollution and waste. Table 9.1 summarises some impacts that transport has on the environment at local, regional and global levels. Figure 9.1 shows for some of the most commonly occurring air pollutants the proportions coming from transport and from other areas of economic activity in 1991.

A global example — carbon dioxide emissions

As an illustration of the importance of the transport sector to atmospheric pollution, carbon dioxide (CO_2), the most common and pernicious of the greenhouse gases, can be used. CO_2 is produced in transport mainly as a by-product of the burning of oil fuels in petrol and diesel engines. Transport accounted for 24 per cent of the UK's total CO_2 emissions in 1991, 21 per

Table 9.1: Some environmental impacts of transport and their distribution

	Local	Regional/National	Global
Air pollution	Exhaust emissions including: 　Carbon monoxide (CO) 　Nitrogen dioxide (NO_2) 　Hydrocarbons (HC_x) 　Sulphur dioxide (SO_2) 　Particulates (soot) 　Heavy metals 　Complex organic compounds (all contribute to various health problems)	Nitrogen oxides (NO_x) and Hydrocarbons contribute to tropospheric ozone and photochemical smog NO_x contributes to acid rain (with a minor contribution from transport sources of SO_2)	Carbon dioxide (CO_2) is the main contributor to global warming and climate change Minor contribution to depletion of ozone layer
Physical effects	Visible smoke Dust, dirt and spray Fuel/oil leakage and spillage Soil contamination Water pollution Staining of buildings Noise Vibration Visual intrusion Severance	Land use changes Vehicle manufacture Infrastructure construction Water pollution	
Health and Safety	Wide variety of medical impacts including: Chest and respiratory ailments and diseases	Increased demand for health and emergency facilities	

Table 9.1: Continued

	Local	Regional/National	Global
	Oxygen deprivation and associated problems Eye, nose and throat irritations Potential carcinogens		Depletion of fossil fuel reserves Consumption of primary materials
	Fear		
	Stress		
	Accidents		
Resources	Land take	Operational and maintenance costs (private and public)	
	Costs of congestion and delay	Distributional effects of car availability	
		Land take	
		Waste (scrap) disposal and recycling	

Source From *The Local Authority Associations and LGMB* (1992), Section J cent from road traffic. These proportions had increased from 15 per cent and 13 per cent in 1981, but during the decade national emissions of CO_2 had increased by only about 1 per cent in total. In 1992, the UK Government signed the United Nations Framework Convention on Climate Change (UNFCCC) committing itself to take measures to return emissions of each greenhouse gas to 1990 levels no later than the year 2000.

Let us assume that CO_2 emissions in every other sector apart from transport can be contained to meet their individual targets. This is achievable as measures already being taken in the other sectors are proving effective. This is indicated by the increase of around 60 per cent in transport's contribution to an only slightly changed total in the eleven years to 1991. For transport, the National Road Traffic Forecasts (NRTF) published by the Department of Transport (DoT) in 1989 (Department of Transport 1989a) showed traffic growth of between 83 per cent and 142 per cent between 1988 and 2025. However, the recession of the early 1990s has led to virtually static traffic levels between 1990 and 1992. Major improvements in fuel efficiency and emission control are not currently expected — perhaps 4 per cent by 2000 and 10 per cent by 2025 — so that increasing travel demand will lead to continuing rapid growth of emissions of CO_2.

Using NRTF projections of traffic growth and a central economic growth assumption of a 2.25 per cent per annum increase in gross domestic product (GDP) between 1990 and 2020 gives the results shown in Figure 9.2. The low growth projection involves a slight fall in real prices of fuel to end users, while the high growth implies a modest real increase. These might reflect the differences between continuing fuel tax policies as they were before the March 1993 budget, and the policy of increasing real levels of fuel taxation introduced in that budget and emphasised in the first unified budget of November 1993. Already, the real rise in fuel prices because of taxation has been increased to over 5 per cent per annum and this is set to continue in future budgets.

However, prior to the 1993 policy changes, projections based on NRTF show that emissions of CO_2 in the transport sector might well rise between 18 per cent and 33 per cent between 1990 and 2000 and could be between 60 per cent and 100 per cent higher by 2025 (LGMB et al. 1992c). Substantial measures will continue to be necessary to achieve the UNFCCC targets, both by government and by consumer action.

In the simple scenarios described, where other sectors succeed in remaining at or returning to their 1990 emission levels,

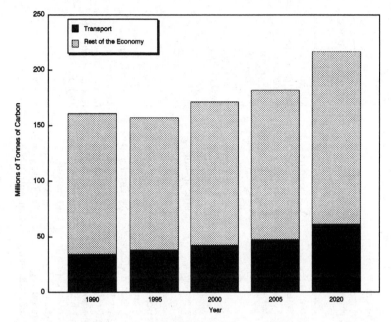

Figure 9.2. Projection of United Kingdom CO_2 Emissions (Lower growth in fuel prices)

growth of road traffic alone could result in the UK breaching its total UNFCCC target by between 4 per cent and 7 per cent. These calculations are simplistic of course. For example, better performance in other sectors may well compensate for transport, or, more likely, the tougher fuel taxation policies and introduction of road charging could limit traffic growth to the low end of the NRTF projections. Equally, there could be breakthroughs in engine, fuel or emission control technology, but these would probably not have significant impacts before the end of the century.

It is salutary that a widely supported environmental measure, the fitting of catalytic convertors to reduce emissions of toxic gases from internal combustion engines, actually reduces engine efficiency and increases the direct output of CO_2 from motor vehicles. However, it is also believed that this may be compensated for as the more noxious gases such as oxides of nitrogen also have

Table 9.2: Effects of some common pollutants on health and the environment

Pollutant	Sulphur Dioxide	Airborne Particulates	Carbon Monoxide	Ozone	Nitrogen Dioxide
Source	Combustion of sulphur-containing fossil fuels. Power stations contribute 72% of UK total. In cities levels can be boosted by smoke from diesel engines.	Vehicles, especially diesels, contribute nearly a half overall and up to 90% in urban areas. Coal burning in power stations and fires.	Incomplete combustion of fuel. 85% from motor vehicles.	A secondary pollutant formed by photochemical reaction between sunlight, nitrogen oxides, and hydrocarbons. The highest levels occur from heavy traffic in hot weather.	Motor vehicles are the major source, emitting 51% of total nitrogen dioxides. Power stations account for a further 28%.
Health	Breathing problems, such as bronchitis. Asthmatics are affected. Most serious is combination with particulates where, with moisture, can form sulphuric acid in lungs. Long	Heavy metals and some complex organic compounds, such as polyaromatic hydrocarbons carried deep into lungs on particulates. These potentially cause cancer.	Deprives body of oxygen by reacting with haemoglobin. Slows thought and reflexes, causes drowsiness and headaches. Increased presure on heart. Fatal at high concentrations.	Although beneficial in the ozone layer it is harmful at ground level. High concentrations severely damage lung tissue and impair defence against infections. Lower concentrations	Increased susceptibility to viral infection, irritates lung tissue, increases risk of bronchitis and pneumonia.

Pollutant	Sulphur Dioxide	Airborne Particulates	Carbon Monoxide	Ozone	Nitrogen Dioxide
	term exposure can increase mortality from cardio-respiratory diseases.		Can retard foetal growth if inhaled by pregnant women.	cause coughing, impaired lung function, eye, nose and throat irritation and headaches, particularly in people who exercise. Aggravates asthma and bronchitis.	
Environmental Effects	The main constituent of acid rain, which damages aquatic life and increases concentrations of heavy metals in acidified water. Injury to plants, both vegetation and trees. Corrosion of buildings.	Soiling of buildings with associated cleaning costs. Reduced visibility. Odour.	Reacts with chemicals which would normally remove 'greenhouse' gas methane, and oxidises to carbon dioxide, another contributor to global warming.		Responsible for about one third of the acidity of rainfall. At low dosages, can stimulate plant growth, but also increases susceptibility to insect attack or frost damage.

Source From *The Local Authority Associations (1990), Section D (Originally from work by Friends of the Earth)* an indirect and longer lasting effect on global warming because of the chemical changes they induce in the atmosphere. Paradoxes such as this, added to the high dependency of society on transport, complicate the task of determining the features of sustainable transport policies

At the individual level, transport has considerable environmental impacts. The effects of some common pollutants on health and the environment are summarised in Table 9.2, which also includes more details of how these are produced. One of the most neglected aspects of transport pollution has been the relationship between transport and health, apart from the obvious concerns with injury from road accidents and the long-standing recognition of the harm caused by atmospheric lead emitted by vehicles burning leaded fuels. Formation of The Transport and Health Study Group, which in 1991 published the important report *Health on the Move* (The Public Health Alliance 1991), has provided a focus for cross-disciplinary debate and research on the issues and problems involved. A good example of the type of transport impact under investigation is the link between allergic reactions of the 'hay fever' type, and the combination of atmospheric pollution from vehicle emissions with hot and humid weather conditions.

What is a sustainable transport system?

The examples quoted above should establish the interdependence of transport with virtually every area of human activity. Transport is a crucially important service, and people are right to expect adequate standards of access (ability to reach the particular activities that they wish to engage in) and mobility (the opportunity to travel, or gain access, without being excessively constrained by the availability of transport). These are relative terms and the equity dimension is also important, so that, by and large, the goals of transport policy makers are often to ensure that reasonable levels of access and mobility are available to all groups within their communities.

Generally transport policies aim to achieve minimum standards for all groups, as clearly the ability to purchase increased mobility, and consequently access to a wider range of opportunities, increases with wealth. Ownership of a luxury car and use of private air transport probably represent the highest levels of personal mobility available for domestic and international travel respectively and can give virtually unconstrained access in transport terms. However, for people with disabilities that limit personal mobility, or who because of age, low income or choice depend on public rather than personal transport, mobility is immediately restricted. Intervention in the market for transport services is therefore necessary to achieve the aim of ensuring reasonable standards of mobility and access for all groups within society.

In view of the high degree of interdependence between transport and the activities it serves and because most transport operations cannot themselves be sustainable, it is more realistic to re-express the task as defining the transport systems necessary to support sustainable communities. Transport policies, therefore, should not be determined independently of economic, social and land-use policies, particularly in urban areas. The amount and type of transport needed is determined by the activities that take place in communities and the form of development that is adopted. These in turn may be influenced by transport as some of the earlier examples show.

Within sustainable development policies, suitable goals for transport might be:

- to provide no more transport than is necessary to sustain the community and its activities;
- to minimise the consumption of land and non-renewable resources for transport purposes;
- to encourage the use of the most environmentally suitable forms of transport, including walking and cycling;
- to maximise the efficiency of energy use;
- to minimise the pollution caused by vehicle emissions.

The policies necessary will depend on what has happened in the past as well as on future needs. For example, it may not be possible to serve low density development efficiently by public transport and private cars may achieve better performance in terms of both fuel consumption and emissions. Future planning may well seek to alter this situation, by intensifying development to enable it to support effective public transport services.

British transport policy in the 1990s

Before considering ways of developing transport policy to support sustainable development we need to examine the current structure of transport in Great Britain.

UK Government policy is that, wherever possible, activities should be transferred from the public sector to the private sector. Thus extensive privatisation of former nationalised or municipal undertakings has taken place in road transport, airlines, airports, ports and bus companies and is being implemented for railways. Together with this transfer of ownership, other activities which require public support are to be secured through contracting, including highway construction and maintenance, socially necessary bus services and, in due course, railway services. Private sector involvement is being encouraged in the financing and management of major new transport infrastructure such as the Manchester Metrolink LRT system (Senior and Ogden 1992) the Channel Tunnel, the Queen Elizabeth II bridge at Dartford, the second Severn road crossing, the Jubilee line underground extension or the London Crossrail and Channel Tunnel High Speed Rail Link projects.

Government transport policies are formulated and put into effect by the Department of Transport (Department of Transport 1993b). Its strategic aims are stated as:

> an efficient and competitive transport market to serve the interests of the economy and the community, with maximum emphasis on safety and the environment, achieved by:
> — opening up new ways to make best use of private sector skills, initiatives and funds;
> — substantial public sector investment where appropriate;
> — getting better value for money from public expenditure on transport;
> — increasing competitiveness;
> — sustaining and improving both the environment and transport safety;
> — using the price mechanism to give users and providers the right signals about the real costs of transport;
> — advancing UK interests in world markets.

Note that, despite the inclusion of references to safety and the environment, these aims are largely concerned with the interests of transport suppliers rather than consumers. The Government believes that the market itself will ensure that consumers are satisfied: if they are not it assumes they can seek alternatives. Further aspects of Government policy therefore include de-regulation on which the DoT says;

> Some regulation is essential in the interests of safety, the environment or competition. Unnecessary or unduly heavy regulation must, however, be restricted and, where it already exists, be removed. (DoT 1993b)

They quote as 'an outstanding example' progressive reductions in the regulation of air services (for which international co-operation is necessary), and go on to say 'The plans for the deregulation of bus services in London illustrate the further contributions that will be made in the transport sector towards the Government's determined drive to ease the burden of regulation'. However, in November 1993, the Government announced that, while privatisation of London Buses Ltd subsidiary companies would go on, with all London routes to be allocated on the basis of tendering for minimum subsidy contracts, deregulation would not proceed in the lifetime of the current Parliament. The reasons for this delay are not entirely clear, but undoubtedly the fear of severe congestion and consequent adverse environmental effects will have played some part.

In terms of the consumer's interests, the DoT's main policy initiatives come through the adoption of charters to protect passengers' interests when using public sector services provided by both British Rail and London Underground Ltd, and, in the near future, for bus services operating under contract to London Transport. Excellent work is also done by the DoT's Disability Unit to raise awareness of the travel problems faced by disabled people in using both private and public transport. However, when the railways are fully privatised, although charters will be required for franchised (generally subsidised) services, the Government will rely again on the market to provide what the consumer wants for fully private 'open access' services, in the same way that they have already done for bus services outside London.

For the environment, the DoT intends:

— using regulation and the price mechanism to send the right environmental messages to the transport system and its users;
— encouraging people to take account of the environment when making their transport choices and, in particular, seeking to reduce congestion in urban areas; and
— seeking to achieve the proper balance between, on the one hand, the conservation and improvement of the environment, and, on the other, the benefits to the economy from an effective transport system and the freedom that comes from personal mobility. (DoT 1993b)

Again these aims rely on the users making appropriate choices rather than direct intervention. Differential rates of fuel duty for leaded and unleaded petrol are an example of use of the price mechanism.

Roads and parking

The DoT is responsible for much (but not all) of the trunk road and motorway network. Local government controls some

96 per cent of the total road length in the country including urban motorways outside London. A few roads are provided privately or by bodies such as the Forestry Commission and the Government aims to increase private involvement as set out in its 1989 paper *New Roads by New Means* (Department of Transport 1989b). In furtherance of the desire to expose users to the costs of their transport choices the DoT is actively investigating the possibility of charging for the use of roads, through research into urban road pricing for London and options in the consultation document *Paying for Better Motorways* (Department of Transport 1993c).

Following the November 1993 Budget the DoT announced that, as soon as the technology is proven, it will introduce electronic charging systems on motorways. Charges will be set taking account of shadow tolls to avoid undesirable transfer of traffic to non-tolled roads. The revenues will be applied to the provision of new motorway capacity, rather than the environmentally preferable alternative of being used to best effect within the transport budget as a whole. But there remains the danger that surpluses from road charges could be added to general tax revenues rather than used for transport purposes as the tradition of British government finance is not to hypothecate tax revenues.

Much public car and lorry parking, both on and off-street is provided or controlled by local authorities. However, in most urban centres, significant amounts of parking are almost wholly outside the local highway authority's influence being provided on a 'private non-residential' (PNR) basis in association with offices, commercial developments or other activities. The only means available to local authorities to influence the amount of such parking is through conditions attached to new planning permissions. As the availability of convenient parking compensates for much of the inconvenience caused by congestion delays, more extensive powers to control both the supply and price of parking may be essential to reduce the amount of car traffic in urban areas.

Public transport

Increasingly, public transport operation is in the private sector, and the remaining publicly owned bus companies must operate on strictly commercial principles. British Rail is being privatised: packages of passenger services will be offered as franchises that private operators will bid for on the basis either of the most cost-effective use of subsidy (the majority) or maximum payment for the right to operate in the few cases (mainly Inter-City) which are profitable. Freight and parcels services will be fully privatised although a new grant regime will encourage transfer of freight from road to rail. Most track, signalling and stations are controlled by a new company, Railtrack, itself to be privatised in due course. Railtrack charge operators for using its facilities. The Railways Act 1993 completed its passage through Parliament in November 1993, but, in common with much recent legislation, is an enabling measure. Many details of how the new arrangements will operate thus remain to be settled by regulations and guidance to be promulgated by the Secretary of State for Transport and decisions by the new statutory officers, the Rail Regulator and the Director of Passenger Rail Franchising (the 'Franchising Director').

Bus services were deregulated in Great Britain outside London in October 1986 (following earlier deregulation of coach services in 1980). Any operator is free to operate any service subject only to registration of intent at least 42 days in advance, although the DoT is consulting on whether to vary this period. Traffic regulation conditions may be applied to control safety or environmental problems but these provisions have been rarely applied by the Traffic Commissioners who are responsible for administration of the registration and operator licensing systems. Socially necessary services not provided commercially can be secured on contract by local authorities after a process of competitive tendering. Authorities can also operate concessionary travel schemes for young, elderly and disabled people, provide passenger facilities such as bus stations, shelters and stops and take measures to promote the use of public transport, including the co-ordination of services. However, all this must be done in ways which do not inhibit competition between operators.

Private transport

Free competition is the norm in road haulage. This largely deregulated industry is split between 'own account' operations (which in practice may be contracted in from specialist operators) and general carriage of goods for hire and reward. Freight transport, including environmental factors relating to depots, is under the jurisdiction of the Licensing Authorities, the same bodies as the Traffic Commissioners for buses and coaches. Taxis and private hire cars are licensed by district councils outside London, and by the Metropolitan Police in the capital.

It might be argued that taxis in particular are really a form of public transport. The DoT is consulting on whether to legislate for a unified system of taxi and private hire car licensing with relaxation of existing regulations governing conduct of the trades (Department of Transport 1993d). Although taxis are shown in DoT statistics (Department of Transport 1993a) to contribute the greatest amount of CO_2 per passenger kilometre and are therefore environmentally suspect, presumably by analysis based largely on London figures, taxis and hire cars provide a very useful alternative to private cars and must be fully considered with public transport in any comprehensive approach to transport planning and management.

The largest component of road traffic, indeed of all passenger travel, is private cars. Although private car travel is largely under individual control, a majority of new cars registered are either purchased by companies for their employees or financed with assistance from employers. As this is facilitated by favourable tax treatment, the extent of which has however been progressively reduced in recent years, there are substantial distortions introduced into the transport market.

Non-motorised transport

Walking and cycling are the principal non-motorised, non-specialist modes and account for a substantial volume of passenger movement, in urban areas particularly. Local authorities are almost wholly responsible for footpaths, pavements and cycleways alongside or integrated with the road network and may have further interests in the development of footpaths, cycleways and bridleways for longer distance, principally leisure and recreational use.

Modal shares

Figures 9.3 and 9.4 show passenger and freight transport by mode between 1951 and 1992, showing the dominance of road transport that accounted for 93 per cent of all passenger kilometres and 61 per cent of all freight tonne kilometres in 1992. Internal air movements are not shown but are growing steadily, accounting for about 0.7 per cent of total passenger kilometres. The national statistics (Department of Transport 1993a) from which the figures in this section are drawn do not include walking.

In passenger transport in 1992, 86 per cent of passenger kilometres were by car, taxi or motor-cycle, 6 per cent by bus

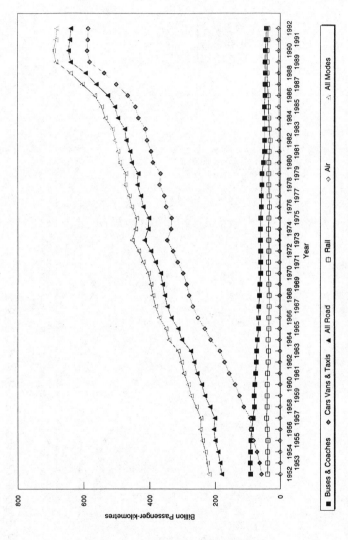

Figure 9.3. Internal UK Passenger Transport 1952–1992 (Billion Passenger-kilometres)

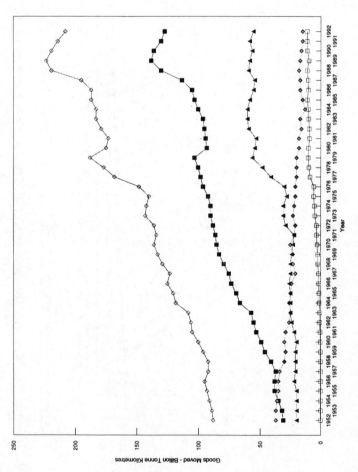

Legend:
Road ■
Rail ◆
Water ▲
Pipeline □
All Modes ◇

Goods Moved - Billion Tonne Kilometres

Year

Figure 9.4. Freight Transport: By Mode 1952–1992

or coach, 6 per cent by rail and 1 per cent by pedal cycle. For freight, 7 per cent of total kilometres moved by rail, 24 per cent by water (coastal shipping with some contribution from canals) and 5 per cent by pipeline (mainly petroleum products).

Patterns of activity are such that, whatever the mode used for the main part of the journey, both passengers and goods must use road transport either at the start or finish of their journeys or both. Because of this it would be very difficult to reduce significantly the number of road journeys (although not the distance travelled by road) without radical changes in land-use and patterns of demand. This reinforces the point made earlier that transport cannot be viewed in isolation from other activities, whether in the economic, social or environmental contexts.

Environmental impacts

Transport's environmental impacts have been summarised already in Figure 9.1 by comparison to other sectors and descriptively in Tables 9.1 and 9.2. Table 9.3 shows for each of the main exhaust pollutants the relative contributions in 1981 and 1991 by road transport, other transport modes and sectors other than transport, together with the percentage changes in volume of pollutants in each case over the decade. This table clearly demonstrates that not only is the environmental impact of transport emissions increasing in relative terms, they are also rising at such a rate as to increase total national emissions, except for black smoke. In the latter case, the lower volume of smoke from coal burning has been replaced to a large extent by the increases from diesel engines, principally lorries.

Transport's threats to the environment are not, of course, confined to atmospheric pollution. Land-take, severance, visual intrusion and noise are also causes for concern, and, particularly in the case of transport infrastructure, may also cause problems for ecology or conservation.

Some interesting paradoxes can arise. For example, major railway structures, condemned by the Victorians at the time they were constructed, are now regarded as heritage sites in their own right, even though in some cases they have ceased to be used for transport purposes. Conversely railway and road embankment and cutting sides and disused railway alignments allow access to urban areas for wildlife and promote the spread of vegetation. In extreme cases, the re-introduction of services on old railway alignments has been opposed because of adverse impacts on natural habitats that have been established since the railways closed following earlier policies of retrenchment in the 1960s and 1970s.

Living with road traffic

As already noted, most passenger and goods trips involve movement by road at least at one end of the journey. Without radical changes in land-use and patterns of activity this situation will not change. Rail alternatives are only effective where large numbers of passengers or high volumes of goods are to be moved. For passenger traffic, Table 9.4 shows the relative energy requirements of different modes of travel — energy consumption being to all intents and purposes directly proportional to the emissions produced. Lightly loaded buses and trains can cause more environmental damage than private cars carrying the same number of trips. However it has to be remembered also that effective public transport requires sufficient capacity for normal peaks and that therefore the presence of unused capacity at other times does not necessarily indicate wasteful use of resources.

Until comparatively recently most measures to reduce the environmental impacts of transport relied on mitigation. Typical actions included screening of highways or railways by high fences or tree planting (to cut noise and visual intrusion), the use of unleaded petrol and desulphurised diesel fuels (the latter not yet widespread in the UK) and the use of three way catalytic converters. Publication in 1989 of the National Road Traffic Forecasts (Department of Transport 1989a) considerably changed perceptions and attention in moving rapidly to managing not only the way transport is used, but also to controlling the demand for movement (see for example Goodwin's editorial in the new journal *Transport Policy* Goodwin 1993).

It has been shown that road transport is responsible for high proportions of most forms of environmental pollution. As around 86 per cent of total vehicle mileage is by private cars, evidently measures to reduce the impact of private motoring will form a major part of any transport measures within sustainable development strategy.

As well as the local effects of environmental pollution from car traffic, it also plays a substantial part in the build up of photochemical smog, acid rain and greenhouse gases. Most atmospheric lead comes from car emissions, but the extent of this problem has been successfully reduced by regulation of the lead content of petrol and, more recently, by differential rates of tax which have successfully ensured that the proportion of

Table 9.3 Changes in pollutant emissions 1981 to 1990 for road transport and other sectors

POLLUTANT	Road Transport			Other Transport			Other Sectors			All Sectors
	1981 % of UK Total	1991 % of UK Total	% Change in Volume 1981–1991	1981 % of UK Total	1991 % of UK Total	% Change in Volume 1981–1991	1981 % of UK Total	1991 % of UK Total	% Change in Volume 1981–1991	% Change in Volume 1981–1991
Carbon Dioxide (CO_2)	13	21	+58	2	3	+87	85	76	−10	+1
Carbon Monoxide (CO)	83	89	+43	1	1	+5	16	10	−1	+32
Nitrogen Oxides (NO_x)	36	52	+78	7	8	+38	57	40	−14	+23
Volatile Organic Compounds	38	46	+43	1	3	+192	61	51	−1	+17
Black Smoke	21	42	+87	1	1	0	78	57	−31	−6

Source *Department of Transport (1993a)* Tables 2.10 and 2.11 (with 1981 figures from comparable tables in 1992 volume)

Notes (i) 1981 and 1991 figures are the percentages of total UK emissions of each pollutant for road transport, other forms of transport (railways, shipping and civil aircraft) and for all other economic sectors.

(ii) % change in volume is the relative change in tonnes of pollutant emitted by road transport, other transport, other economic sectors and all sectors combined. + indicates an increase in emissions, − a decrease, and 0 that the change is not significant to the nearest 1%.

Table 9.4 Relative energy consumption of different travel modes

	Assumed Number of Persons Carried	Energy Used (Mj) per Passenger Mile	Energy Used (Mj) per Passenger Mile - if fully laden
Cars and Motorcycles			
Petrol: under 1.4 litre	1.5	2.79	1.05
1.4 - 2.0 litre	1.5	3.21	1.20
over 2.0 litre	1.5	4.96	1.86
Diesel: under 1.4 litre	1.5	2.42	0.91
1.4 - 2.0 litre	1.5	2.96	1.11
over 2.0 litre	1.5	3.93	1.47
Motorcycle	1.2	3.13	1.88
Moped	1	1.31	1.31
Buses & Coaches			
Double-decker bus	25 (33% full)	0.83	0.28
Single-decker bus	16 (33% full)	1.40	0.47
Minibus	10 (50% full)	1.15	0.57
Express Coach	30 (65% full)	0.61	0.40
*Rail**			
InterCity (100 mph electric)	338 (60% full)	0.77	0.46
InterCity 225 (125 mph electric)	289 (60% full)	1.04	0.62
InterCity 125 (diesel)	294 (60% full)	0.95	0.57
SuperSprinter (diesel)	88 (60% full)	0.89	0.53
Electric Suburban	180 (60% full)	0.70	0.42
Air: (Boeing 737)	100 (60% full)	3.90	2.34
*Non-Motorised**			
Bicycle*	1 person	0.10	0.10
Walk*	1 person	0.25	0.25

Source *The Local Authority Associations (1990)*, Section D (based on work by Hughes)
Notes: Carbon dioxide emissions correspond, to a first approximation, to primary energy consumption.
   *   Very little carbon dioxide, or other pollutants, produced
   **   Electrified rail travel produces less carbon dioxide emissions if an increased non-fossil fraction is employed by the electricity supply industry.

Table 9.5 Journey lengths and mode of travel

Percentage of Journeys at each length	Journey Length			Percentage By Mode
	Short Under 10 Miles	Medium 10 to 50 Miles	Long 50 Miles or More	
Walk	11	–	–	9
Local Bus	10	3	–	9
Train and Underground	1	7	11	2
Non-local Bus	–	1	6	1
Other Public	2	1	–	1
Car Driver	45	55	44	46
Car Passenger	27	32	33	28
Other Private	4	3	6	4
ALL MODES	100	100	100	100

Source From *Department of Transport (1993e)*, Table 9.3
Note. Totals do not all add to 100 because of rounding.

unleaded fuel used in the UK had grown to about 47 per cent by 1992 and will continue to increase as all new cars must be capable of using unleaded fuel.

The DoT's national roads programme set out in the White Paper *Roads to Prosperity* (Department of Transport 1989c) aims to remove heavy traffic from congested town and village centres through the construction of by-passes and improvement of overloaded inter-urban road links. The public perception because of the contribution of heavy lorries, buses and coaches to noise and vibration, and the higher proportion of visible pollution from black smoke from diesel engines, is that heavy vehicles are the main problem. However, the capacity provided by new roads is largely used by passenger cars and it is these, because of their higher speeds and parking requirements, that contribute most to both land take and congestion.

For example, each mile of 3 lane motorway designed for a 70mph maximum speed requires 25 acres of land, while the length of peak periods in many cities has doubled in little over a decade and, in the worst cases, traffic volumes do not significantly vary during most of the working day. Such conditions mean that the concentration of pollutants increases, particularly in hot and humid weather, and the number of occasions on which air quality falls below acceptable levels in British cities is growing rapidly.

Although the car is seen as the principal cause of environmental problems from transport, and reducing the need for car travel must therefore have a high priority, this is not the same thing as restricting car ownership. Car ownership significantly improves personal mobility and access and there are very many trips which cannot be made efficiently by public transport. What is required is to achieve a balance in the provision of roads and public transport which enables the public to make the most appropriate choices for their journeys. The UK Government believe that this will be achieved largely through the market, but a substantial body of both professional and public opinion believes that intervention and guidance is necessary to achieve the desired results.

The local authority role

Most transport is local. Table 9.5 shows the distribution of trip lengths and means of transport, including walking, from the National Travel Survey 1989/91 (Department of Transport 1993e). Local authorities have a pivotal role in managing both transport demand and supply. They are responsible for strategic planning and for detailed development control; they provide and maintain much of the road network; they have powers to regulate traffic movement; they are responsible for subsidising and promoting public transport services and provide facilities such as bus stations, shelters and stops; they have worked with British Rail to develop the role of both freight and passenger services. As major employers, local authorities are themselves major users of transport, and, perhaps most importantly, by advocacy education and example they can encourage the adoption of good practice in the use of transport services.

The strategic approach

Recognising the inextricable links between land use, economic and social activity and transport, the various local authority associations have each produced policy documents calling on the Government to overhaul the way in which resources are allocated for transport and transport systems are managed. The Association of County Councils for example, has put forward the six point strategy for transport shown in Figure 9.5 (Association of County Councils 1991).

The Association of Metropolitan Authorities in its transport policy statement *Changing Gear* (AMA 1990) called for a 'package approach' to transport investment. This involves common mechanisms for the appraisal of costs and benefits of road and public transport expenditure, and returning the discretion to allocate resources between different types of project to local authorities by allowing flexibility in the use of grants and spending approvals rather than the rigid mechanisms that had evolved during the 1980s. While there are still considerable constraints imposed by the local government financial system, the DoT has, after considering a trial package submitted jointly by the six metropolitan district councils and the passenger transport authority in the West Midlands, adopted the package approach for allocation of transport supplementary grants and credit approvals with packages being phased in from 1994/5 onwards. Authorities can bid either singly or in partnership for package allocations covering urban areas. While this falls short of the AMA's original proposals which would have looked at resource allocation on a conurbation or sub-regional basis, ideally within a new financial regime, it does allow much more scope for shifting resources between roads and public transport.

At the local level, many councils are developing comprehensive transport strategies, often in association with unitary development plans or structure plans and complementing environmental

Figure 9.5 The ACC's six point strategy for a sustainable transport strategy

1. TRANSPORT AND LAND USE
Objective   The recognition of the interrelationship of land use and transportation and the adoption of mechanisms, techniques and procedures to ensure that all transport decisions are made in the full knowledge of their major implications for land use and the development of the local and regional economy, and vice versa.
Action   Secure better co-ordination of land use and transportation decisions at Central and Local Government levels by DoE and DoT and by County and District Councils through a re-examination of the adequacy and distribution of powers of decision, implementation and control.
2. MANAGEMENT OF DEMAND
Objective   The acceptance of the inability in environmental and economic terms to meet all of the likely future demand for individual mobility and access through the provision of additional road space and the need therefore to move to a regime of demand management designed to make effective and environmentally acceptable use of existing and new transport infrastructure.
Action   A public information and awareness campaign on the need to restrain the unbridled use of the private car and recognise the true costs of travel; a review of existing planning policies to achieve reductions in the need for travel; the development of advanced traffic management policies to optimise the use of the limited transport resource and a research project to establish the criteria for the new road building which will be possible.
3. PUBLIC PASSENGER TRANSPORT
Objective   To make public passenger transport an attractive and viable alternative to the private car in order to

Figure 9.5.—Contd.

achieve its optimum use and facilitate the modal change from the private car to public transport.

Action   Institute research into new, innovative and improved forms of public transport; review current taxation and pricing mechanisms to encourage modal change and provide additional investment in public transport infrastructure.

4. MOVEMENT OF FREIGHT

Objective   To complete and sustain an adequate main road network for the movement of freight and to seek the transference of freight from road to rail (and water) and reduce the impact of freight distribution on the urban and rural environment.

Action   Review taxation and pricing mechanisms to encourage further use of rail and water infrastructure and investigate ways by which the penetration of the lorry into towns and villages may be discouraged, e.g. by freight distribution centres and the use of smaller delivery vehicles.

5. ENVIRONMENT AND SAFETY

Objective   To improve and safeguard the standard, quality and safety of life in both town and country.

Action   Institute a programme of public education to build on the growing awareness of environmental issues, resource and expedite further research into such matters as new technology, noxious emissions and noise pollution; set targets for the achievement of environmental standards and increase investment in schemes with a high 'environmental' return, such as by-passes, and which achieve pedestrian preference and personal safety.

6. INVESTMENT IN TRANSPORT

Objective   To secure the most cost-effective allocation (in environmental and financial terms) of public and private sector investment at the maximum affordable level (in social and economic terms).

Figure 9.5.—Contd.

Action	Review appraisal techniques to permit a truer comparability for decision making (the level playing field concept); review taxation and pricing mechanisms to achieve policy objectives (re: e.g. demand management, public transport and freight); increase investment and redress the imbalance and inequity of public highway and transport allocations as between central and local government expenditure.

Source: ACC 1991

strategies. A good example is the Leeds Transport Strategy jointly developed by Leeds City Council and the West Yorkshire Passenger Transport Authority (through Metro its Passenger Transport Executive) working in consultation with Leeds Development Corporation (the Government development agency formed to promote regeneration in parts of the city). Development of the Transport Strategy forms an integral part of the City Council's Green Strategy. Its objective is:

> To promote the development of an improved urban transport system to support economic development and achieve a range of environmental objectives, contributing to an overall vision for the city's future.

The strategy is based firmly on partnership, and political and public consensus: it was prepared by a joint members' working party representing all parties on the City Council, WYPTA and Leeds Development Corporation, and full consultation was carried out. The consultation process comprised:

- a major local opinion survey;
- 3 citywide public consultation exercises;
- discussion with key local organisations (including the Civic Trust, Chambers of Commerce and Industry, and Chamber of Trade) and close involvement of the Leeds Initiative (the city's public–private sector partnership organisation).

The Transport Strategy proposals encompass:

- improvements to existing rail and bus systems including guided bus;
- a new light rail system;

- a programme of 'bypass' road schemes with environmental/ economic objectives;
- traffic management (including calming);
- a package of city centre transport initiatives;
- emphasis on the needs of people with disabilities and others with mobility problems.

The balanced package adopted will reduce future pollution (through minimising traffic growth), improve road safety and create opportunities for pedestrianisation and other physical enhancement. Many of these benefits will be difficult to measure and will only be apparent in the longer term. By increasing the capacity and quality of transport, accessibility and environmental quality will be enhanced, increasing the appeal and attractiveness of the city centre and supporting economic development and employment in the city generally.

The strategy is now being pursued through a wide range of constituent projects whose progress is being kept under review. Environmental aspects of traffic will be monitored through mechanisms being developed in the city's Green Strategy. Public transport patronage is monitored by Metro, traffic volumes and accidents by the City Council. The capital cost of all the measures necessary to implement the Strategy over 20 years has been estimated at £800m. Some of this is already planned (e.g. Government road proposals, TPP schemes) but much depends on investment by railway and bus operators, and on Government support for new public transport initiatives.

Another important advance in relation to the encouragement of more strategic approaches to land use and transport has been the completion of the study of land use and transport undertaken for the Departments of Environment and Transport as a commitment following publication of *This Common Inheritance* (Department of the Environment 1990). A draft Planning Policy Guidance Note 13 has been circulated for comment which makes clear the necessity to maximise the use of existing transport assets in locating new development and ensuring that where new transport infrastructure or services are required these can be provided as efficiently as possible.

The results of consultation were being considered at the time of writing, one of the main concerns of local authority consultees has been to ensure that the guidance will reflect as fully as possible the situation that most transport is, or will be, provided by private companies. Therefore, robust procedures must be developed to reconcile commercial, social and environmental objectives in the development planning process.

Assessing transport impacts

Proposals for large transport projects, including major road schemes, new railways and airports are required to include an environmental statement. This is to enable the predicted impacts of the project to be identified, their importance assessed and any measures necessary to mitigate them to be determined before planning permission is granted. Environmental Assessments (EAs) are now regarded as a standard part of scheme appraisal alongside economic and financial assessments. There is a strong case for extending the discipline to evaluation of the environmental consequences of transport policies and programmes through the related technique of Strategic Environmental Assessment (SEA).

A good example of the way in which Environmental Assessment is used is to be found in the Environmental Assessment Handbook produced by Kent County Council and now routinely used for major transport proposals in the county. The procedures used are contained in Figure 9.6 (LGMB *et al.* 1992c). Kent have also taken a lead in mitigating the effect of railway routes leading to the Channel Tunnel and together with neighbouring authorities is contributing to the cost of noise barriers to screen neighbouring households.

Figure 9.6 The environmental assessment process followed by Kent County Council

1. ***Area of Search***
    Having established that new highway construction may be required, an area of search is identified within which the environmental and planning implications must be considered, and includes the following:
    *   Nature conservation, landscape, agriculture
    *   Conservation areas, listed buildings and ancient monuments
    *   Foothpaths, water gathering grounds, local plan designations, etc.
    Initial comments from 'in-house' experts are also collected, regarding, for example, archaeology, ecology, landscape or architecture.
    This initial environmental evaluation is required if a scheme is to be included in the county structure plan.

Figure 9.6.—Contd.

2. *Alternative Routes*

The decisions on possible routes are then made balancing environmental, engineering, traffic and economic considerations in the determination. Work done at this stage can prove useful in the environmental assessment and can avoid further work at a later stage. Where critical decisions have to be made, some statutory consultees may be asked to advise.

3. *Public Consultation*

The various scheme options determined through the previous processes are exhibited to the public giving all relevant information. All planning and environmental issues relating to the scheme are accurately shown. This forum proves to be an ideal opportunity to gather local knowledge of environmental issues relating to a scheme and is often called a 'scoping exercise' in environmental assessment practice. All advantages and disadvantages of the scheme are identified and form the basis of the environmental appraisal. It is following this stage that the preferred scheme is selected.

4. *Integration with Structure and Local Plan*

Once selected, it will be necessary to check with the planning department to ensure that the route is included in the structure and local plans. Consideration of need, alignment, land use and environmental implications of the route may be discussed at structure plan or local plan inquiry.

5. *Detail Design*

Having identified in the earlier stages of investigation the likely environmental effects of the scheme, the mitigating measures proposed to offset these effects are developed and become part of the scheme design. All the information is provided for each proposal whether or not an environmental statement is required. Consultation between highways and planning is continuous, ensuring that all aspects of the scheme are dealt with including the need for discussions with all people and groups concerned. This process not only reduces the work needed at a later date but also avoids the situation where an application is returned due to an inadequate statement.

Figure 9.6.—Contd.

6. ***Submission of the Planning Application***
    The consultation process and detailed appraisal of the
    scheme becomes the responsibility of the planning
    department, which organises the necessary visits and
    public meetings. Teamwork, however, continues with
    further information being supplied by highways as and
    when required.

7. ***Public Inquiry***
    The detailed information in the statement and appraisal
    process provides a good basis for the evidence required
    at planning, compulsory purchase or side road order
    inquiries. The cost of an inquiry is about £10,000 per
    day, so any study which provides information for the
    environmental statement and can save a day of inquiry
    time has to be considered.

It is important that the financial and environmental impacts
of major transport projects can be brought together. For major
highways projects, cost benefit appraisal is used with predicted
benefits to users and the community counted in full against the
costs of the scheme. The Standing Advisory Committee on Trunk
Road Appraisal (SACTRA) (Department of Transport 1992) has
considered ways of valuing environmental costs and benefits for
incorporation into such appraisals. For public transport schemes,
the approach is somewhat different as it is assumed that users
will pay through fares the full value of the benefits that they
received. However, the Government will allow benefits such as
the relief of congestion to be counted in appraisal of public
transport schemes and is involved jointly with local authority
associations in a study of investment appraisal criteria. Ideally,
the same basic appraisal frameworks incorporating appropriate
means of assessing environmental impacts should be used for
both roads and public transport investment if properly balanced
transport strategies are to be developed.

Managing impacts

In towns and villages where through traffic is intrusive and causes
congestion and other environmental damage, by-passes offer the

opportunity of relief, although they may also create adverse impacts in surrounding areas. The Department of Transport and local authorities are collaborating in a three year 'By-pass Demonstration Project' involving six towns:

Berkhamsted, Hertfordshire;
Dalton in Furness, Cumbria;
Market Harborough, Leicestershire;
Petersfield, Hampshire;
Wadebridge, Cornwall;
Whitchurch, Shropshire.

In each case the changes in traffic flows resulting from the completion of a by-pass will be monitored, and the effects of complementary measures such as traffic calming and screening evaluated.

By their nature, transport corridors such as roads and railways dominate large areas of country. Careful management of the corridor 'between the fences' can do much to enhance the local environment and to reduce the impact of the transport facility. Measures include appropriate planting of verges, cuttings and embankments: several highway authorities for example have taken the opportunity to provide habitats for wild flowers or animals, while comprehensive improvement of derelict land in railway corridors has been undertaken by the Groundwork Trust in various areas.

Controlling the ways in which cars are used, particularly in residential and busy shopping streets, is an essential part of managing the impact of traffic in towns. Often streets are called upon to fulfil functions for which they were not designed, including parking, short cuts and rat runs. Traffic calming and parking control measures, such as residents parking schemes, are therefore being widely introduced.

One problem with traffic calming has proved to be its impact on bus services. Many through streets in which traffic calming measures are proposed are also bus routes. Road humps that are effective in controlling car speeds can cause severe discomfort, even when negotiated at low speed, to drivers and occupants of buses and emergency vehicles. Some bus companies have reported problems of back injury as a result. Where possible, other measures such as chicanes combined with bus boarders (which allow buses to pull right alongside the stop without interference from parked cars) might be used to achieve similar effects. Rather than continuous road humps, 'cushions' over which buses can pass without jolting offer an alternative.

Projects such as by-passes, corridor management and traffic calming and others such as area traffic management and control schemes and pedestrianisation are all part of the range of measures available to control the environmental impact of current and projected traffic. They can easily be assimilated into wider transport and environmental strategies for the areas concerned.

Paying the price

One of the main problems in achieving balanced transport strategies is that public transport users pay directly for their journey on each trip they make. For motorists, only the marginal costs are perceived directly and the costs of the highway itself are met from general taxation. In recent years attention has turned increasingly to methods of removing this disparity and several proposals for road pricing have been developed. The simplest involve payment to enter a particular area such as the city centre or to drive on a section of road or motorway. More sophisticated techniques involving electronic beacons and in-car meters would allow the charging to be more directly related to the time and distance travelled.

Mention has already been made of the DoT's research and proposals. Cambridgeshire County Council had proposals for a congestion charging scheme in the intensively developed City of Cambridge, but this was abandoned late in 1993 in favour of applying the capital required to improving public transport. It is proposed that the revenues from such schemes should be used to improve transport facilities, for example by providing funds for public transport improvements in cities, or motorway schemes in the case of the Department of Transport's consultation paper *Paying for Better Motorways* (Department of Transport 1993c).

At a more immediate level, parking policy is an important tool for managing road traffic. Both the level of charges and time restrictions can be used effectively to alter patterns of demand. However this only applies where the local authority can control a significant proportion of parking space. In many towns and cities the amount of private non-residential parking means that controls in the public sector have only limited impact.

Promoting public transport

Sustainable development will inevitably require a considerable increase in the proportion of trips made by public transport. This means that people must be persuaded that they have no need to use their cars because public transport offers them convenient, fast and reasonably-priced alternatives. Exposing car users to their full economic and environmental costs by road pricing would be an enormous help in this, but is not likely to be available in the short to medium term. Therefore public transport has to compete on price (perhaps assisted by subsidy) and particularly quality.

The quality of a public transport trip is determined by a wide range of elements. Waiting conditions at the stop or station, the availability of timetable information, both in planning the journey and during it, the convenience and ease of use of the fares system, including matters such as transfers between services without separate payment, the amenity of the vehicles themselves, the possibilities for interchange to other services and modes including park and ride, are all important in addition to the basic attributes of frequency of service and journey speed. Production of effective services will depend on partnership between the authorities responsible for highways, service subsidies and often information too, and the operators themselves. The aim has been described as to provide 'seamless' journeys, and, as public transport must compete in a literal sense with car travel, a strong marketing approach is appropriate (Stokes *et al*. 1991).

Rail systems, including light rapid transit (LRT) and further modernisation and expansion of the suburban and inter-urban networks around major cities will have a substantial part to play. However, it has to be acknowledged that the bus is, and will remain, the most readily available form of public transport. Outside London, almost 90 per cent of public transport trips are carried by bus. Unfortunately the bus at present suffers from a poor image. The industry is still settling down after deregulation in 1986 and public confidence in the stability of services is low. Financial returns are poor for many companies resulting in a rapidly ageing fleet which is being renewed at only half the rate most bus operators consider acceptable, although several operators, often from the larger groups, but usually enjoying monopolistic or oligopolistic trading conditions, are succeeding in reinstating substantial vehicle replacement programmes.

Despite current problems, both the industry itself, through the operators' association, the Bus and Coach Council, and the local authority associations are working hard to promote buses. The Department of Transport has responded by establishing demonstration programmes for funding bus priorities and promotion measures, and the introduction of the package approach will also help the implementation of traffic measures to assist buses.

Access to vehicles is an important consideration. Improving accessibility helps most users, not just those who are disabled. The Disabled Persons Transport Advisory Committee (DPTAC) has produced guidelines for features that can improve access to existing designs of buses. They are also leading advocates for the introduction in the UK of new designs for low floor buses, trials of which will be carried out in Merseyside, Tyneside and London.

Promotion of public transport is therefore not concerned only with information, but rather with developing the concept of a complete network of services — corresponding to the road network – fully co-ordinated and with improving standards not only of vehicles but also features such as bus shelters, stops, information displays (including 'next bus' electronic information in due course), interchanges, park and ride and so on. The highway network must be managed so as to improve bus performance and recognise the enormous advantage the high capacity of buses gives them in making efficient use of road space.

Walking and cycling

In terms of sustainability, walking and cycling perhaps approach the optimum forms of transport. Not only do they achieve transport objectives they also provide healthy exercise. Much can be done to promote walking and cycling by careful attention to detail in planning and maintenance.

Well designed networks of pavements and footpaths providing direct links between key points, including bus stops, with high standards of lighting and visibility are essential. The local authority associations have developed the 'Feet First' programme of demonstration projects (The Local Authority Associations 1993) which incorporate new approaches and standards of design for securing high levels of amenity, safety and security for journeys on foot.

These schemes involve the local community in the planning and development process, and move the whole subject of catering for pedetrian movement on from earlier initiatives which were largely concentrated on town centre pedestrianisation schemes.

Provision of cycling can be seen as having five complementary aims:

- Traffic aims
    — in the long term a shift from car to cycle travel for short journeys should be encouraged to reduce pollution, congestion and parking problems;
    — to reduce the high level of accidents involving cyclists, taking advantage of the low cost of works for cyclists relative to works for motor vehicles.
- Leisure aims
    — cycling should be encouraged as a contribution to people's health, fitness and recreation;
    — access to appropriate open spaces and to the country-side should be provided to increase environmental and recreational awareness.
- Other aims
    — tourism and economic development can be enhanced by making people aware of cycling provision and the contribution it can make to limiting the environmental intrusion caused by growth in motor traffic.

The extent of cycling is obviously influenced by topography and, to some extent, tradition so that cities such as Cambridge, Derby, Oxford and York have higher than average proportions of cycling. The aims quoted above were produced to guide the development of a cycling strategy for Derby. Measures taken in the implementation of that strategy include shared bus and cycle lanes, cycle tracks alongside main roads and avoiding roundabouts, special links through culs-de-sac and road closures and contra flow access to one way streets. Shared pedestrian and cycle facilities are also included.

Nationally, the charitable company SUSTRANS has developed extensive stretches of cycleways mainly on disused railway alignments, often for leisure use but also giving traffic free access to urban or suburban centres in some cases (The Local Authority Associations 1990).

Public involvement

Consumerism and the speed of modern media and communications mean that members of the public not only feel they have the right to know but in many cases they also wish to contribute to the decision making process. There is a perceived frustration that even locally elected representatives are remote. The answer to such tensions is good consultation on projects and good information and public awareness programmes generally.

Two particular ways of increasing public awareness of environmental issues have been found to be effective: pollution monitoring programmes mounted by local councils and reported on in the local press or newsletters and schools resource packs and liaison programmes. Such initiatives can be broadened to inform the public generally and young people in particular of the environmental and social costs of their transport choices.

The European dimension

As a member of the European Union, Britain plays a part in shaping European policies on transport and the environment. Transport infrastructure projects, such as the East Coast Main Line electrification and many industrial access roads, that promote industrial, economic or social development in assisted areas have received assistance from the European Regional Development Fund (ERDF).

In December 1992, the EU published a White Paper, *The Future Development of a Common Transport Policy: A Global Approach to the Construction of a Community Framework for Sustainable Mobility* (The European Commission 1992). This highlighted the imbalances and inefficiencies in the transport system that have led in all member states to high congestion levels and large contributions to environmental pollution. It ascribed these problems to the lack of awareness by transport users of the full costs that their activities impose and the rate of provision of new transport infrastructure which has lagged behind demand for transport.

In this analysis, the EU confronted the potential conflicts between the economic policies of the Community which encourage further liberalisation of transport and construction of major new links in the road and rail systems and new or expanded airports and port facilities, all generating further traffic particularly by road and air, with social and environmental policies which recognise the inequalities of access to existing transport systems and the harm that unmanaged growth may inflict.

The EU believes that economically efficient transport policies will meet social and economic mobility needs whilst also safeguarding against the harmful environmental effects of increased transport. In this, they may have in mind the policies being pursued in Alpine countries — Austria and Switzerland (which are not members of the EU) and, to a lesser extent, Italy — to couple regulations to reduce traffic in sensitive areas with major infrastructure improvements to promote combined transport, such as new railways designed to transport lorries through the mountains on trains, or the successful packages of car restraint and improved public transport pursued in several major cities in continental Europe. To be successful within a market-led economic union, such approaches require that the cost of transport, by whatever mode, reflects in full the costs it imposes on society.

National authorities, particularly regional and local governments, are seen by the Commission as playing the lead roles in developing and implementing policies and programmes for sustainable mobility. The Commission identifies a role for itself in ensuring compatible development across its member states of regulations and technological development to achieve these ends. Particular functions that the Commission believes should be undertaken at Community level include:

- introducing the concept of a 'citizens' network' of transport services subject to quality charters;
- research into the development of new technologies;
- clarification of the scope for state aids for collective (public) transport.

From a local government perspective, the EU White Paper has much to commend it, although it can be argued that it is wrong to put emphasis on the desirability of increased mobility in itself rather than first considering the levels of accessibility to goods and services that are required to achieve economic and social objectives. Although the potential conflicts between market solutions and environmentally and economically sustainable transport provision are recognised, the EU perhaps overestimated the extent to which the market will produce acceptable solutions without intervention, even if new pricing mechanisms adequately reflect environmental and non-renewable resource costs.

Thus far, much European financial assistance for policy and management development has been channelled to research into advanced technologies which will also assist manufacturers in Europe to compete against non-European countries. Thus the DRIVE programmes, for example, involve 'leading edge' research into the application of information technology to areas such as route guidance, real-time information at the individual user level, computer control of networks and payment technologies. This valuable research will undoubtedly lead to significant new methods, but initially only a few of the largest and most prosperous cities and regions are likely to be able to use them as they will be expensive and prototype testing and development will be necessary before series production at lower cost can commence.

It is hoped that the next generation of European Research and Development grants will assist transfer of best practice between member states as many isolated examples of good traffic management or new public transport operating or promotional techniques can be identified but have never been widely disseminated. Such lower level research and exchange of experience is likely to be extremely cost-effective.

There are tensions between the UK Government and the EU about the extent to which the European Commission and Parliament should intervene in matters which are essentially local, and the principle of subsidiarity is likely to be the focus for continuing debate. However, as the effects of transport decisions do have global implications, it is obviously right that the EU as a pan-national grouping should aim for consistency of approach by all member states. Clearly, there are many further issues that could be raised in the European context but only a brief treatment can be given in a survey such as this.

Conclusions

Transport does not have a particularly good environmental record. Without a considerable shift in both national and local policies and in public opinion, car traffic will continue to grow and congestion and environmental pollution will continue to get worse. Attention has concentrated on the evaluation and alleviation of adverse impacts from major projects such as new roads and rail links at the expense of consideration of more local problems arising from the changing patterns of urban and rural development and activities and the resulting traffic growth.

At both national and European levels, there is a tendency for an almost doctrinaire adherence to the principles of the totally free market to cloud the need for action to control unwarranted traffic growth and increases in pollution. One person's freedoms are often another person's constraints or even penalties. Indeed, often the regulation to create or protect the free market exceeds that required to restrict its adverse effects. An example is to be found in the widespread agreement between many bus operators and local authority co-ordinators that the bureaucracy involved with bus services since October 1986 is greater than that under the regulated, but liberalised system, that operated between 1980 and 1986.

With a 22 per cent fall in passenger journeys by buses in Great Britain outside London between financial years 1985/86 and 1991/92, despite a considerable increase in bus mileage operated, the validity of such a policy in terms of sustainability must, in any event be open to question. With the detailed implementation of rail privatisation still to be settled, and deregulation of buses in London at least deferred, the UK Government has the opportunity to rethink at least some of its policies in a more pragmatic way.

Despite the temptation to be critical, there are many examples of successful action to reduce traffic impacts and develop transport systems that support moves towards sustainable development. The key theme is partnership, public authorities with private transport operators, national with local government, all three with each other, as advocated for the bus industry in *Bus Routes to Success* (The Chartered Institute of Transport 1993), in order to provide systems in which members of the public can make informed choices of the most appropriate means of transport for their journeys. To such initiatives must be coupled action at the European level, and, perhaps most important of all, public awareness and education programmes to develop understanding of the consequences of transport decisions for the environment and a sustainable future.

10 Ecological planning

David Goode

This chapter is concerned with the role of ecology in the work of local authorities, particularly within the fields of nature conservation and environmental greening. For many local authorities this is an area of work which has developed rapidly in recent years and has become a central component of environmental policy. By its very nature such work crosses departmental boundaries, involving planning, leisure services, land management and education. It is characterised by many new innovations at the local level and often by considerable commitment from local government politicians. Local authorities have, in fact, been in the forefront in developing new approaches and new practices which are radically different from the well established science-based rationale for nature conservation, developed in the UK over the past forty years. This is particularly true in the case of urban local authorities where many new ideas and approaches have germinated.

In view of the fundamental changes in philosophy and practice, this chapter commences with a brief historical view of the main elements involved and goes on to illustrate how nature conservation strategies and policies have been developed and implemented at the local level. This is followed by consideration of broader aspects of environmental greening, together with community involvement and partnerships. Reference is made throughout to examples of good practice in the UK. The chapter concludes with an appraisal of how ecological approaches can be further developed to meet the needs of local authorities in developing effective policies for sustainability.

Historical perspective

Looking back over the past twenty years it is evident that a number of important changes have influenced the role of ecology within local authorities. Such changes include increased professional input from ecologists, the broadening of the philosophical basis of nature conservation, especially within towns and cities, the development of new constituencies through partnerships and involvement of local communities, and also the development of new techniques for habitat creation and ecological rehabilitation.

During the early 1970s the professional input of ecologists to local government was, with some notable exceptions, extremely limited. Not only were relatively few ecologists employed directly by local authorities, but those who were tended to be in junior positions with insufficient influence on policy making. Furthermore it was apparent from a number of studies that ecological information was not readily used by the planning profession, largely because of the way such information was presented (Holdgate and Woodman 1975). A study undertaken by the Institute for Operational Research (Friend and Hickling 1975) identified a significant 'communication gap' between the two professions. The need was recognised for intermediaries who would interpret ecological science in a way which could be understood and used by professionals involved in planning and land management. Equally important, of course, was the need for ecological advice to be fully understood by political decision makers at all levels.

Since then considerable progress has been made, not only in the number of ecologists now employed by local authorities, but also in the effectiveness of the dialogue between all the professions concerned. A significant increase in the number of ecologists employed by local authorities has occurred over the past twenty years. Cheshire County Council was apparently the first to appoint an ecologist in the early 1970s. By 1974 about a dozen such posts existed throughout the UK and it was then that the Working Panel of Local Authority Ecologists was formed. By 1978 it had a membership of 80 people working in ecologically orientated posts in districts, counties, regions, New Towns and National Parks (Sheldon 1978). Some counties were already developing ecological units to provide detailed ecological information and advice as in Merseyside and South Yorkshire (Handley 1984). Local environmental records centres were also established within local government as in West Yorkshire. By 1986 it was estimated from a questionnaire survey that some 280 officers in 440 local authorities had particular responsibility for nature conservation (Tyldesley 1986).

In some areas the number of ecologists employed by local authorities increased dramatically during the 1980s. To give just one example, when the Greater London Council decided to develop an ecological dimension within its planning and land management functions in 1982, hardly any of the 33 London boroughs employed an ecologist and at that time the Greater London Development Plan (GLC 1976) made no mention of either ecology or nature conservation. A survey in 1992 identified at least 45 posts occupied by trained ecologists and a further 20 officers trained in planning or landscape design who have specific responsibility within local authorities for work on nature conservation in the Greater London area. The analysis of the role and performance of local authorities in nature conservation (Tyldesley 1986) suggested that employment of professional staff to work on nature conservation is probably the most important resource allocation local authorities can make in this field. The need for such staff is now generally recognised, though it is frequently the case that such officers are not sufficiently senior to effectively influence policy making. A clear lesson from the past ten years is that for good practice to be implemented it is essential that qualified ecologists are appointed at a sufficiently senior level.

A second major change over this period has been a broadening of the philosophy of nature conservation and the development of entirely new initiatives by local authorities. Perhaps the most significant change in this respect was the development of non-statutory designations for protection of sites of value for nature conservation. Twenty years ago, with the advent of County Structure Plans, it became customary for county authorities to incorporate Sites of Special Scientific Interest within strategic plans and that was frequently the full extent of input on nature conservation. The development of new non-statutory designations by local authorities, such as 'Sites of Nature Conservation Value', at County or District level has involved a fundamental change of philosophy and practice. Local authorities have taken it upon themselves to develop a broader approach to nature conservation which differs in many respects from the top-down national system of SSSIs. These differences are reflected in greater emphasis on the value of natural areas for people to enjoy, the community-based bottom-up approach involving numerous local partnerships and the recognition that programmes for nature conservation have a rightful place in local democratic processes.

Many local authorities have acted as facilitators in developing such new programmes and partnerships, but there have been a number of quite different strands in the development of this new philosophy.

The emergence of urban nature conservation has been one of the most powerful forces for change over the past ten years (Goode 1989b). Urban nature conservation differs in a number of ways from traditional approaches. While the importance of rare or endangered species or habitats is recognised, considerable weight is also given to the value of ordinary wildlife. Completely new criteria for conservation have been established and accepted as part of the planning system, criteria which include social factors and an acceptance that quite unassuming habitats can be of great importance to local residents. One is no longer dealing with a system based entirely on scientific criteria for assessing 'intrinsic value'. In developing programmes for nature conservation in urban areas, local authorities recognise that appreciation and enjoyment of nature is one of the crucial factors contributing to the overall quality of life for urban residents. It is also generally recognised that urban nature areas offer considerable scope for environmental education (Goode 1989a).

Another difference is that many of the habitats in urban areas have developed relatively recently on derelict or disused land. They are very different in kind from long-established semi-natural habitats such as ancient woodland or heathlands but their value in the urban context is now firmly established.

Urban nature conservation goes even further in the sense that it addresses the opportunities for habitat creation, habitat enhancement, and even the incorporation of entirely new habitats within the built environment. A conference on Green Cities held at Liverpool in 1984 was an important milestone in promoting many of the ideas which are now becoming widely adopted. Ecological approaches to the greening of towns and cities are now much more widely accepted and the techniques are becoming available even in the built environment (Johnston and Newton 1993).

Over the same period there have been rapid developments in the field of habitat creation in both urban and rural areas. No longer are we dealing just with protection of existing important habitats, though these should always take priority, but the opportunities for creation of new habitats are now well-established. This is reflected in a whole range of initiatives from the landscapes of school grounds to agricultural set-aside.

How does all this affect local government? It provides significant opportunities for partnerships in environmental projects, in the spirit of Local Agenda 21. It provides new inspiration and a new and developing agenda which can enable local authorities to play a key role in environmental protection and enhancement.

Strategies and policies

The development of strategies for nature conservation by local authorities has been one of the most important advances in recent years. These provide an overall framework for policy development, explaining why nature conservation is important and how it can be implemented. Such a strategy contains a clear set of objectives, it lists the necessary policies to achieve those objectives, and identifies sites worthy of protection. Recent examples of such strategies have also dealt at considerable length with the necessary mechanisms for the implementation of policies, either through the planning process or by means of partnerships of various kinds.

A strategic approach of this kind has been adopted by many local authorities. In a survey carried out by the London Ecology Unit for English Nature in 1992 it was found that about half of all county authorities in England had either a subject plan or strategy for nature conservation identifying sites of importance (Waite *et al.* 1992). Some of the earliest examples were for metropolitan areas such as Greater Manchester (Greater Manchester Council 1986), Tyne and Wear (NCC 1988), Greater London (GLC 1984) and the West Midlands (West Midlands County Council 1984). These early examples were not only significant locally, but also provided important models for use elsewhere. The main aims of these strategies, summarised in Table 10.1, illustrate the newly developing values of urban nature conservation in that they all place considerable emphasis on the local value of nature to residents of urban areas. Common strands running through all of these are the need for protection of habitats of value, enhancement of existing areas of open land for wildlife and the creation of new habitats in areas deficient in wildlife. These strategies also identified the need for an ecological database for planning purposes.

The range of programmes developed in London over the period 1982–1986 is described in detail elsewhere (Goode 1989a), but it is worth mentioning as it illustrates very well the range of work which can be incorporated within such a strategy. The

Table 10.1: Examples of nature conservation strategies in urban areas listing the main aims in each case

Greater Manchester 1986	West Midlands 1984	Tyne and Wear 1988
Protect valuable sites from adverse developments	Ensure that all residents in the county have reasonable access to habitats of wildlife interest	Identify rare habits and rare species and promote their protection and proper management
Reduce to a minimum the impact of development on other sites	Protect and enhance a basic network of open-spaces and wildlife corridors	Identify opportunities for nature conservation and use these to create new wildlife sites, or enhance and improve existing areas
Ensure that local authorities and other public agencies give due weight to natural history interests when drawings up their own plans	Improve the suitability of the County's undeveloped land for wildlife	Create and protect a network of wildlife corridors which link sites and encourage the movement of plant and animal species throughout the county
Encourage the improvement of existing valuable areas and the development of new ones	Protect rare habitats	Make areas of wildlife interest accessible to all people within the county.
Provide an information and research service for the whole of Greater Manchester	Protect the habitats of nationally rare species	Generate interest in natural history and encourage community involvement in the creation, management and enjoyment of sites
Maintain a forum for consultation with and between natural history organizations	Promote the significance and encourage the consideration of the County's wildlife	
Ensure that the enjoyment of wildlife is available to all, by making suitable wildlife sites accessible to the public		

Source Goode 1989a

GLC decided in 1982 to develop an ecological perspective in all aspects of its work, especially through strategic planning and through the management of Council owned land. The Council also promoted a series of innovative projects including ecology parks at Camley Street near King's Cross and Tump 53 in Thamesmead, and established the London Ecology Centre as a public venue in Covent Garden. Details of these new initiatives were described in the first of a series of popular handbooks (GLC 1984). This first handbook set out the strategy for nature conservation in London which has been implemented in considerable detail over the past ten years. This strategy has been based on a multi-disciplinary approach in which input to strategic planning is only one element. Other aspects include provision of advice on habitat creation and encouraging community participation in wildlife projects. Another vital element is the development of sites for environmental education.

It is notable that many of the recent strategies for nature conservation such as Peterborough's Strategy for People and Wildlife (Peterborough City Council 1992) or the Nature Conservation Plan for Hackney (Hackney Borough Council 1993) place considerable emphasis on community liaison. They demonstrate very clearly the role now adopted by local authorities working in partnership with other bodies to encourage community participation. Another, earlier, example was St Helens which, having identified nearly 100 sites of wildlife interest in its policy for nature, stated that 'the Council will actively encourage voluntary groups and local communities to participate in the management of sites of existing and potential wildlife interest' (St Helens Borough Council 1986).

The advantages of such strategies are not only that they provide a clear input to the planning process, though undoubtedly this is one of the most important advantages, but also that they provide a framework facilitating local people to become involved in nature conservation projects. Such strategies also provide a firm commitment on the part of local authorities, often as part of their environmental charter.

Policies for the identification and protection of sites of value for nature conservation are an integral part of such a strategy. These policies provide the essential nature conservation element of county structure plans and unitary development plans. The importance of having clear and effective nature conservation policies in such plans cannot be overstated. In London the set of model policies developed in 1984 and published in the first ecology handbook (GLC 1984) was crucial to the successful development of a nature conservation programme. Subsequent inclusion of these, or similar, policies in many of London's local plans was instrumental in ensuring that nature conservation became an integral part of planning in the capital (Pape 1989). This set of policies has been refined over the years and recently the London Ecology Unit produced detailed policies for inclusion in the new unitary development plans (UDPs) for individual London boroughs. Virtually all the boroughs have now included chapters on nature conservation in their UDPs and many have adopted the policies proposed by the Ecology Unit. These model policies were published jointly with other bodies in a report entitled *Green Capital*, which provides guidance on all aspects of open space planning in London (Countryside Commission 1991). In recommending policies to the London Boroughs the London Ecology Unit has emphasised the need for strong protection policies for the most important sites. The following extract from *Green Capital* illustrates the approach adopted:

> Recommended Policy:
>
> Development will not be permitted which may destroy or adversely affect a Site of Special Scientific Interest (SSSI), a statutory Local Nature Reserve (LNR), or other site of nature conservation importance.
>
> Some boroughs may not wish to make such a strong commitment to their SSSIs, LNRs and other sites of nature conservation importance. If this is the case, it is strongly recommended that the minimum level of protection will be afforded by a presumption against development. Hence the policy would read: 'There will be a presumption against development which may destroy . . .'

Although this is the minimum level of protection recommended by the London Ecology Unit the DoE has been reluctant to accept even this policy wording in some recent local plans. The Unit emphasises that sites need to be identified in the plan and to be defined on the proposals map along with other categories of protection. In implementing strategies for nature conservation many local authorities have adopted non-statutory designations as a system of site protection. In its recent analysis of such systems the London Ecology Unit (Waite *et al.* 1992) found that all county authorities in England use such a system. Of 38 counties analysed 25 referred to such sites in the County Structure Plan and in 30 cases the sites were defined in District Plans or UDPs. An analysis of the role of local authorities in developing 'non-statutory' systems for protection of sites is provided by Collis and Tyldesley (1993).

Non-statutory systems of protection developed by local authorities are sometimes referred to as 'second tier sites', because such sites are of 'lesser quality' than the statutorily protected SSSIs. It is preferable to regard such a system as complementary to the national series of SSSIs, the non-statutory sites often performing a rather different function. The selection of a series of non-statutory sites requires first of all an adequate comprehensive survey of the overall resource by means of a 'phase one' habitat survey. It also requires the development of a philosophy for site assessment and evaluation appropriate to the local area. Finally, it requires a standardised system of gradings within the geographical area concerned, a county generally forming the basis for such a system (Dawson and Game 1987).

The London Ecology Unit has developed such a system for Greater London. Sites are categorised according to their significance at a London-wide, borough or local level. Sites of London-wide significance are referred to as metropolitan sites which are either the best example of each major habitat type in London, or places of special significance for wildlife and its enjoyment on a London-wide basis. Some sites are given this status because they are the best examples of natural habitats close to the centre of London and have special value to many people (even though their intrinsic biological interest may be less than that of sites nearer the periphery of London). A total of 125 sites of metropolitan importance have been identified and these have been endorsed by the London Ecology Committee of 23 London boroughs. Sites of borough importance are defined as the best examples of habitats within each borough. Such a category is particularly relevant as the boroughs now form the administrative units for all aspects of planning. In outer boroughs, many such sites are good examples of semi-natural vegetation, but in inner boroughs most are artificial habitats, i.e. places which have become unintentionally wild. Since 1988 sites of borough importance have been divided on the basis of quality into two grades.

Sites of local importance are those which are, or may be, of particular value to nearby residents or schools. These sites may already be used by schools for nature study or be run by management committees mainly composed of local people. Where a site of metropolitan or borough importance is also used in this way it acts as a local site, but further sites are given this designation in recognition of their role. Local sites are particularly important in areas otherwise deficient in nearby wildlife sites. Built-up areas more than one kilometre from an accessible metropolitan or borough site are defined as areas of deficiency. Further local sites are chosen as the best available to alleviate this deficiency. Where no such sites are available, it is recommended that opportunities should be taken to provide them by habitat enhancement or creation, by negotiating access and management agreements, or by direct acquisition.

An important feature of this whole approach is that different categories involve cleary defined 'areas of search' within which the assessment is made. It is also important to recognise that the categories perform rather different functions. So, although the same range of criteria is used throughout for site assessment (see Table 10.2), the balance of emphasis will vary according to the categories concerned. Thus criteria relating to intrinsic biological features (e.g. ancient character, richness of species, or rarity of species) tend to be of greater significance at the metropolitan level, whilst criteria related to social factors (e.g. value for educational use or local amenity) tend to be most important at borough or local level. In producing these strategies the London Ecology Unit undertakes considerable public consultation to ensure that the views of local people are taken into account, and to ensure that local knowledge is fully utilised.

Using these categories the London Ecology Unit has now published detailed nature conservation strategies for 16 London boroughs, recent examples being those for Islington (Waite and Archer 1992) and Sutton (Yarham, Barnes and Britton 1993). Each of these is published as a handbook which performs the dual function of providing necesssary input to planning for the UDP and provides a popular account of the natural history of each of the boroughs. An analysis in June 1993 of 24 boroughs for which such data were complete revealed a total of 125 sites of metropolitan importance, 241 sites of borough importance (grade 1), 287 sites of borough importance (grade 2), and 333 local sites, totalling 992 sites in all these categories. Extrapolated to the whole of Greater London this would provide a total of just over 1300 sites of nature conservation value.

The result is that a system has been widely established in the capital for protection of sites of nature conservation value right down to the local level. At least 25 of the 33 London boroughs have adopted the London Ecology Unit's nomenclature for sites of metropolitan importance and have used this term in their unitary development plans. Most of the boroughs for which individual strategies are published have adopted the proposals as the basis for the nature conservation section of their UDPs. It should be pointed out that although widely adopted there has

Table 10.2: Factors considered in the evaluation of sites for nature conservation importance

---

- Representation
  The best examples of each major habitat type are selected as Metropolitan sites. Typical urban habitats are considered, e.g. abandoned land colonised by nature.
- Habitat rarity
  Some sites are selected because a particularly rare habitat is represented.
- Species rarity
- Habitat richness   } All these factors may contribute to the quality of
- Species richness   } particular sites.
- Size
  Larger sites are usually more important than smaller sites (e.g. they allow for species with special area requirements), and they are likely to accommodate more habitat variation.
- Important populations of species
  Some sites are important because they hold a large proportion of the London population of a species (e.g. waterfowl populations or colonial birds such as herons and jackdaw).
- Ancient character
  Some sites have ecological characteristics derived from their long standing such as ancient woodland and traditionally managed meadows.
- Recreatability
  In addition to the biological reasons why certain habitats cannot be recreated (e.g. ancient woodland), many sites are not capable of being recreated because of practical reasons such as land availability and cost.
- Typical urban character
  e.g. canals, abandoned wharves, and railway sidings colonised by nature. The juxtaposition of the man made with the wild provide these areas with particular ecological and visual qualities. Such areas are often useful for the study of plant colonisation and succession.
- Cultural/historic character
  Sites such as historic gardens with semi-wild areas and old Victorian cemeteries which have reverted to the wild have a unique blend of cultural and natural history.
- Geographical position
  This is also an important consideration in selecting sites of local importance.
- Access
  An important consideration in urban areas.
- Use
  The importance of a site could include its established usage (e.g. for education), including interpretative facilities or nature trails.
- Potential
  Sites may have potential for habitat enhancement through management. They may have potential for increased educational and amenity use. Where such potential is readily capitalised it is considered important.
- Aesthetic appeal
  This is difficult to assess objectively, but often indication is given by the number of people using the site.

Source: London Ecology Unit 1989

been no statutory requirement for local authorities in London, or elsewhere, to develop such strategies. The Nature Conservancy Council encouraged adoption of such strategies in its guidance to local authorities on the preparation of UDPs (NCC 1987) and the DoE also recognised their value in its circular on nature conservation (DoE 1987) in which strategies were listed as one of the initiatives undertaken by local authorities. The series of Ecology Handbooks forming the nature conservation strategy for London was referred to by the Secretary of State in his Strategic Guidance to local authorities in London prior to production of unitary development plans (DoE 1989). There has, therefore, been some encouragement from national agencies and central Government, but it is, nevertheless, remarkable how much has been achieved by local authorities in implementing non-statutory systems of site designation for nature conservation in the absence of specific duties or legislation. The fact that such designations are now widely adopted in structure and local plans gives considerable force to this very significant element of nature conservation through the planning process.

A further category of designation of particular relevance to local authorities is the Local Nature Reserve (LNR). This is a statutory designation under Section 21 of the National Parks and Access to the Countryside Act 1949. In recent years the number of LNRs designated by local authorities in Britain has increased considerably. In 1986 there were 101 LNRs in England (Tyldesley 1986). By March 1993, 337 LNRs had been declared by local authorities in England and about 50 more have been proposed. The increase is even more dramatic in the case of London where only 2 LNRs existed until 1986 but at least 10 each year have been designated since 1990 and by June 1993 46 LNRs had been declared within Greater London. Seven more have been agreed by English Nature but are not yet declared by the local authorities concerned, and a further 45 sites are currently under consideration by London boroughs.

The advantage of designating a site as an LNR is that it has a specific designation within the planning system and therefore arguably has greater security against development. It is also possible for the local authority to introduce by-laws specifically for nature conservation on such sites. Other less obvious advantages are the increased commitment on the part of local authorities to the selection and management of such sites and the undoubted civic pride which accompanies such designations. For further details concerning LNRs see English Nature (1991).

Greening the city

Turning now from planning to design it is worth looking at what has happened in cities over the past ten years in developing innovative approaches to nature conservation. The greening of the cities has a very different philosophical basis from traditional approaches to nature conservation. Here we are involved in the art of the possible and much of the stimulus has come from landscape designers who could see the value of working with nature. Amongst the leaders in this field were Nan Fairbrother whose seminal work *New Lives, New Landscapes* (1970) still provides a stimulus for urban planning and design. Another pioneer was Ian McHarg whose *Design with Nature* (1969) is equally significant. More recently, Spirn (1984) described the ecological basis of cities and there has been considerable progress in this field over the past ten years. A joint UK and North American conference on Green Cities held in Liverpool in 1984 provided the stimulus for many of these initiatives. For the first time this brought together a range of disciplines including planners, landscape designers, ecologists and park managers concerned with city greenspace. A similar conference in Toronto in 1986 also provided vital impetus in this field (Gordon 1990).

Like the word 'sustainability', the phrase 'greening the city' means many different things to different people. At a fundamental level it may mean reversing the trends by which urban dwellers have become divorced progressively from nature. It can involve everything from window boxes and roof gardens to extensive tracts of community forest. Many local authorities in Britain have been involved in such initiatives. A national campaign for green cities stemming directly from the Liverpool conference, produced action packs for local authorities with examples of good practice in urban greening. One of the best of these was produced jointly with Manchester City Council (Think Green 1986). Other initiatives have included the development of green chains and city wildlife walks. Some of the most notable successes have been in the establishment of urban nature areas for local communities and especially for use by schools. The London Ecology Unit reviewed a range of such initiatives and published a guide to the creation and management of *Nature Areas for City People* (Johnston 1990). The keys to success described in this document were the result of direct experience in the establishment of Camley Street Natural Park at King's Cross, together with other case studies of various kinds in London.

Greening of towns and cities includes a wide range of initiatives which individually and in combination have a significant part to play in achieving sustainability. The development of new habitats on buildings may not at first seem particularly relevant. However, it has been demonstrated that green roofs and vegetation on walls, can have considerable influence on the energy budget of buildings. Green roofs may also reduce run-off rates of water from the built environment, which can be particularly beneficial during storm conditions. These advantages are in addition to the straightforward value of bringing nature into the urban fabric. Considerable progress in this field has been made in Germany and Holland in recent years and the London Ecology Unit has recently published a technical guide on how to establish such vegetation in the built environment (Johnston and Newton 1993).

At the other end of the scale are the new community forests which have been promoted by the Countryside Commission in recent years. Such forests have been proposed in about fifteen locations, generally on the fringe of urban areas. They include East London, Swansea, South Staffordshire, South Tyne and the central belt of Scotland. Other new woodlands include the Black Country Forestry Project and the new National Forest in the Midlands. All of these offer considerable opportunities for nature conservation through the design of new landscapes. It is vital that a strategic approach to the design and planning of these forests is developed from the outset. This is compatable with the Forestry Authority's newly-developing system of Indicative Forestry Strategies which is based on a broad assessment of landscapes (Price 1993). In this way an ecological dimension is brought into the planning of such forests from the start. In so doing it is possible to identify areas of existing wildlife value which should not be forested and secondly to use ecological guidelines in the detailed design of the new woodlands. An example of this approach is provided in *Nature Conservation in Community Forests* (Marsh 1993) which used the East London Community Forest as a case study.

Many aspects of the basic philosophy of greening as illustrated by Nicholson-Lord (1987), Goode (1990) and Spirn (1984) are entirely compatable with principles of ecological sustainability, towards which many local authorities are now striving. For successful implementation of sustainability it is often necessary, however, to separate individual components so that clear objectives can be identified. In her inspirational treatment of city ecology Spirn provides both analysis and recipe for action. We are now seeing many of her ideals being converted into reality.

Partnerships and the role of the community

Establishment of new partnerships across a wide spectrum of society has been crucially important in the development of nature conservation in recent years. Such partnerships are of many kinds at many different levels. Some are institutional, providing new frameworks for more effective action between the agencies responsible for nature conservation. Others enable local people to become directly involved so that nature conservation has become part of the daily lives of many ordinary people.

At the institutional level successful partnerships have long been established in the rural environment. Farming and Wildlife Advisory Groups have encouraged better understanding of nature conservation within the farming community through the work of specialist advisory officers. In particular they have made examples of good practice more widely known and have encouraged awards for innovative new projects. Other well established partnerships are the Groundwork Trusts, the first of which was established at St Helens in 1981. In 1993 there were 35 Groundwork Trusts in towns and cities throughout the UK. They are remarkably successful in bringing about improvements in environmentally derelict areas, especially in the urban fringe, through stimulating and setting up partnerships between diverse sectors of the community. The work of these Trusts has included many innovative nature conservation projects, especially through the creation of new habitats as part of environmental improvement schemes.

Yet another example of local partnerships is the establishment of Pocket Parks. A scheme for making small areas of land accessible to people living in rural areas was first developed by Northamptonshire County Coucil. It involved a partnership between the County Council and local communities to identify appropriate areas and to negotiate access agreements. Many Pocket Parks have an important nature conservation function, providing an opportunity for people to have immediate contact with nature. The need for such areas is just as great in the agricultural landscapes of eastern England as it is for town dwellers.

Local communities have become increasingly involved in environmental projects over recent years. Examples include the production of parish maps identifying all significant features of the local scene from ancient trees to old horse troughs. Involvement of residents in such schemes has lead to greater commitment in defending vital elements of the parish landscape. In towns and cities residents have taken responsibly for the design and development of community wildlife gardens. The success of such schemes has depended entirely on the commitment of local people working with facilitators, frequently through a partnership with the council.

Community action has been one of the key factors in the rapid development of urban conservation and this has depended to a large extent on the establishment of partnerships with local authorities. In many cases local authorities have given the lead by developing nature conservation strategies or by publishing environmental charters. But the most effective progress has been made where local authorities have established some form of environmental forum, involving local organisations and residents. In London the formation of borough ecology or nature conservation committees has been instrumental in ensuring that ecological issues are given proper recognition on the political agenda. Many London boroughs now have such a committee or forum, which have a vital role in developing green plans or environmental charters and in considering local environmental issues. These committees generally include elected councillors, officers from planning and parks department, and representatives from a wide range of voluntary groups and local residents. Establishment of an effective dialogue by means of these committees has been a crucial factor in promoting nature conservation in London (Goode 1989b).

The most productive environmental committees are those which are constituted as sub-committees of the council and chaired by either the chair of planning, leisure or environmental services. In this way the work of an environmental forum is automatically reported through the council's main committees and the forum can more easily influence decisions which are crucial to nature conservation. Some of the better forums address all aspects of environmental concern with sub-committees to deal with specific topics such as recycling, energy, traffic, etc. Some have adopted less formal arrangements whereby local amenity groups meet to discuss environmental issues with council officers in attendance, but on the whole such arrangements are less effective than having formal links with coucil committees.

The establishment of formal arrangements of this kind has allowed local authorities to make considerable progress in this field. By promoting a dialogue with local amenity societies and local residents, such committees ensure that local expertise is more readily available to the council. But it goes much further than this. An environmental forum provides a vital institutional framework which facilitates effective grassroots action at the local level. The framework is a catalyst for a vast array of local initiatives, many of which would not occur in its absence. The whole process is very different from the long established 'top-down' approach of national agencies dealing with nature conservation in the wider countryside. One of the obvious benefits is that elected members attending such committees become more closely involved in ecological and environmental issues.

With growing commitment and increasing knowledge on the subject they are in a more effective position to influence the council's decisions. Such committees also provide an opportunity for those councillors with specific interest or training in ecology to have direct input to policy making (Goode 1993).

The Nature Conservancy Council increasingly recognised the importance of establishing more effective partnerships for nature conservation. NCC's Partnership in Practice initiative grew out of a conference on this subject in 1987 and the NCC subsequently supported a range of projects including regional rural strategies, support for community action, environmental networks, and the establishment of industry and conservation associations. The NCC deliberately placed emphasis on support for local schemes as a means of facilitating a 'bottom-up' approach. Provision of grant aid through the community wildlife scheme has been an effective means of encouraging local action.

More recently one of NCC's successor authorities, English Nature, has placed even more emphasis on community involvement in its *Strategy for the 1990s*. It has recognised that enjoyment of nature is part of the justification for nature conservation alongside the scientific rationale and states that it will involve local communities in identifying natural areas and in setting conservation objectives and continue to support community involvement through grant aid (English Nature 1993).

Future directions

Following the adoption of Agenda 21 at the United Nations Conference on Environment and Development (UNCED) 'The Earth Summit' held in Rio de Janeiro in 1992, local authorities are faced with daunting problems in applying principles of sustainable development at the local level. The development of 'green plans', audits and 'environmental charters' is part of this process and it is clear that ecology has a major role to play in developing sustainable solutions. Local authorities are encouraged to adopt a Local Agenda 21 for their community, in effect to define a strategy for sustainable development at the local level. Sustainable development has been defined as 'development which improves people's quality of life, within the carrying capacity of the earth's life support system'. There are links between Local Agenda 21 and the commitment to safeguarding biodiversity also stemming from the Earth Summit.

The development of strategies and programmes of local action for wildlife conservation is central to the implementation of Local Agenda 21, in the sense that wildlife conservation and maintenance of biodiversity are crucial aspects of both quality of life and long term biological sustainability. Substantial progress has already been made in the UK regarding the development of strategies and programmes as described in this chapter. However, if we are to make progress in achieving local sustainability, it is essential that success is measured against clear objectives. We need to be clear as to what constitutes good practice and to have a means of measuring success in achieving these objectives.

It is necessary for all the professions involved in planning and land management to consider the implications of sustainability to ensure that political decision making at all levels takes full account of these issues. There are already indications that the principles of sustainability are now being considered at national and regional level in relation to strategic planning. The Draft Regional Planning Guidance for the South East (DoE 1993a) and the Draft Advice on Strategic Planning for London (LPAC 1993) both contain significant shifts in policy in an attempt to take account of sustainable development. However, there is still a considerable gulf between the proposals contained in official documents such as these and the exploration of sustainable alternatives by non-government organisations, good examples of which are Friends of the Earth and the Town and Country Planning Association.

Greater integration between the professions is essential if sustainability is to be achieved in all aspects of planning and land use, in both urban and rural areas. This will require understanding and application of environmental economics, together with co-operation between professions such as ecology, planning, landscape design, forestry and agriculture in the implementation of new approaches. In the built environment more emphasis will need to be placed on community architecture and sustainable principles in building design. Ecology has much to offer across all these fields, but it is essential that common ground between the professions is explored and new approaches developed in a co-operative manner, applying fundamental principles of sustainability. A good example of such progress is in *Building Green* (Johnston and Newton 1993) which examines ways of establishing ecological methods of design in the built environment. Extension of now well-established approaches to 'community nature conservation' in both urban and rural areas will be an important feature of future work.

For substantial progess to be made in the field of ecological planning it will be necessary to make rapid progress in implementation of GIS systems containing selective ecological information specifically for planning purposes. Such an ecological database for planning purposes is long overdue. It is particularly important that such a facility is available for nature conservation purposes in order to assess the effectiveness of current policies in relation to both the Biodiversity Treaty and Local Agenda 21.

If real progress is to be made in sustainability, it will be necessary for partnerships to be established capable of achieving rather different objectives than hitherto. Such partnerships will of necessity include several sectors of society and it is essential that programmes of action are related closely to the needs of local communities. So, not only must there be closer working partnerships between the professions to ensure that the necessary expertise is available, but there is the need for partnerships which include the private sector, local communities and local authorities.

The environmental committees and forums of local authorities could be a crucial element in implementing Local Agenda 21. Existing environmental committees of the kind described earlier provide a model which could be applied to the current challenges facing local authorities in developing effective policies and programmes for local sustainability. Their interdepartmental composition and close links with both the local community and specialist environmental bodies gives such partnerships a unique role in this rapidly developing field. It would, of course, be necessary to ensure that the business community is fully involved and that the whole approach is developed in such a way that results are achieved on the ground.

From recent experience it is clear that there are limits to the extent to which local action can provide all the answers. Those local authorities which have been in the forefront in this field are now experiencing serious barriers to progress as they reach the limits of their areas of influence. Whilst such authorities have developed well-established environmental practices in nature conservation and other topics such as recycling, they are finding considerable constraints because of national policies on other environmental issues such as energy and transport. In the same way that local authorities can act as facilitators for grass roots action at the local level, so it will be essential for national government to provide an effective framework for sustainability at the national level if Local Agenda 21 is to really mean sustainable development in the next century.

11 Energy and local authorities

Paul Fleming

Most scientists now agree that the greenhouse effect threatens our global climate to an unprecedented extent. The effects of climate change may differ from region to region and the exact impact on different parts of the world is unpredictable, but no part will be invulnerable to its impact. This could range from severe flooding in coastal areas to millions of refugees fleeing ecological disasters. The impact of this will stretch local (and national) authorities to their limits.

Local authorities can do something to alleviate the effect of climate change. Many local authorities in North America and Europe are taking action to reduce emissions of greenhouse gases. They have greater jurisdiction and powers than UK local authorities, and can profoundly influence the production, distribution and consumption of energy within their areas. Local authorities in the United Kingdom should be assuming a wider role and having a greater influence over all energy related decisions taken within their area. They should be working closely with the electricity and gas utilities to deliver substantial energy efficiency improvements in the industrial, commercial and domestic sectors as well as working on their own buildings.

Local authorities have a strategic role to play in reducing carbon dioxide emissions. The Government will be unable to achieve its own CO_2 reduction target without the assistance of local authorities. Government should be working in partnership with local authorities in order to achieve their targets. By using energy more efficiently and maximising the use of renewable energy resources such as wind, solar, wave, hydro, geothermal and biomass, the contribution that energy consumption makes to global warming can be reduced. Technologies exist that could reduce local authority energy consumption by between 33 per cent and 50 per cent by the year 2025. Local authorities can meet this challenge but need the appropriate resources and management structures to implement the technologies.

Environmental concern

The burning of fossil fuels releases carbon dioxide and other pollutants into the atmosphere. These greenhouse gas emissions are the largest single contributor to the growing environmental crisis of climate change, or global warming. The main greenhouse gases are water vapour, carbon dioxide, methane, nitrous oxide and chloro-fluoro carbons (CFCs). Apart from CFCs these gases occur naturally in the environment. Their presence in the atmosphere has the effect of trapping heat leading to a global rise in temperature. Carbon dioxide is by far the most significant human produced greenhouse gas. Its contribution to global warming is as much as all the other human produced greenhouse gases combined. 'Greenhouse gases' are responsible for controlling the mean global temperature at 15°C. Without this layer of gases reducing the amount of heat radiating from the earth's surface into space, this would be − 18°C.

It was during the 1970s that scientific concern about the greenhouse effect and global warming began to grow worldwide. Subsequent international and national conferences have led to a broad consensus among scientists that human activities are the main cause of the emission of greenhouse gases and their increasing concentration within the atmosphere. Unless we take action to reduce CO_2 emissions, their concentration will grow to twice the pre-industrial level by the year 2050.

The concentration of carbon dioxide in the atmosphere has been rising since the nineteenth century, especially since the Industrial Revolution and has been accelerated by increased deforestation. It is now rising at an increasing rate. Mathematical models suggest that this increase, combined with greater emissions of other greenhouse gases, will result in a higher mean global temperature, which will in turn significantly affect the environment, possibly within a few decades. This is likely to produce rising sea levels, more erratic and variable weather patterns and the flooding of agricultural land in developing countries. It may therefore have disastrous global economic, political and social repercussions. Livelihoods of large sections of the world's population may be threatened.

Despite not knowing the exact causes and effect of climate change, enough scientific detail exists to demand immediate political action. The rise in mean global temperatures of 33°C (from − 18°C to 15°C) has been caused by natural greenhouse gases of which water vapour is the most significant. The other naturally occurring gases include carbon dioxide, methane and nitrous oxide. It is the human production of greenhouse gases and the emission of CFCs (that do not occur naturally) that should be reduced in order to help prevent climate change.

The impact of the greenhouse effect will probably vary globally from region to region and the following may occur:

- a tendency towards greater climatic extremes;
- warmer air masses over the continents than over the coastal regions;
- the northern hemisphere will experience greater warming of its lower air masses than the southern hemisphere, because of its larger land masses;
- long, hot dry periods during the summer;
- all inland communities will be affected, resulting in threats to forests, vegetation and water resources; water will become more scarce and the threat of massive forest fires more likely;
- greater monsoon rains, high tides and floods during the winter;
- in the short term, some regions may appear to benefit from the greenhouse effect due to longer growing seasons, this will be short lived.

The knowledge and understanding of the causes of the greenhouse effect have now reached such a high degree of certainty that lack of knowledge is no longer seen as a reason for not undertaking political measures.

In 1988 the Toronto Climate Conference set the goal of reducing CO_2 emissions worldwide by 20 per cent by the year 2005 and 50 per cent by the year 2050. In 1992 the United Nations Conference on Environment and Development in Rio de Janeiro did not stipulate reduction targets, instead the nations that signed the Climate Convention, committed themselves to stabilise CO_2 emissions at levels which will not effect the climate system. This is a more severe target than most people realise, and the UK Government have interpreted this as reducing emmisions by 10 million tonnes by the year 2000, that is, aiming to stabilise CO_2 emissions at the 1990 level. The international community now need to make every effort to reach the UNCED goals.

Worldwide, the developing nations are likely to continue to increase emissions of CO_2. Thus it is for the wealthy nations, who are responsible for the majority of CO_2 emissions, to substantially reduce their energy consumption. It is not just national governments that need to take action. Local authorities have a decisive role to play in helping to solve environmental problems, as they and their communities are the ones affected by air, water or waste pollution. Local authorities have been taking the initiative to solve such environmental problems for many years, long before national governments or international bodies.

The impact of global warming on the environment, is not merely a function of a temperature rise. It is the rate of this rise that is critical. The earth's ecosystems can only have a chance to adapt to the change if the speed of the temperature rise can be reduced. Local authorities should take immediate action now to reduce CO_2 emissions, improve the quality of life for the people living and working in the authority's area and at the same time, realise financial benefits.

At UNCED, representatives of some 178 governments discussed environmental issues. This was the largest ever conference held on reducing environmental threats. The outcome was documents on the following:

- Rio Declaration
- Agenda 21
- Convention on Biological Diversity
- Principles for a Global Consensus on the Management, Conservation and Sustainable Development for all Types of Forests
- Framework Convention on Climate Change

All the documents directly addressed the problems of climate change, but it was the Climate Convention that focused on joint action to try and alleviate these problems.

It established an international legal basis for the protection of the global climate and was the outcome of over five years of intensive research undertaken by thousands of scientists, environmentalists and experts. The convention was negotiated within 15 months under the auspices of the United Nations.

The signatories to the convention agreed upon:

- stabilising the concentration of greenhouse gases at a level that would prevent dangerous human interference with the climate system;
- that this level must be reached in sufficient time to allow ecosystems to adapt to changes, the threat to food production to be eliminated and economic development to continue in a sustainable way;
- the commitment to take measures to limit human produced emissions of greenhouse gases and enhance greenhouse sinks and reservoirs (oceans and forests).

The Convention on Climate Change does not specifically address the role of local authorities but they have considerable potential for action in terms of reducing energy consumption in their area. Local authorities should consider the well-being of their citizens and proceed to set targets instead of waiting for governments to formulate their national climate protection programmes. Governments in turn should work with local authorities to help them accomplish their goals which should encourage local initiatives.

The European Community also signed the Framework Convention on Climate Change at the UNCED. However, without a substantial change in policy, they are going to find it very difficult to meet the commitment to reduce CO_2 emissions to a level acceptable to global ecosystems, because existing policies are actually increasing energy consumption. Environmental policy has failed to be integrated into the entire decision making process of the Commission. The European Single Market encourages greater transportation of goods over longer distances and EU estimates of economic growth and traffic volume could wipe out any carbon dioxide emission savings due to improved energy efficiency.

The free trade of electricity and gas could mean the end of municipal energy supplies in the member states which have them. Energy can be used most efficiently at this municipal level rather than that of the large power generating plant. That is, cities should have combined heat and power (CHP) systems to provide hot water for domestic and industrial processes and electricity for consumers. The most wasteful use of energy is in electricity generating power stations, where two thirds of the energy content of the fuel input into the power station is thrown away as waste heat. EU policies should be encouraging and supporting city-wide CHP, rather than supporting the free trade of electricity and gas. The price of energy within the EU remains low and this gives very little incentive to people to improve their energy efficiency.

Energy efficiency in the UK

Energy efficiency has traditionally had a relatively low profile in the United Kingdom. Most larger local authorities first appointed fuel efficiency officers, or energy managers, in the 1970s as a response to ever increasing fuel bills following the 1973 Yom Kippur War and the threat of diminishing fuel reserves. Their primary aim was to reduce energy costs and this was easily achieved by switching off heating at unwanted times, changing energy tariffs and increasing staff awareness of energy efficiency.

In 1985, the publication of the Audit Commission report *Saving Energy in Local Government Buildings* provided a greater impetus for the local authority energy manager. It recommended that local authorities should employ one member of staff to deal with energy for each million pounds of energy spent and invest the equivalent of 10 per cent of their energy spend in improved energy efficiency measures. It also put energy management higher up the political agenda. The report provided the independent justification for energy managers to successfully argue for more staff and larger investment budgets. However, subsequently, the cost of energy in real terms fell and the influence of the energy manager declined in many authorities.

Following the 1987 election, the Government appeared to lose interest in energy efficiency. They placed greater emphasis on 'market mechanisms' to promote it. Several promotional and grant schemes were ended or 'targeted more tightly' and funding for Energy Managers' Groups and the Energy Efficiency Office budgets were cut. The urgency to reduce energy consumption seemed to disappear despite many successful and cost effective energy efficiency investments in buildings. The Government believed that its 'Monergy' campaigns had been successful, that the benefit of investment in energy efficiency was self evident and that funding was therefore no longer needed. However, a Department of Environment survey in 1991, *Attitudes to Energy Conservation in the Home* showed that people remain ill informed of the need for, and benefits of, increased energy efficiency.

This situation improved between 1989 and 1990 with the increasing awareness of environmental issues and in particular, the threat of climate change. Friends of the Earth produced their

Environmental Charter for Local Government which gave high prominence to energy. This was followed by many local authorities producing their own charters and responding to Friends of the Earth. Energy was now on the environmental agenda. The momentum was maintained by the publication of the White Paper *This Common Inheritance*, the two editions of the Local Authority Association's *Environmental Practice in Local Government* and the endorsement in November 1991 by the Local Authority Associations of a target to reduce energy consumption by 15 per cent over a five year period.

In 1992 the Government published *Our National Programme for CO₂ Emissions* and embarked upon a consultation programme with industrial, transport interests and the domestic and public sectors. A conference in May 1993 considered the response to this consultation and this will form the basis of the Government's future measures.

In the short term, energy efficiency is now recognised as the single most cost-effective way of reducing carbon dioxide emissions and the energy manager now has an integral role in the development and implementation of local authority environmental protection strategies. One of the major barriers to increased energy efficiency is the lack of legislation and consequently inadequate standards for thermal insulation, heating control and domestic appliances etc. Whilst the 1985 Audit Commission report greatly assisted the energy manager's role in local authorities, there are few examples of any other positive action until the revision of the Building Regulations in 1990. This resulted in improving the thermal insulation standards for new houses. However, these are still no tighter than those adopted in southern Sweden in the 1930s — an area with temperatures very similar to northern Britain.

Local authorities have virtually no influence over the energy standards of new buildings, unless constructed on their own land, when standards in excess of building regulations can be imposed. The standards used by Milton Keynes Development Corporation in 1986 for developers of both domestic and non-domestic buildings is probably the best example. The Development Corporation insisted that all new dwellings meet a certain energy efficiency standard for domestic dwellings — now the National Home Energy Rating (NHER) — and a similarly improved standard for non domestic buildings — Chartered Institute of Building Services Engineers (CIBSE) Energy Code, less 40 per cent. Although the Development Corporation was not a local authority and also had considerably more powers, local authorities can impose similar standards on development of their own land and recommend the adoption of these standards for other developments. Similarly local authorities can adopt good energy efficiency standards for their own refurbished buildings, and recommend these standards for other refurbishment. Advice to potential developers, or to people altering or extending their houses could also be given via building control. This could be either one to one advice or by distributing leaflets to applicants seeking building control approval.

Local management of schools (LMS) has helped greatly to motivate schools to take energy efficiency far more seriously. This is because the lower the energy spend, the more money is available for other educational items. However, in many local authorities, LMS has resulted in the loss of an authority-wide central monitoring role. The energy group no longer centrally monitors schools' energy consumption nor the effectiveness of any energy efficiency investment. Yet the information is needed by all local education authorities in order to monitor progress towards the target of reducing energy consumption by 15 per cent over the next five years.

All local authorities have been affected by the privatisation of the electricity and gas utilities, and energy managers are spending a greater proportion of their time dealing with revised tariff structures. Whilst tariff changes may show cost savings, there are no comparable environmental savings, that is consumption is not reduced, only cost.

Inadequate legislation to promote energy efficiency is most apparent in the generation of electricity. This is the single most inefficient use of energy in the UK, and is, unfortunately, outside the influence of local authorities. For every 1 giga joule (GJ) of electricity generated 2 GJ are wasted. Using this waste heat to heat buildings can improve the overall efficiency of power stations from 30 per cent to up to 80 per cent. In Denmark all new electricity generation plant must be either CHP or via renewable energy resources. Legislation is needed in the UK to ensure that new power stations do not waste the heat. Such CHP plants provide a great environmental benefit. Small scale CHP units are now widely used in local authority swimming pools and other buildings with a relatively high summer heating consumption, but as yet Nottingham's city-wide CHP scheme is the only one in the UK. The economics of these large city schemes, in particular the cost of laying mains and the selling price of electricity, have so far prevented other city-wide CHP schemes being implemented. The Sheffield scheme operates successfully as a heat only scheme and is planning to introduce electricity generation. A scheme in the City of London is currently underway and the Southampton geothermal scheme is introducing CHP to its network.

It is the European Community that is leading the way in increasing energy efficiency through its proposed legislation. The energy efficiency regulatory programme (SAVE) proposed during 1991 covered measures such as efficiency standards for boilers, energy labelling for domestic appliances, energy certification of buildings, and energy audits of 5 per cent of government building stock per annum.

These are precisely the type of measures that many local authorities have been unsuccessfully pressing the UK Government to implement. Unfortunately, the original proposals of 1991 have been affected by the arguments over subsidiarity. The SAVE Framework Directive will set out where progress could be made, but leaves the precise details of how to implement them to member states.

Local authority strategies to reduce greenhouse gas emissions

An effective strategy to reduce the emission of greenhouse gases must include an analysis of the 'energy system' of a particular local authority as well as the factors that determine the energy services and their impact on energy use. The local authority should develop a 'climate protection plan' that outlines an effective strategy that focuses on reducing CO_2, the most important greenhouse gas. This local action plan should include the following:

1   identifying local energy demand and use pattern;
2   identifying appropriate measures that could be taken to reduce CO_2 emissions;
3   evaluating and prioritising these measures;
4   establishing a specific carbon dioxide reduction target;
5   developing policies and programmes to implement these measures.

An example of a plan, proposed by ICLEI is presented in Figure 11.1. The CO_2 emissions should include the emissions as a result of energy consumed by buildings, vehicles and industry. They must be those which are produced over the entire lifetime (that is, lower efficiency systems will produce far more CO_2 than high efficiency systems), for example, the very inefficient use of energy in conventional electricity generating power stations. The

Figure 11.1 A local energy plan/climate protection plan

Step 1 — develop a municipal energy profile

- Determine the emissions of CO_2 and other pollutants for the base line year. Undertake an inventory of energy use and CO_2 emissions associated with this energy use for this year. Calculate the amount of energy used in each sector (residential, commercial, industrial and transportation). This could be measured as energy per unit of floor area or energy per vehicle per kilometre travelled.
- Develop a scenario for the future. Choose a future target year and forecast energy use. Assume a business as usual scenario based upon accepted rates of growth.

Step 2 — identify measures to reduce CO_2 emissions

- Identify the technical measures (such as insulation, heating control, etc.) that reduce CO_2 emissions by reducing energy consumption, promoting cleaner fuels, and taking advantage of renewal energy. Identify measures, such as awareness raising, that reduce CO_2 emissions by changing people's attitudes.

Step 3 — evaluate and select measures

- Identify which measures need to be included within a local action plan.
- Consider the following criteria:
  - Does the local authority have power to implement the measures?
  - What proportion of CO_2 emissions does the measure effect?
  - How well defined are the cost and benefits of the measure?
  - Do institutional or market barriers make the measure difficult to implement?
  - Will the measure achieve many environmental or social benefits?
  - Does the measure lead to the development of trade partners?
  - Can the measure gain popular political support?

Figure 11.1—Cont.

Step 4 — establish a CO_2 reduction target

- A realistic forecast is essential to the setting of a specific CO_2 reduction target. The target could be expressed relative to the level of CO_2 released during the base line year. It implies a reduction from a level in the future forecast by the business as usual scenario.

Step 5 — develop a local action plan

- The plan should include the policy and programme options the local authority proposed to use to implement the CO_2 reduction measures that have been selected.

Figure 11.1 A local energy plan/climate protection plan
Source: International Council for Local Environmental Initiatives

heat that is thrown away from these power stations should be used to heat industrial and domestic properties.

In the UK local authorities have no influence over energy supply and distribution, since this is left to the privatised electricity and gas utilities. In many other European municipalities, local authorities have a strategic relationship with the fuel utilities. A dialogue between UK local authorities and the utilities is needed in order to achieve a successful CO_2 reduction strategy. Local authorities should be instigating this dialogue.

Domestic, commercial and industrial consumers of energy do not want to buy kilowatt hours (KWH) of electricity or gas, they want heat to keep warm in their buildings and they want light and power. Electricity and gas are a means of providing that service. However, the energy service can be provided more efficiently by reducing the amount of heat required to keep a building warm (via thermal insulation), or by providing more electricity efficient appliances or more energy efficient modes of transport rather than providing more kilowatt hours. Advice and information, coupled with grant aid, is required to enable people to make these choices.

Land use and transportation infrastructure issues are major concerns in reducing carbon dioxide emissions. Planning authorities should be taking strategic decisions to minimise the use of energy consumption by encouraging higher population densities that can take advantage of distributing energy and heat; also by encouraging people to travel by foot, bicycle or public transport rather than more energy inefficient forms of transport such as the private motor vehicle. The development of a new settlement is an ideal opportunity to optimise these features in order to minimise energy consumption.

State-of-the-art energy management

The state-of-the-art practice in energy management is a comprehensive approach across all disciplines. This can be divided into three main areas of practical action.

- Standards — ensuring that good energy standards are applied and met for all new and refurbished buildings.
- Monitoring — ensuring that buildings are performing as they should be. Detecting and reducing any excessive consumption, by monitoring utility bills and setting consumption targets.
- Maintenance — ensuring that buildings and building services are maintained at optimum efficiency.

A massive reduction in carbon dioxide emissions would be achieved by the adoption of a state-of-the-art approach to energy management in UK local authorities. UK research suggests that CO_2 reductions of 33 per cent are achievable, yet the Government is slow to help local authorities realise this reduction by not allowing them to invest sufficient money in energy efficiency improvements. However, the provision of additional supplementary credit approval for local authority administrative buildings for 1993/4 is a step in the right direction.

Many local authorities have been monitoring their energy consumption for over a decade. Central Government started this in 1991, with the setting of a target of a 15 per cent reduction in consumption for government buildings in the next five years. The Local Authority Associations have also accepted this target and, with the necessary resources, should be able to achieve it, although they will find it far more difficult than the Government since many local authorities undertook the easy measures ten years ago.

Although many local authorities have an enviable record in energy efficiency, others could and must achieve far greater success. Most authorities can still easily identify the occasional overheated building, the building where lights are left on when no-one is using it, the building where heating is left on at night or at weekends or the recently constructed building that does not have lighting control or low energy lamps installed as standard. Unfortunately this list can be almost endless.

This encouragement to others to use energy efficiently can take many forms. It could include establishing a demonstration building that clearly explains what energy and environmental improvements are possible in buildings and provides advice and information. Making sure the public see that the council 'practices what it preaches' is also critical. It should be a priority to install low energy lamps in public areas, and these areas should be kept at a comfortable temperature and not overheated. Low energy lamps should also be offered for sale to council tenants. Road shows, seminars, energy plays and pantomimes should be organised, guidebooks produced and advice centres created or modified to provide energy advice. Combined with energy efficiency campaigns these measures should raise public awareness about energy efficiency.

Improved energy efficiency also has considerable social benefits. Ensuring that housing is constructed and refurbished to a high standard of energy efficiency helps to alleviate fuel poverty and provide affordable warmth. This is of greater importance, now that the Government has imposed VAT on domestic energy supplies and standing charges.

In order to achieve the comprehensive local authority strategy to reduce carbon dioxide emissions, an integrated approach is required. This needs to include energy management, transportation planning, land use planning, and finance. An effective action plan also requires full co-operation of key officers and of members. Without full political support, the strategy will not succeed.

The major items in any action plan should ensure that:

- the construction of CHP stations to distribute heat to district heating schemes and sell electricity to electricity companies or other organisations is a priority;
- when agreeing briefs for new or refurbished buildings, energy efficiency standards should be set *higher* than current building regulations;
- a programme exists to bring existing buildings up to this standard wherever possible;
- higher thermal insulation and heating control standards are adopted and applied to council and private dwelling;

- the potential of renewable energy resources to power council buildings is regularly reviewed as new developments alter the economics of such systems;
- small scale combined heat and power units are installed where appropriate (e.g swimming pools and district heating schemes);
- energy efficiency is given a high political priority with positive member support;
- advice is provided to the public and local businesses.

If local authorities are trying to reduce CO_2 emissions within their area, they need to be setting a very positive example to both people and businesses. It is thus essential that the local authorities own offices, housing, buildings and transport fleets are as energy efficient as possible.

Investment in the infrastructure within the local authority also needs to be taken for environmental rather than economic reasons. Purchasing policies within a local authority need to ensure that only energy efficient goods and services are purchased. Architects and engineers who design schemes for local authorities should be designing the most energy efficient solutions to the problem.

Urban form has an indirect impact on energy use and CO_2 emissions. Any areas with high population and employment densities can take advantage of energy efficient distribution systems such as combined heat and power. They can also take advantage of energy efficient forms of transportation such as walking, cycling and public transport. Where urban densities allow people to live, shop and work in the same area cars tend to be left at home. Local authorities should be using long term land use transportation plans to influence the urban form and so minimise CO_2 emissions.

Energy supply

In the United Kingdom it is the regional electricity companies, British Gas, British Coal and oil companies that supply most of the energy requirements of their area. At present, the attitudes of these companies appear to be to sell more of their product rather than to conserve it. Local authorities need to influence these companies to encourage them to make money from selling energy efficiency improvement measures rather than selling energy. Investments in energy efficiency could yield more profit than simple investments in more energy supply. Energy suppliers should give the same priority to investments which reduce energy demand as they do to investments in new energy supply. Energy efficiency is almost always cost effective in the long term. It should thus offer an excellent rate of return for the utilities.

The regulators (OFGAS and OFFER) should amend utility regulation to make it more profitable to sell 'energy efficiency' rather than more units of energy. This would provide the greatest incentive for utilities to work with local authorities to deliver energy efficiency. Local authorities should also be arguing for higher energy taxes, because the present lower fuel costs discourage investment in energy efficiency. The revenues raised from such taxation should be used to both provide grants for energy efficiency improvements and for additional benefits for those living in the most energy efficient homes. Improved regulations are required that set good standards of energy efficiency for buildings and transport and also to persuade the energy supply industry to move towards an energy service industry.

To significantly reduce the CO_2 emissions from transport, local authorities need to be able to switch traffic (both goods and people) from private vehicles to systems of transportation that produce less CO_2. When planning and investing in new transportation systems, they should give priority to environment friendly means of transportation such as walking, cycling, buses, trams and railways. It is this that should be the basic transportation function within a local authority and should be available to everyone. The private car should thus become a supplementary vehicle which would be reserved for use only when none of the other modes of transport can do the job. The most important measures include:

- traffic calming, reducing the speed in non-main arterial road and declaring roads in residential areas as 'residential streets';
- imposing a larger proportion of the social cost on private vehicles by introducing economically cost covering parking and charging for entering city centres;
- establishing greater pedestrian areas in centres of cities;
- planning and establishing a cycle infrastructure with fast bike access between city centres and residential areas;
- offering attractive public transport for example, by expanding routes for bus, tram and railways, establishing points to switch modes between public transport, bicycle and

car, speeding up the bus and tram traffic and introducing attractive fares and conditions for public transport.

In the long term, local authorities must reduce dependence on fossil fuels not only by increasing efficiency but also by a massive switch to renewable energy. Whilst the economics are not yet advantageous, advances in technology may soon result in financially viable schemes. These could include photovoltaic roof and wall panels, small scale wind and hydro schemes to provide electricity, and the use of passive solar design in new and refurbished buildings. Local and central government could do much to encourage the rapid development of renewable energy technologies.

Government action

The Government, as a response to its signing the United Nations' Framework Conventional Climate Change, embarked upon a novel method of consultation in its document *Climate Change — Our National Programme for CO_2 Reduction*. Rather than simply requesting people to comment upon the document, it arranged a series of workshops over a two day period, inviting people from all sectors to discuss the issues of climate change and to identify measures that the Government, local government, industry and the individual should take to reduce CO_2 emissions.

The workshops concluded that a broad range of measures need to be implemented in order to reduce CO_2 emissions and that the voluntary action alone would not be effective. The Government must be a lead player if the CO_2 programme is to be effective, but it was felt Government had not yet shown its commitment to taking the issue as a serious priority. The targets should be seen as long term ones and such policy commitments should be clearly signalled to corporate decisions makers. No single solution will bring success. Success will depend upon an integrated programme of action across all disciplines including both 'sticks and carrots'.

The workshops agreed that the market alone would not deliver the CO_2 emissions assessed by the Government. Lack of finance was felt to be a major disincentive, and longer payback periods should be accepted. The relative cheapness of energy was highlighted as a major barrier, but simply raising taxes, without an energy efficient investment programme was felt to send the wrong signals. Unfortunately it is existing central government policy that is causing much of the problem. For example, policies on deregulating the systems within industry has resulted in less integrated transportation systems within cities, older less energy efficient buses on the roads and higher fares resulting in people preferring to use the private motor vehicle rather than public transport.

Policies on the privatisation of the electricity and gas industries have caused similar problems. The electricity and gas industries appear to concentrate on maximising profits from selling energy rather than conserving energy. In particular the electricity industry appears to be obsessed with generating electricity efficiently rather than using energy efficiently. The continued concentration of investments on roads rather than other means of transport causes further problems.

The Government have also announced the formation of the Energy Saving Trust, an independent body, under the chairmanship of Lord Moore, set up by the Government, British Gas, twelve regional electricity companies in England and Wales, Scottish Power and Scottish Hydro-Electric to propose, develop and manage new programmes to promote energy efficiency. It is intended that a levy on electricity and gas prices should be imposed and the funds resulting from this levy be invested in the various measures identified by the Energy Saving Trust. The Energy Saving Trust thus provides virtually the only opportunity for grants towards energy efficiency through domestic and small business customers. Its initial schemes include grants for condensing gas boilers, pilot local energy advice centres, combined heat and power in residential buildings and a grant for low-income households.

In other countries that operate similar schemes, local authorities are an integral part of the Trust. For example in Holland, it is the local authorities that are instrumental in identifying the measures that are eligible for grants under the scheme. In the UK, however, it is a different situation, there is no local authority representative on the Energy Saving Trust.

It is the local authority, in conjunction with all other sectors, that should be developing the Local Action Plan and implementing measures to reduce carbon dioxide emissions. The utilities and the Energy Saving Trust have a role to play in providing support for the successful implementation of the measures. Local authorities should be monitoring the success of the action plan and identifying the most cost effective measures undertaken to date. They should also be providing regular information to the public and to businesses as to the success of the climate change policies within their areas. The Energy Saving Trust will not achieve its

CO_2 reduction targets without the support and partnership of local authorities.

It is widely acknowledged that energy prices within the UK are relatively low. Thus the move to increase the price of energy should be welcomed in principle, since it should stimulate additional investment in energy efficiency measures. However, the Government's imposition of VAT on domestic gas and electricity without introducing any other measures is a mistake. Energy prices should be higher, but the revenue raised from increasing prices should be re-invested in energy efficiency measures. VAT on domestic energy consumption will hit those least able to afford it most since it is people on low incomes who tend to live in the most energy inefficient houses.

What the Government should have announced was VAT on energy plus a comprehensive grant system (administered through local authorities) to improve the energy efficiency of domestic dwellings. The measures would include, not only loft insulation, hot water tank insulations and draught proofing, but also heating control improvement and grants towards efficient heating appliances and other electrically consuming appliances. In this way, the effects of increased energy costs would not adversely affect people on low incomes. In addition, transitionary relief should be introduced for those homes unable to immediately carry out energy efficiency improvements.

With the trend towards centralisation, government support is a major factor in assisting local authorities to improve their energy efficiency. Other examples of government assistance over recent years are limited to the housing sector. The Department of the Environment has given a greater priority to energy efficiency within its Estate Action Programme and also introduced a Greenhouse Energy Efficiency Demonstration Programme to improve the energy efficiency of local authority housing and has issued guidance for the Housing Investment Programme. The Home Energy Efficiency Scheme(HEES) continues to offer grants towards loft insulation, hot water tank insulation and draught proofing for people in receipt of certain state benefits. The Energy Management Assistance Scheme (EMAS) providing grants to businesses commenced in 1992. This scheme will help with the cost of consultancy for instigating energy efficiency projects in small and medium sized businesses, who may not have their own in-house energy management facilities.

Improvement grants for the private sector include a discretionary element for energy efficiency measures but unfortunately energy is not part of the basic fitness standard. A publicity campaign

'Helping the Earth Begins at Home' was launched in 1991 and leaflets identify energy saving measures for householders in order of cost effectiveness. A greater local authority contribution is envisaged. Such partnership is essential to 'get the message across', but will fail unless grant aid is provided at the same time.

The Government established the Central and Local Government Environment Forum during 1991. This forum set up a number of working groups to look at various environmental issues. The Energy Working Group met during 1991 and recommended a series of actions, subsequently adopted by the forum which are outlined below.

Summary of recommendations of the Central and Local Government Environment Forum

- The Local Authority Associations should agree a target of 15 per cent over five years for reductions in energy use in local authorities. Individual authorities should agree their targets and maintain annual monitoring to assess their progress.
- The Local Authority Executive should back the objectives of the energy manager, and raise the profile of their work.
- The often inadequate training of energy managers should be pursued with the Local Government Management Board.
- Local authorities should consider increasing general staff awareness of energy efficiency by using publicity/promotional activities.
- Best practice advice on the structure and the financial arrangements of effective energy management units should be featured in any future editions of *Environmental Practice in Local Government*.
- Contract energy management should be seriously considered as an alternative arrangement.
- Local authorities should give higher priority to energy efficiency within their budgets and should consider setting up an energy fund which allows them to recycle their energy savings.
- The need for capital expenditure on energy efficiency measures should continue to be taken into account when central government departments assess and allocate capital resources.

- The Department of Energy should discuss with OFFER the unfavourable tariff offered for Local Authority Combined Heat and Power—generated electricity.
- OFGAS should be consulted about the pricing structure which discourages the efficient use of gas.
- The Department of Energy should also explore with OFFER and OFGAS the problem of data-tape billing.

Conclusions

There is now a scientific consensus that the threat of climate change is real and that we must take action to reduce its impact. Many governments have signed the Framework Convention on Climate Change and committed themselves to reduce carbon dioxide emissions to a level acceptable to the planet's ecosystems. Governments cannot achieve this target alone and need to work in partnership with local authorities.

Government has a vital role to play in setting the framework for local authorities, businesses and individuals to work within, in order to achieve substantial carbon dioxide emission reductions. Local authorities need to be working to this framework and developing plans for their area to reduce the emission of carbon dioxide through improved energy efficiency. Energy efficiency improvements need to be on the supply side (for example, CHP), on the demand side (energy efficient buildings and appliances), and on the transport side (energy efficient integrated public transport systems).

There are few technical barriers to increased energy efficiency in local authorities. A major barrier to implementation however is lack of appropriate management information. Energy managers should be setting the energy budgets for large local authority buildings and providing financial information to building managers, and to finance committees. Once awareness is raised about the financial as well as the environmental benefits, this will help decision makers to make the commitment of investing in energy efficiency.

The ability of authorities to invest in energy efficiency improvements is significantly affected by government restrictions on local authority spending. The Government should provide local authorities with additional finance to spend on energy efficiency improvements. For example, if a carbon/energy tax is introduced, authorities should be allocated a large proportion of the funds raised both to improve the energy efficiency of their own buildings and to give grants to the domestic and commercial sectors to enable them to improve the energy efficiency of their buildings. Energy efficiency improvements will not be gained without some financial inducement for building owners.

By maximising the use of renewable energy resources considerable CO_2 reductions can be achieved. In the long term, local authorities look to Government to reverse decades of lack of investment in renewable energy and develop less environmentally damaging energy supplies. In the short term, energy efficiency improvements remain the best solution.

The Government should set the framework for others to follow in order to achieve the carbon dioxide abatement target. This would need to include:

- regulation (of buildings, appliances, vehicles etc.);
- advice (campaigns, awareness raising, energy efficiency training etc.);
- financial incentives (energy taxes, vehicles fuel taxes, grants, subsides etc.);
- research and development (research into both energy efficiency technologies and into renewable energies).

This framework should include Government actions to:

- further revise building regulations to allow both improvements in the overall thermal properties of all buildings and temperature control of individual rooms and offices to restrict winter over heating and summer under cooling, lighting and water control;
- provide grants towards the cost of replacing old inefficient plant and equipment with new, energy efficient ones;
- provide grants towards the establishment of city-wide combined heat and power schemes to more than double the energy efficiency of power stations from 30 per cent to up to 80 per cent;
- establish energy labels for domestic appliances, industrial plant and equipment, houses etc.;
- incorporate renewable energy measures in standards for new and existing buildings;
- improve appliance efficiency standards;
- encourage more energy efficient modes of transport.

The role of local authorities is wider than their own buildings. At present, many local authorities are developing energy plans for their areas involving not only the public sector, but also the private sector and utilities. With this comprehensive overview, it is then possible to identify measures that can be implemented to achieve carbon dioxide reduction targets. The Government should be encouraging more local authorities to develop such plans, working closely with the utilities and the business sector. It is the utilities that should be playing the greatest role in reducing energy consumption. The regulators should ensure that the utilities have a greater incentive to promote energy efficiency and to carry out energy efficiency measures on domestic and industrial buildings, rather than simply selling more energy.

The local authority programme for reducing carbon dioxide emissions needs to be integrated into all the decision making of the local authority. That is, it needs to be an integral part of the planning process, economic development, and advice and education. The role of the local authority in assisting the Government and the United Nations to meet their climate change targets, cannot be over emphasised. Only with effective balanced partnership between central and local government and the business and domestic sectors, will it be possible to deliver the measures that will result in reducing the emissions of carbon dioxide to those which the global environment can cope with.

12 Local environmental policy for the 21st century

Julian Agyeman and Bob Evans

We hope that the chapters in this book have clearly demonstrated that local environmental policy is thriving in contemporary Britain, despite the difficult political and economic climate within which local government and other local organisations are currently having to operate. There can be little doubt that this is due to the energy, commitment and vitality of the local authorities, local authority associations, community organisations and pressure groups who have led the way and forced the pace for change, with little or no encouragement from central government.

However, although much is currently happening, much also needs to be done. In many parts of the country there is still only restricted local environmental action, and it is clear that many, if not most, people in Britain still perceive environmental problems in a limited and detached manner. This is of course unsurprising, since problems such as unemployment, poverty, racism or homelessness affect individuals and communities with an immediacy and force which tends to marginalise environmental questions.

Nevertheless, there is cause for a degree of optimism. The Rio and Maastricht agreements have established an international framework which will continue to place pressure upon signatory governments to move towards sustainability, and although it is necessary to have a cautious assessment of what Agenda 21 and 'Towards Sustainability' might bring, it is clear that they are important vehicles for organising and pressing for policy change. It is for environmentalists both inside and outside of local government to utilise these agreements to prod and push their legitimate claim for environmental action.

Given these circumstances, what of the future? We do not wish to crystal ball gaze here, but on the basis of the preceding chapters, we feel that it is appropriate to briefly emphasise a number of points which we feel will be central to the development of local environmental policy into the next century and which will undoubtedly be the focus of political action and controversy. In particular, we would like to comment upon the points which we raised at the end of Chapter 1 as the contributory themes which inform and contribute to the principle of sustainability.

Community environmental education

We put this first because of its centrality. It will be impossible to secure popular support for policies designed to secure sustainability without a massive programme of public education. This is not an optional, add-on extra. It is fundamental to the success of policy since, as we have already argued, sustainability must be viewed as an inherently undemocratic principle which requires that many people in countries such as Britain act against their perceived short term interests.

We see community environmental education as a life-long process which seeks to empower people such that they develop an empathy with the aim of sustainability. The task therefore is to enable people to develop the attitudes, confidence, knowledge and skills necessary to make informed choices about the local and global environment, their role within it and their life and workstyles, either as individuals or collectively, such that they minimise their impact upon it.

Part of this process is clearly related to the existing, formal educational system, from nursery to tertiary level, associated with a programme of public information and awareness conducted through the media and community educational programmes, similar to those undertaken by the health service such as the anti-smoking and Aids/HIV programmes. However, it is more than this. It is also a process which requires dialogue, patience and tolerance, and perhaps most importantly, time. There can be little doubt that the changes in public attitudes which all this requires are immense, and that there are many powerful and established interests who will seek to frustrate and undermine such a programme. Nevertheless, it is clear that without a commitment to CEE at national and local levels, there can be little expectation of significant long term achievements in local environmental policy.

Democratisation

We have already argued the centrality of this in Chapter 1, but we make no apology for emphasising that greater democratisation and involvement in policy making is fundamental to the acceptance and achievement of policy objectives in this field. Moreover, if democracy is integral to sustainability, it is equally clear that sustainability also implies some measure of sharing common futures and fates and hence some degree of perceived equity. This two-pronged and overtly political agenda will clearly cause some difficulties, particularly for those of an 'environmentalist' persuasion who see environmental problems as being amenable to managerialist solutions, not involving questions of power, control or financial interest.

Sustainability and the new environmental agenda imply more than simply providing an opportunity for citizen participation in decision making. As the Agenda 21 agreement makes very clear, both empowerment and capacity building are central to the environmental policy process. There has to be a programme of education and encouragement which will not only prepare people for informed participation in the decision making process, but also mechanisms which will enable and assist in building the capacity to actually deliver policy and programmes in partnership with other agencies.

As we have already seen, there is little evidence to suggest that the UK Government is at present prepared to offer more than tokenism with respect to these two notions. Nevertheless, despite the dismal prospects for the early implementation of any kind of empowerment or capacity building, we wish to emphasise the essential contribution that these objectives have for environmental policy, and the complementary purposes that exist between community environmental education and democratisation.

Balanced partnership

In emphasising the notion of balanced partnership, we are seeking to stress the importance of co-operation and collaboration at the local level between statutory agencies, including local government; the private sector and 'the community'. There may be other players, perhaps national pressure groups or the local authority associations, but it is likely that the main partnerships for local policy will have to be between locally based agencies and institutions. As we have already indicated in Chapter 1, we are using the term 'balanced partnerships' to emphasise the need to avoid links and associations which principally benefit existing established interests and stakeholders.

It is clear that 'partnership' is a central plank of some areas of current government policy, notably urban regeneration in the form of the City Challenge programme, and it is equally clear that the arrangements as currently structured tend to disadvantage the majority of ordinary residents in favour of a few larger organised groups, the private sector and local authorities. We have no illusions over the form and character of current partnership agreements. Instead, we are simply recognising the need to involve all key local organisations, views and approaches into the environmental policy process as the only way of progressing towards sustainability.

Holistic and integrated policy making

Our final 'contributory theme' has run throughout this book and is a simple reflection of the need to adopt policy mechanisms which mirror the complex and interdependent character of environmental problems. The need for local policy making which is integrated and holistic, and which transcends traditional, professional and departmental boundaries is clear, and many local authorities have already adopted such approaches, either partially or completely. What is still lacking is a national system of environmental plans, incorporating land use, pollution control, resource management, transport, water, energy and all the other components of environmental policy.

As we have seen, many local authorities have prepared such plans, but they currently have no statutory force, and they lack the vital element of regional and national co-ordination. The need for such a national and regional environmental planning framework is becoming more evident by the day.

We are very conscious that the above may be read as a naive and hopelessly utopian 'wish list', and we have no illusions as to the likely implementation of many of these suggestions in the immediate future. However, we think it is essential that environmental policy is continually contextualised, so that achievable, 'realistic' policy initiatives are always understood and placed within a larger, longer term set of objectives. Within the day-to-day compromise of local environmental policy and politics 'the art of the possible' may rule supreme, but there is always the need to keep the spirit and purpose of the long term goal firmly in view.

Finally, we would like to end by praising and emphasising 'the local'. To think globally and to act locally is an important maxim which is beginning to bear fruit. It is local action which is likely to develop enduring concern and involvement, and it is local action which will be needed to secure commitment and facilitate democratic control. Moreover, it is 'the local' which can enable experimentation and permit diversity. Although there must be international, national and regional frameworks and guidance, it is local policy and action which will ultimately deliver sustainability. The examples in this book demonstrate that we are moving in the right direction. The task is to continue to do so.

Bibliography

Adams, L.W. and Leedy, D.L. (eds) (1987), 'Integrating man and nature in the metropolitan environment', *Proceedings of the National Conference on Urban Wildlife*, National Institute for Urban Wildlife, Columbia, Maryland, USA.

Agyeman, J. (1988) 'A pressing question for green organisations', *Town and Country Planning*, **57**, No. 2, pp. 50–52.

Agyeman, J. (1993), 'Please go away, we're saving the world', *The Independent*, 21 June.

Agyeman, J. and Tuxworth, B. (1994) *Local Authority Environmental Publicity Guide*, Central and Local Government Environment Forum / DOE, London.

Association of County Councils (1990) *County Councils and the Environment*, ACC, London.

Association of County Councils (1991) *Towards a Sustainable Transport Policy*, ACC, London.

Association of District Councils (1990) *Pollution*, ADC, London.

Association of Metropolitan Authorities (1989) *Action for the Future Priorities for the Environment*, AMA, London.

Association of Metropolitan Authorities (1990) *Changing Gear: Urban Transport Policy into the Next Century*, AMA, London.

Association of Metropolitan Authorities (1993) *The AMA and the Environment*, AMA, London.

Audit Commission (1992) *Citizens' Charter Performance Indicators*, HMSO, London.

Bardos, R.P. *et al.* (1991) *Market Barriers to Materials Reclamation and Recycling*, Recycling Advisory Unit, Warren Spring Laboratory.

Barnes, M. (1990) 'Putting the world to rights', *Local Government Chronicle*.

Bell, S. (1993a) *Local Authority Pension Fund Yearbook, Environmental Investment*, PIRC, London.

Bell, S. (1993b) *Muck and Brass: The UK Waste Management Industry* PIRC.

Blowers, A. (ed.) (1993) *Planning for a Sustainable Environment*, Earthscan, London.

Boaden, N., Goldsmith, M., Hampton, W. and Stringer, P. (1982) *Public Participation in Local Services*, Longman, Harlow.

Bowman, C. and Asch, D. (1987) *Strategic Management* Macmillan, London.

Bristol Energy and Environment Plan (1992) Avon and Bristol Energy Action Committee.

British Standards Institution (1992a) *BS7750 Specification for Environmental Management Systems*, BSI, London.

British Standard Institution (1992b) BS5750 *Quality Management Systems*, BSI, London.

British Standards Institution (1993) BS 7750 *British Standard on Environmental Management*, BSI, London.

CAG Consultants, (1993) *Initial Statement on behalf of UK Local Government*.

Campbell, Converse and Rogers (1976) *The Quality of American Life* New York, Russell Sage Foundation.

Capel, J. (1991) *The James Capel Green Book*, James Capel.

Carson, R. (1962) *Silent Spring*, Hamish Hamilton.

Central and Local Government Environment Forum (1993) 'Eco-Auditing in Local Government', *Environment Forum* Issue 3.

The Chartered Institute of Transport (1993) *Bus Routes to Success*, London.

Clarke, M. and Stewart (1992) 'Empowerment : A Theme for the 1990s' *Local Government Studies*, **18**, No.2, pp. 18–26.

Collis, I. and Tyldesley, D. (1993) *Natural Assets Local Government Nature Conservation Initiative* Hampshire County Council, Winchester.

Commission of the European Communities (1985) Directive 85/337, *Environmental Assessment*, CEC.

Commission of the European Communities Directive (1991a) *Draft Directive on Assessment of Plans*, CEC.

Commission of the European Communities Directive (1991b) *Proposal for Civil Liability for Environmental Damage*, COM (91) 217, CEC.

Commission of the European Communities (1992a) *Towards Sustainability: The Fifth Environmental Action Programme*, CEC.

Commission of the European Communities Directive Regulation (1992b) *Eco-Management and Audit* (COM (91) 459, CEC.

Commission of the European Communities Directive Regulation (1992c) *Eco-Label* (COM (91) 880, CEC.

Commission of the European Communities (1992d) *EIA for Policies, Plans and Programmes*, CEC.

Countryside Commission (1991) *Green Capital: Planning for London's Greenspace*, Technical Report Series, Countryside Commission, Cheltenham.

County Planning Officers' Society (1993) *Planning for Sustainable Development*.

Dawson, D. and Game, M. (1987) *Biological Survey for Nature Conservation Planning*, Unpublished report, London Ecology Unit, London.

Deakin, N. and Edwards, J. (1993) *The Enterprise Culture and the Inner City*, Routledge, London.

Deelstra, T. (1986) 'National, regional and local planning strategies for urban green areas in the Netherlands: an ecological approach', Int. Seminar, Urban Green Areas, Barcelona, MAB, UNESCO.

Department of the Environment (1987) *Nature Conservation, Circular 27/87*, HMSO, London.

Department of the Environment (1988) *Town and Country Planning (Assessment of Environmental Effects) Regulations*, HMSO (SI 1988/1199).

Department of the Environment (1989) *Strategic Planning Guidance for London*, HMSO, London.

Department of the Environment (1990) *This Common Inheritance: Britain's Environmental Strategy*, HMSO, London, (CM 1200).

Department of the Environment (1991a) *Recycling, Waste Management Paper No. 28*, HMSO, London.

Department of the Environment (1991b) *Policy Appraisal and the Environment: A Guide for Government Departments*, HMSO, London.

Department of the Environment (1991c) *Competing for Quality*, HMSO, London.

Department of the Environment (1992a) *PPG 12 Development Plans and Regional Policy Guidance*, HMSO, London.

Department of the Environment (1992b) *PPG 1 General Policy and Principles*, HMSO, London.

Department of the Environment (1993a) *Consultation Draft: Regional Planning Guidance for the South East*, DOE, London.

Department of the Environment (1993b) *UK Strategy for Sustainable Development Consultation Paper*, HMSO, London.

Department of the Environment (1993c) *Landfill Costs and Prices: correcting possible market distortions*, a study by Coopers & Lybrand, HMSO, London.

Department of the Environment (1993d) *Climate Change — Our National Programme for CO_2 emissions*, HMSO, London.

Department of Trade and Industry/Department of the Environment (1992) *Economic Instruments and Recovery of Resources from Waste*, A study by Environmental Resources Limited, HMSO, London.

Department of Transport (1989a) *National Road Traffic Forecasts (Great Britain)* HMSO, London.

Department of Transport (1989b) *New Roads by New Means*, HMSO, London.

Department of Transport (1989c) *Roads to Prosperity*, HMSO, London.

Department of Transport (1992) *Assessing the Environmental Impact of Road Schemes: Report of the Standing Committee on Trunk Road Appraisal*, HMSO, London.

Department of Transport (1993a) *Transport Statistics Great Britain 1993*, HMSO, London.

Department of Transport (1993b) *The Government's Expenditure Plans for Transport 1993/94 to 1994/95*, HMSO, London.

Department of Transport (1993c) *Paying for Better Motorways*, HMSO, London.

Department of Transport (1993d) *Taxis and Private Hire Vehicles*, HMSO, London.

Department of Transport (1993e) *National Travel Survey 1989/91* HMSO, London.

Dobson, A. (1990) *Green Political Thought*, Harper Collins, London.

Energy Efficiency Office (1993) *Organisational aspects of Energy Management*, Best Practice Programme, BRECSU, Watford.

English Nature (1991) *Local Nature Reserves in England*, English Nature, Peterborough.

English Nature (1993) *Strategy for the 1990s*, English Nature, Peterborough.

The European Commission (1992) *The Future Development of a Common Transport Policy: A Global Approach to the Construction of a Community Framework for Sustainable Mobility*, European Commission, Brussels.

Evans, B. (1993) 'Why we no longer need a town planning profession', *Planning Practice and Research*, **8**, No. 1, pp. 9–15.

Fairbrother, N. (1970) *New Lives, New Landscapes*, Architectural Press, London.

Fines, K.D. (1968) 'Landscape Evaluation, a Research Project in East Sussex', *Regional Studies*, 2.

Fraser, J., Hamm, H. and Jessup, P. (1993) *Saving the Climate — saving the cities*, ICLEI, Toronto.

Friend, J.K. and Hickling, A. (1975) *Environmental Sciences in Regional and Structure Planning: the Design Phase in Retrospect*, Unpublished Report I0R/860, Institute for Operational Research, Coventry.

Friends of the Earth (1988) *Environmental Charter for Local Government*, FOE, London.

Gaster, L. (1991) 'Quality and decentralisation are they connected' *Policy and Politics* 19, No.4 pp. 257–267.

Geddes, M. (1993) *Local Strategies for Environmentally Sustainable Economic Development*, Paper presented to the Urban Change and Conflict Conference, Sheffield, September.

Geeson, T. and Hansard (1990) 'Devolved management – the Berkshire experience' *Local Government Studies,* January/February 1990, pp. 393–410.

Goldsmith, M. (1992) 'Local government', *Urban Studies*, 29, pp. 393–410.

Goode, D.A. (1989a) 'Urban nature conservation in Britain' *Journal of Applied Ecology*, 26, pp. 859–873.

Goode, D.A. (1989b) 'Learning from the Cities', *Ecos.* 10, No. 4.

Goode, D.A. (1990) 'A green renaissance' in Gordon, D. (ed.) *Green Cities: Ecologically Sound Approaches to Urban Space*, Black Rose, Montreal.

Goode, D.A. (1993) 'Partnerships in the town hall', *Bulletin of the Institute of Ecology and Environmental Management*, 7.

Goode, D.A., Machin, N. and Dawson, D. (1992) 'Habitat and species protection in the UK' in Stewart, J. and Hams, T. (eds) 1992 op. cit.

Goodwin, P. (1993) 'Bridging the gap' in *Transport Policy* 1993 1, No.1, pp. 3–5, Butterworth-Heinemann, London.

Gordon, D. (ed.) (1990) *Green Cities: Ecologically-sound Approaches to Urban Space*, Black Rose, Montreal.

Greater London Council (1976) *Greater London Development Plan* Greater London Council, London.

Greater London Council (1984) 'Ecology and nature conservation in London'. Ecology Handbook No.1, Greater London Council, London.

Greater Manchester Council (1986) *A Nature Conservation Strategy for Greater Manchester. Policies for the Protection, Development and Enjoyment of Wildlife Resources*, Greater Manchester Council, Manchester.

Guinee, J.B. *et al.* (1993) 'Quantitative life cycle assessment of products' *J. Cleaner Prod.* **1**, No.1, pp. 1–13.

Hackney Borough Council (1993) *Nature Conservation in Hackney: a Strategy for Wildlife and the Community*, Hackney Council, London.

Hambleton, R. (1992) 'Decentralisation and democracy in UK local government', *Public Money and Management*, July–September 1992, pp. 9–20.

Handley, J.F. (1984) 'Ecological requirements for decision making regarding medium-scale developments in the urban environment' in Roberts, A.D., and Roberts, T.M. (eds) *Planning and Ecology*, pp. 224–238, Chapman and Hall, London.

Henke, H. and Sukopp, H. (1986) 'A natural approach in cities. Ecology and Design in Landscape' Ed. by Bradshaw, A.D., Goode, D.A. and Thorp, E.H.P. *Symposium for the British Ecological Society*, pp. 307–24, 24, Blackwell Scientific Publications, Oxford.

Heseltine, M., Rt Hon, (1992) *The Greening of Money*, The Gresham College Lecture, DOE.

HMSO (1994) *Sustainable Development: The UK Strategy*, HMSO, London.

Hogget, P. (1992) 'A new management in the public sector?', *Policy and Politics*, **19**, No.4, pp. 243–256.

Holdgate, M.W. and Woodman, M.J. (1975) 'Ecology and planning: Report of a workshop', *Bull, British Ecological Society*, **vi**, No 4, pp. 5–14.

Horton, C. (1992) 'Vive La Devolution', *Local Government Chronicle*, May.

Houck, M.C. (1991) 'Metropolitan wildlife refuge system: A strategy for regional natural resource planning', in Adams, L.W. and Leedy, D.L. (eds), *Wildlife Conservation in Metropolitan Environments*, National Institute for Urban Wildlife, Columbia, Maryland.

Hughes, A. (1991) *Attitudes to Energy Conservation in the Home* Department of the Environment, HMSO, London.

ICC (1991) 'Guide to effective environmental auditing', *ICC Publication 483*.

IDG (1992) *An Integrated Approach to Environmentally and Economically Sustainable Waste Management: the Adur Project*, Institute of Grocery Distribution.

International Union of Local Authorities (1992a) *Common Declaration*, IULA, The Hague.

International Union of Local Authorities, (1992b) *The Curitiba Commitment*, IULA, The Hague.

Jacobs, M. (1991) *The Green Economy*, Pluto, London.

Jacobs, M. (1993) *Summary of Requirements of BS7750 and the Eco-Management and Audit regulation: Environmental Auditing for the Small and Medium Sized Organisation*, CAG Consultants.

Jacobs, M. and Stott, M. (1992) 'Sustainable development and the local economy' *Local Economy*, 7, No.3.

Johnston, J.D. (1990) *Nature Areas for City People, Ecology Handbook 14*, London Ecology Unit, London.

Johnston, J.D. and Newton, J. (1993) *Building Green: A Guide to Using Plants on Roofs, Walls and Pavements*, London Ecology Unit, London.

Keating, M. (1993) *Agenda 21 — A Plain Language Guide*.

Kirklees Metropolitan Council/Friends of the Earth (1989), *State of the Environment Report*.

Lancashire County Council (1992a) *Lancashire's Green Audit*, LCC, Preston.

Lancashire County Council (1992b) *Structure Plan*, LCC, Preston.

Lancashire County Council (1992c) *State of the Environment Report* LCC, Preston.

Langley, A. (1988) 'The roles of strategic planning' *Long Range Planning*, 21, No. 3.

Lee, N. and Walsh, F. (1992) 'Strategic environmental assessment: an overview', *Project Appraisal*, 7, No.3, Beech Tree Publishing.

Leicester City Council (1990a) *Environment City*, LCC.

Leicester City Council (1990b) *Energy Action Plan*, LCC.

Lenz, R.T. and Lyles, M.A. (1989) 'Paralysis by analysis: is your planning system too rational?' in Readings Asch, D. and Bowman C. (eds) *Strategic Management* OU.

Levett, R. (1993) *Agenda 21: A Guide for Local Authorities in the UK* LGMB, Luton.

Lindblom, C.E. (1959) 'The Science of Muddling Through' in Pugh, D.S. (ed.) *Organisation Theory* (2nd. Edn 1984), Penguin.

The Local Authority Associations (1991) *Feet First: a Programme of Demonstration Projects*, Association of Metropolitan Authorities, London.

Local Government Commission (1992) *Local Government Re-organisation in England*, HMSO.

Local Government Management Board *et al.* (1990) *Environmental Practice in Local Government*, LGMB, Luton.

Local Government Management Board (1992a) *Statement to UNCED*, LGMB, Luton.

Local Government Management Board (1992b) *The Local Agenda 21 Initiative in the UK* LGMB, Luton.

Local Government Management Board *et al.* (1992c) *Environmental Practice In Local Government* (2nd edn) LGMB, Luton.

Local Government Management Board (1993) *Declaration on Sustainable Development on behalf of UK Local Government*, LGMB, Luton.

Local Government Training Board (1989) *Environmental Practice in Local Government*, LGMB, Luton.

London Ecology Unit (1989) *Sites of Metropolitan Importance for Nature Conservation*, London Ecology Unit, London.

London Planning Advisory Committee (1993) *A guide to Draft Advice on Strategic Planning Guidance for London*, London Planning Advisory Committee, London.

London Resource Centre (1993) *The London Energy Study.*

Marsh, S. (1993) *Nature Conservation in Community Forests Ecology Handbook 23*, London Ecology Unit, London.

McHarg, I. (1969) *Design with Nature*, Doubleday Natural History Press, New York.

McLaren, D.P. (1993) *Sustainable Cities or Cities for Children*, Friends of the Earth, London.

Meadows *et al.* (1972) *Limits to Growth: A Report for the Club of Rome's project on the predicament of mankind*, Potomac.

Mellor, M. (1992) *Breaking the Boundaries: towards a feminist green socialism*, Virago, London.

Mendip Borough Council (1993) *An Audit for Mendip.*

Messent, E.J. and Wilkinson, F. (1938) 'The "Hyganic" method of refuse disposal', *Journal of the Institute of Municipal and County Engineers*, pp. 1910–17.

MORI (1992) *Financial Research Fund Managers Views*, MORI, London.

Morphet, J. (1993) *Towards Sustainability — A Guide for Local Authorities*, LGMB, Luton.

Murdoch, J. (1993) 'Sustainable rural development: towards a research agenda' *Geoforum*, **20**, No.3.

National Institute of Adult Continuing Education (1993) *Adult Learning and the Environment*, NIACE, Leicester.

National Rivers Authority (1992) *Policy and Practice for Protection of Groundwater*, National Rivers Authority.

Nature Conservancy Council (1987) *Planning for Wildlife in Metropolitan Areas: Guidance for the Preparation of Unitary Development Plans*, Nature Conservancy Council, Peterborough.

Nature Conservancy Council (1988) *Tyne and Wear Nature Conservation Strategy*, NCC, Peterborough.

Newcastle Upon Tyne City Council (1992) *Energy and the Urban Environment Strategy for a major Urban Centre Newcastle Upon Tyne UK*, Newcastle Upon Tyne City Council.

Nicholson-Lord, D. (1987) *The Greening of the Cities* Routledge and Kegan Paul, London.

O'Brien, M. (1993) 'Environmental Culture? The Social Organisation and Disorganisation of the Environment,' Paper presented to the Interdisciplinary Research Network on Environment and Society Conference, Sheffield, September.

O'Laoire, D. (1993) *Environmental Management Systems — A Strategy for Regional Development*, EMA.

Open University (1993) *Watch your Waste at home and at Work*, OU, Milton Keynes.

Pape, D.P. (1989) *A Strategic View of Nature Conservation in London*, unpublished report, London Ecology Unit, London.

Parston, G. (1991) *Managing for Social Results: A New Framework for Public*.

Pateman, C. (1970) *Participation and Democratic Theory*, Cambridge University Press, Cambridge.

Pensions and Investment Research Consultants (1989) *Towards a Green Portfolio* PIRC, London.

Pensions and Investment Research Consultants (Date needed) *Pension Fund Investment and the Environment* PIRC, London.

Peterborough City Council (1992) *Peterborough's Strategy for People and Wildlife*, Peterborough City Council, Peterborough.

Piel, G. (1992), 'Agenda 21: sustainable development', *Scientific American*.

PIFA (1993) *Valorisation of used flexible packaging*, Packaging Industrial Films Association/Oriented Polypropylene Film Manufacturers Association.

PIRC (1993) *What Shade of Green?: A report to local authority pension funds on UK Company Environmental Policy* PIRC.

Poracsky, J. (1991) 'The Portland–Vancouver natural areas inventory: photo interpretation and mapping', In *Wildlife Conservation in Metropolitan Environments*, National Institute for Urban Wildlife, Columbia, Maryland.

Price, G. (1993) *Landscape Assessment for Indicative Forestry Strategies*, Forestry Authority, Cambridge.

Quinn, J.B. (1980) *Strategies for Change: Logical Incrementalism*, Irwin.

Reade, E. (1987), *British Town and Country Planning*, Open University Press, Milton Keynes.

Ruff, A. (1993) 'The Greening of Local Planning', Paper presented at the Annual Conference of British Geographers, Egham, January.

SEC (1989) *A Community Strategy for Waste Management*, 934 Final.

Senior, J. and Ogden, E. (1992) *Metrolink* Transport Publishing Company.

Serplan (1992) *Waste — its reduction, re-use and disposal: regional waste planning guidelines* SERPLAN.

Sheldon, J. (1978) 'Who and what are the ecologists in local government?' *Ecology and Planning in Scotland*, Unpublished Seminar Report, Nature Conserancy Council, Edinburgh.

Shiers (1989) 'Metro Rochdale "Putting the Rhetoric into Practice". A Radical Approach to Decentralisation', *Going Local*, November.

Shiers (1992a) *Earth summit: Rio 92 — Information Pack for Local Authorities*, Local Government Management Board, Luton.

Shiers (1992b) *Local Agenda 21. Earth Summit: Rio 92 Supplement No.2* Local Government Management Board, Luton.

Skeffington, A.F. and Committee on Public Participation in Planning (1969) *People and Planning: Report of the Committee on Public Participation in Planning*, HMSO, London.

Spirn, A.W. (1984) *The Granite Garden: Urban Nature and Human Design*, Basic Books Inc., New York.

Stewart, J. and Hams, T. (1992) *Local Government for Sustainable Development the UK Government Agenda for the Earth summit*, LGMB, Luton.

St Helens Borough Council (1986) *A Policy for Nature*, St. Helens Borough Council.

Stokes *et al.* (1991) *Buses in Towns* The Transport Advisory Service, Preston.

The Public Health Alliance (1991) *Health on the Move: Policies for Health Promoting Transport*, Birmingham.

Therivel, R., Wilson, E., Heaney, D., Thompson, S. and Pritchard, D. (1992) *Strategic Environmental Assessment*, Earthscan, London.

Think Green (1986) *Community Landscapes* Manchester City Council and Think Green Campaign. Manchester.

Thompson, S. and Therivel, R. (1991) *Environmental Auditing* Paper 1. Oxford Polytechnic and USA Environmental Protection Agency, 1985, *Environmental Audits*.

Toyne, P. (1993) *Environmental Responsibility: an Agenda for Further and Higher Education*, Department for Education, London.

Twiss, B. (1974) *Managing Technological Innovation*, Longman, Harlow.

Tyldesley, D. (1986) *Gaining Momentum: an Analysis of the Role and Performance of Local Authorities in Nature Conservation*, British Association for Nature Conservation.

UNEP-UK (1992) *Good Earth Keeping* UNEP-UK, London.

United Nations Commission on Environment and Development (1992) *Agenda 21* UNCED.

United States v. Allied Chemical Corp. 420 F Supp 122 (ED VA 1976).

Waite, M. and Archer, J. (1992) *Nature Conservation in Islington Ecology Handbook 19*, London Ecology Unit, London.

Waite, M., Goode, D.A. and Machin, N. (1992) *Site Designation Review* Unpublished report to English Nature, London Ecology Unit, London.

Walker and Bayliss (1993) 'The Environmental Monitoring Implications of Planning for Sustainability', Paper presented at the Annual Conference of the Institute of British Geographers, Egham, January.

Wallace, A. (1993) *Shareholder Responsibility*, Speech to PIRC Corporate Governance Conference, Convenor, Central Regional Council Superannuation Fund.

WARM (1992) *The WARM System: a Proposal for a Model Waste Recovery and Recycling System for Britain*, a Gateway Foodmarkets Report.

West Midlands County Council (1984), *The nature conservation strategy for the County of West Midlands*, West Midlands County Council, Birmingham.

Williams, C. (1993) *Sustainable Development 1012*, Planning Ambit Publications.

Wittig, R. and Schreiber, K.F. (1983), 'A quick method for assessing the importance of open space in towns for urban nature conservation', *Biol. Conserv.* **26**, pp. 54–64.

World Commission on Environment and Development (1987) *Our Common Future* (The Brundtland Report), OUP, Oxford.

World Wildlife Fund *et al.* (1991) *Caring for the Earth: A Strategy for Sustainable Living*, WWF.

Yarham, I., Barnes, R. and Britton (1993) *Nature Conservation in Sutton. Ecology Handbook 22*, London Ecology Unit, London.

Index